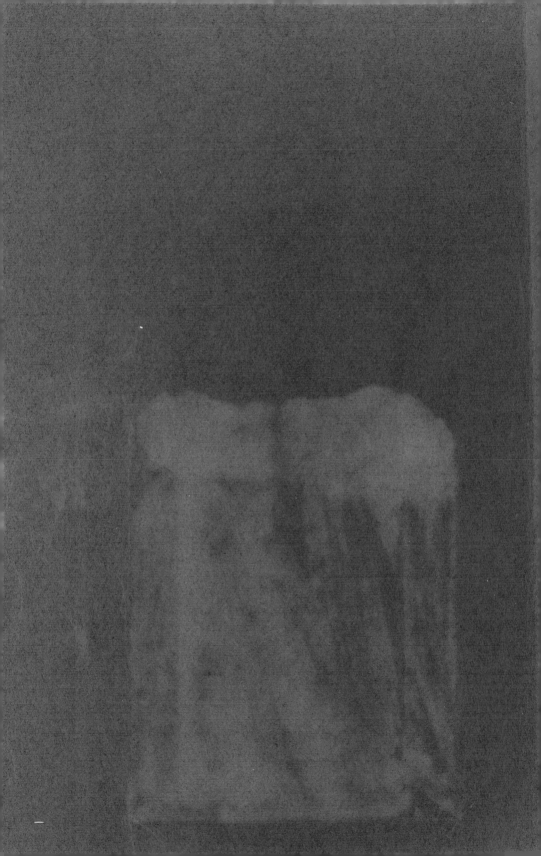

IN SEARCH OF ROOSEVELT

IN SEARCH OF

ROOSEVELT

Rexford G. Tugwell

HARVARD UNIVERSITY PRESS

CAMBRIDGE, MASSACHUSETTS · 1972

PREFACE

These essays are attempts, made since Franklin D. Roosevelt's death, to explore his influence, to assess the means he used, and to penetrate some of the hidden places of his character. He was one of those individuals who, because he rose to leadership in national and world affairs in times of crisis, threw a long shadow. His was perhaps the longest, even though his massive contemporaries Churchill and Stalin outlived him; and his shadow lay over America for a long time in the sense that his absence was felt and comparisons with him persisted. He will continue to be a point of reference even when the inevitable processes of change have extinguished the problems he was so well suited to tackle.

This is the way it is with a few others of our past presidents—Washington, Jefferson, Lincoln, and Wilson, for instance. Roosevelt has become one of the company of those who showed the way to our future and demonstrated the methods of reaching it peculiar to us. This identifying of a national destiny, made lively in the American mind, never stops; but there are times when leaders appear with so commanding a grasp of what is essential, and so persuasive a power to remind us of our duties, that during their administrations our hopes and possibilities are brought into focus and made sharp and clear even to the less certain and more fearful minds among us. Direction is newly defined, courage is aroused, and the resources are found to achieve measures we suddenly know are essential to the realization of our vague ambitions for ourselves.

How strangely diverse these personalities have been! Washington, the patrician planter and soldier; Jefferson, the philosopher, artist, and diplomat; Lincoln, the prairie lawyer; Wilson, the university professor and administrator; and Franklin D. Roosevelt, the improbable son of a quietly aristocratic Hudson Valley family. All had in common that gift for seeing what must be done to make more secure a people's government; but their ways of establishing the pattern in others' minds and of persuading an electorate to support it were notably different. Washington gave example and set a style that would never be much modified; Jefferson called men to the realization of their rights and duties as democrats; Lincoln made a symbol of our Union we shall never abandon; Wilson took us into the world we had to enter if we were not to become an island besieged; and Roosevelt, following as an example an earlier Roosevelt who was a gifted leader too, extended Jefferson's principles into the modern society and enlarged Wilson's commitment to make the world tolerable for democracy.

For years after Roosevelt died at Warm Springs, Georgia, in April of 1945, the ordinary individuals from whose approval his political mandate came carried a sense of grievous loss. This, of course, was deadened by the passing of time. Other men, other events, occupied our minds. They had to, because the men seemed so inadequate and the events so sinister. It was only slowly that men gave up the habit of asking what Roosevelt would have done. Election campaigns, all having their own excitements, continued to be dominated by the Roosevelt image, the Democrats claiming his imagined approval, the Republicans adducing the dangers of his policies.

His shadow was indeed long. It seemed especially so to those who visited the shrines at Hyde Park or at Warm Springs; but it lay as well over Albany, where he had been governor for four years, and Washington, where he had been president for more than twelve. That is to say, comparisons were still made, and regrets were still voiced. People were living, during the postwar years, in terrible disturbance, and most of the time in dangers so deadly they could not actually be realized except as a kind of somber anguish below the level of consciousness. Now it was not only necessary to think of defining and defending ideals, it had become imperative to find ways of ensuring continued existence. The wish for a Roosevelt, who might have solved this problem too, lingered in many minds. Its insubstantial, even ghostly, nature was recognized; but it was still there.

The attempt to understand how such a powerful force in human affairs was organized and how it attained its hegemony over American minds is surely relevant. It happened that I had a better chance to observe, had more material for speculation, than many other of his contemporaries. Some whose opportunities were equally good have made contributions, many of them penetrating. Taken as a whole they constitute an exploration more extensive than other figures, even those of equal consequence in human affairs, have provoked. Even predecessors whom we honor loyally enough are not known as Roosevelt already is. Yet it is literally true that there are mysteries we are quite helpless to penetrate; and we begin to see that we shall probably never be more certain. For such matters there are no measures for analysis, no rules for judging. We know what was done. When we set it against what might have been done or ought to have been done, we are no better off. We do not know what was in his mind except by inference; and inference can always be challenged; and what was the intention is often the most important information we could have.

I have felt, however, that we ought to go as far as we can in the attempt to understand. His effect represents a phenomenon so vital to democracy that its study is essential. It is true that what we shall come to know will not be of the nature a generation inclined to quantification would rather have; but respect for a different kind of generalization will have to be learned—one that depends on insight and inference as well as documentation and measurement.

These essays are inevitably tinged with nostalgia. I was a contemporary and exposed more than most to the tragedy of his removal. I was his governor in Puerto Rico when he died. It was an outpost assignment, but it allowed me to continue certain intimacies. There began at once after he had gone a sort of nagging desire to deepen my understanding of his character and his intentions.

It has been said that various of my studies, in spite of my friendship, have evidenced a certain detachment. I hope this is true; but I am well aware that, as a political observer, I cannot claim this as a considerable virtue in what I may say about him. I must rest on the hope that I have made some contribution to an understanding of him even if I have obviously never been indifferent.

With the exception of Chapters 7 and 8, the pieces that follow have appeared previously; they are here revised to varying degrees. The original publication is noted at the beginning of each chapter. I am indebted to the journals involved for permission to reprint.

R.G.T.

CONTENTS

IN SEARCH OF ROOSEVELT

1

EPISODE BELOW

DOWDELL'S KNOB

Twenty-two years before (in late November of 1934) I had driven along this same way. Or, I should say, had *been* driven; and by a President of the United States. It would not have been strange if my recollection was somewhat hazy; taking a ride with a President is an event likely to leave memories of the man but not of the scenery. I have heard others say of similar experiences that they could recall afterward what he did with his cigarette in its long holder, how he shifted his useless legs, how he monopolized the talk, and even the color and pattern of the tie he wore; but that the surrounding circumstances had been blotted out. After a while they could not be certain what month or even what year it had been. But the head tossed back, the unexpectedness of being addressed by first name, and the puckish grin—these they would not forget.

I should have been long past that wide-eyed stage when we took that ride. I had, after all, been working for and with him for two and a half years, often very intimately. I had never seen him in Georgia; and I had been taken on one of these drives only a few times; but I had studied him and I should have been more relaxed than I seem to have been, and more sensitive to the surroundings. Still, I had just been abroad for some weeks; and meantime the election of 1934 had given him an entirely new stature. It had not been a presidential election of course; but the victory had shown how widely his leadership had been accepted.

NOTE. This essay appeared in the July and September 1968 issues of *The Center Magazine,* a publication of the Center for the Study of Democratic Institutions.

The enhanced power thus acquired had been borne in upon me every day of my journey in other lands. Some of the prestige had been transferred to me and I had been treated accordingly. I was now revisiting its source with a bit of the awe I had felt on first contact. That had been on the front porch of the Executive Mansion in Albany when he had been only a potential candidate. I had been sufficiently impressed then; but now he was President, and, judging from what I had learned in a wasted and tired Europe, much more than that in the regard of the world, actually a man looked to for leadership.

What I do recall is that it was a bright, warm, dry day, with a fresh breeze brushing the uplands of this western Georgia. Leaves wrenched from the trees were blowing across the roads. The whole impression was one of fall brownness and smoky air. The car we were in was open—one of a succession of manually controlled automobiles he had had both here and at Hyde Park. All were small by American standards—that is, they were Fords or Plymouths. And Roosevelt drove well; his useless feet and legs did not prevent him from controlling the car with the negligent ease of a practiced and confident driver; and we went along steadily enough with frequent stops for short lectures about the countryside. The yellow dirt roads were slithery and rutted, and the Secret Service men behind us had a fog of dust to travel in. But the sun struck us, out in front, with almost a summer glare.

These rather general recollections returned all these years after as I traveled the same roads. Not all came back to me sharply; most needed some sort of confirmation; but they were something to go on. Only so short a time after his death, the President had become an enigma to historians, mostly because of conflicting evidence, and I was trying to make my own assessment.

The leisureliness of our progress on that day (and the ones succeeding) was not owed to the defects of the roads. Going about the Hyde Park estate, on woods tracks that were hardly passable, as we had done many times, he had always kept about the same pace as he kept now in the Georgia country. Such outings obviously had for him a double utility. They were convenient for exchanging confidences—some of what I afterward regarded as the most intimate exchanges we ever had took place in these circumstances—and, at the same time, they allowed him the obvious pleasure of savoring the sights, the sounds, and the smells along the way.

Western Georgia was new to me then—it was almost the only part of the country that was—and he was telling me about its peculiarities. This he obviously enjoyed—it was the same penchant that made his press conferences so successful. I once told him that he should have been a high school teacher. He responded that the trouble with high school teachers was that they really did not take in what they saw. "So," he said, "if they don't take it in, how can they give it out?" He finished this off with a very characteristic phrase; they were "too booky."

He was very knowledgeable about Georgia, and he conveyed it well. For political purposes, he spoke of the state as his "second home"; but actually, like me, he was a native New Yorker, and an upstater at that—and with me he did not have to pretend. This southern country was not like our own; we were, the fact was, strangers here, almost tourists, although he now liked to consider himself an old-timer. I was not only a stranger, but one who, somewhat like himself, had a special feel for country scenes.

He had come here first in 1924, and in time had fathered an institution for the treatment of polio convalescents. He had also acquired a farm, and had added to it until it had become a demanding, almost an embarrassing, enterprise.

It yielded no profit; it seemed always to require expenditure for wages, for upkeep, for improvements, and for extensions; but it was a delight nevertheless, until the heavy days of war made any attention to it impossible. It pleased him so much because it offered a challenge. He always tended to believe that something could be done with apparently hopeless enterprises. The more difficult the problem, it often seemed, the more the satisfaction in maneuvering for improvement. There can hardly ever have been a more dismal prospect than was offered by farming that ridge of Pine Mountain. All his efforts would come to very little in the end; but he had not yet—at the time I speak of—accepted the inevitable. He was still hopeful.

Anyway, to be out that day in the dry and resinous air was a pleasure. There were views across broad valleys to other ridges, there were stretches of woody road, and there were reminders everywhere of local lore that he could impart to a newcomer. We visited the farm, and later went on up to Dowdell's Knob. Each stop tapped a vein of explanation; his gestures were wide; his tales traditional. He knew very well I believed only half of it; but that was part of the fun.

But now I was taking a later drive along the same roads, and I tried as I went to eliminate the awareness I had had that the story teller was a President. I tried also to sort out what he had all the time been telling me. On other days in the same car, and in the same country, we had talked of great matters. I had had a preview of policy changes that would affect the whole nation. There had been, for instance, an anticipatory glimpse of what became the Works Progress Administration, the National Youth Administration, the Resettlement Administration, the Social Security System, the yardstick policy for regulating the power industry, the menace of Hitler—and other matters destined to have something done about them before long.

But on this day the talk had all been about farmers and their problems. I was now recalling, or trying to, what it was he had told me about what he had had in mind for this eroded and bedraggled upland, so hardly used, so worthless now to its farmers For some time I had been asking around, from those who ought to have known, what it was that he had been up to. I could bring back a little of what he had told me; but the others I had made inquiries of had been neither very plausible nor very consistent. What they recalled was all mixed up with what they had thought of since. I was on my way now to see Otis Moore. He might be able to straighten me out.

It was the same fall landscape. Twenty-two years had changed it some. The road was now a black hardtop, no longer the dusty yellow-red it had been. On some of the cutover land nearly matured trees had grown, but a localized cyclonic storm a few years before had torn up many of them and mutilated others so that there was no visible gain. The fields once cultivated now had a crop of weeds but not much else.

What a drive in the country means for such a man as Roosevelt is something only those with senses adjusted approximately as his were will understand. A mere glimpse in passing, a faint scent, a muffled sound, will suggest a webbing of linked phenomena. To one not similarly constituted, the images of response will be unfathomable and the conclusions drawn will be bewildering.

Different trees have sharply different outlines; soils do not look alike even to the casual inexperienced eye. A country in drought has a feverish aspect; it wants a drink. The hoot of an owl, the crow of a pheasant, the scolding chatter of a squirrel, or the noises made by domestic animals have significant things to tell. Just as an experienced physician sizes up a patient almost unconsciously, a countryman estimates what he sees. He may feel that all is normal; he may feel, on the contrary, that something is not quite right. Then his mind will run on to remedies.

It was one of the President's characteristics that he was sensitized to a wide range of such data, and that his mind processed it instantaneously, coming up effortlessly with conclusions amounting, sometimes, to an intricately elaborate scheme of action. He relied on these conclusions and had no hesitation in allowing them to shape his attitudes. He had become a powerful person; what he deduced was apt to become not merely a personal conviction but a public policy.

It was one of the curious facts of his life, evident even at that earlier time, that he had about him very few helpers who were tuned as he was to the various appeals of the American environment. One result of this was that they often did not understand how he had come to the conclusions he held. Some who seemed hopelessly stupid about such matters had specialized feelers that were very highly developed about people. So Louis Howe, for instance, who was frankly bored by anything having to do with agriculture, shared with the President an appreciation of political nuances equaled by none of the rest of us. A professional politician was to him an elementary book to be read at a glance. Steve Early had the same gift for knowing the world of reporters and publishers. And Harry Hopkins read the faces of the poor. But there were many who were simply mystified by the operations of his mind. They spoke of it as superficial, or, if they were friendly, as amazing. Others said of him that he was "very complex" and let it go at that; Frances Perkins had once said that in a kind of hopeless way.

That was a time—in 1934— when there was much to be done and when some first efforts had already failed. The powerful men of the decade just past had been insensitive about many things—either that, or they had been incredibly callous. The evidences of decay in the midst of growth, of the wastes and injuries covered by the froth of false prosperity, were obvious enough to some; but actually there were not many who had seen them. Roosevelt had. He knew that nature had been outraged and people exploited. When the land was eroded and its fertility lost, when the rural population was living on its capital and the rest were ill-fed and insecure, his senses not only conveyed the evidence but processed it.

Roosevelt had been late in coming to the presidency. He ought to have arrived there in 1924 or 1928 instead of 1932. But as a New York legislator, and later as governor of the state, he had done what he could. In Georgia, he had been, since his first visit, a twice-yearly visitor. Much of his impulse to reconstruct during that time had been absorbed by the special polio program at the Warm Springs institution. But this was only one specialized exhibition of his penchant for perceiving a need and doing something to meet it. His awareness of a countryside's lacks as he passed through it was a much older and more developed sensitivity. It went back to his childhood, to rides and walks with his father, to play in the Hyde Park meadows and woods, to instruction from those who tended him in a lonely childhood, governesses and tutors.

It was the most natural thing in the world that, set down in this Georgia environment, his impulse to build and change and improve should have begun to work. That he should have acquired a farm and some forest land, as well as a polio establishment, was not all surprising. But I did feel that I might make more definite what it was that he had felt he ought to do. It was for this that I had come back all these years later and had started belated inquiries.

As we moved up the road, I seemed to hear echoes of old conversations that had taken place in this same scene. Recollections boiled up. But sorting them out in any orderly way proved as baffling as it had in other circumstances. The kaleidoscope refused to make a stable pattern.

Only the main headings and the drift of my talks with him would come back. But it was amazing how vividly I recalled the country sights and sounds I had not really been looking at or listening to. That might be, I thought, because I had known how sharply the eyes and ears of the man beside me had been working. I had always suspected that he tolerated the airing of my opinions about large affairs because we shared a precious awareness of smaller ones. He listened to them much more often than he acted on them, of course; but then he had more considerations in mind than I knew about.

Pine Mountain was actually an elevated ridge. The road stretched along its top and dipped, when the ridge turned, down to lower levels and went southward toward the city of Columbus. At a certain point the ridge angled toward the west and ran in that direction for miles. From below, it presented itself as a noble escarpment which, every so often, jutted out boldly above a wide valley. These rocky heights were, in picturesque local language, called "knobs." Dowdell's Knob was one of them, the closest to Warm Springs, an easy trip for an evening picnic or for a withdrawn hour or two.

In 1934, the time I was trying to recall, it had been ten years since the President had first come to west Georgia. Most of the improvements since then concerned the Warm Springs institution back of us at the foot of the north slope where the heavily mineralized warm water poured perpetually from thirty-five hundred feet down in the fractured earth. But up here on the mountain it was not the same either. The application of the restless Rooseveltian creativeness to the raw and reluctant land might have implications for what would be done elsewhere as well. He had said it would; and I had believed him.

Now, all these years later, I looked back somewhat grimly at the hopefulness of those days. It was true that some of the projects had been begun and finished; but some had been begun and abandoned; and others, long pursued, had come to nothing in the end. But there were some that had broken crusts of custom and, although they were no longer identifiable in themselves, had merged into general improvements. Along the ridge now there stretched a state park, very much like thousands of such recreational areas set aside all over the country and improved by the Civilian Conservation Corps. They had been assembled mostly from lands submarginal for agriculture on which an old way of life had been coming to a miserable end. The Pine Mountain Community Project in the valley below the ridge had been an attempt to save small farming; it had been begun as part of the Rural Rehabilitation Program of Harry Hopkins' first organization, the Federal Emergency Relief Administration. But even with expert advice and assistance, it had not prospered. Anything called a community risked being thought communistic, and support had been withdrawn. Its little farms were pathetic reminders of once high hopes.

Apart from the community in the valley, I had wondered for a long time what the President could have in mind for all that land he had bought up there on the ridge where doing anything at all in a farming way seemed so hopeless. I had paid very little attention in the old days when I could simply have asked him. Or perhaps he had told me and I had forgotten before I had reached a time when everything about the workings of his mind had begun to seem important as part of our history. The best I could do now was to inquire of others who had been involved in his enterprises. In this way, guess might be reduced to inference; my interest might be appeased; and historians might be made happier.

So I was looking for Otis Moore. Otis seemed to have been neglected by everyone who should have been concerned to hear his account. He had lived on and operated the Roosevelt farm for some eleven years—there were different reports about the exact number. This haziness was something Roosevelt biographers often had to contend with. Ordinary folk do not keep records or write diaries. They depend on recollections; and these are never dependable. Several otherwise perfectly reliable people had told me about exchanges they had had with the President. The accounts differed in detail, but the origins were recognizably the same. Some of these had obviously been picked up from reading, because they had long since been published. Others had resulted from the President's habit of using stories over and over as parables, telling them a little differently each time to suit the situation. At a distance of twenty years those recounting the incidents were convinced that they had been involved as principals. Some of these incidents I knew to have been reporters' inventions in the first place, born of the pressure for on-the-spot news when actually there was none, or when the reporter was too lazy to do legwork.

Roosevelt's own inventions usually purported to be from his experience. When he found a good one he used it over and over, improving it at every telling. Merriman Smith spoke of this in *Thank you, Mr. President,* and adduced some excellent illustrations of the genre; so did Fred Storm in *When the New Deal was Young and Gay.* The core of the incident may have been very slight or even imaginary; its elaborations may have been intricate. When various individuals, having heard the story from him or from others, or having read it, associated themselves with it, and told it over and over, it took on a kind of significance quite unrelated to reality. It would be a mistake to say that such tales (told of or by all men much talked or written about) have no value for historians. They do indicate something about the mythical man who is being created and who will gradually crystallize in a popular stereotype. But for one attempting a serious study of character, they can be bewildering and misleading. They have to be taken for what they are; and they are not fact, they are parables.

The Warm Springs environment seemed to favor the spawning of these apocrypha, perhaps because most of those who had known the President there had been aware of his immense power and had not had the sophistication to understand its source or its uses. A polio victim is generally self-centered. So much concentration on bodily rehabilitation over so long a time as is required of him is bound to exclude most other interests. And the close little community of a treatment center generates little intellectual intercourse. One of the main therapeutical efforts is to combat this inward-turning; but it seldom succeeds in going further than generating intense interest in other personalities. The President was regarded at the Warm Springs institution as a creature from a strange outer world with a glamorous penumbra. Other strangers came there to see him. They came and went without being much noticed.

It was somewhat the same in the other part of Warm Springs, the village and the countryside. There were several townsfolk who, since his death, had made a kind of career of an imagined intimacy. They had given interviews—still did—and had even published ghost-written accounts of the trivia recalled from watching him at a picnic, at a patient's celebration, or as he was transferred from automobile to train at the railroad station. Not many had ever exchanged words with him, much less any of importance. At Warm Springs, as elsewhere, he was on show except with a few medical men or assistants.

There was *some* difference in Warm Springs. He did seem to relax a little more in that environment. And then, too, he had from the first been the premier physician. No one had known much about polio in the early days, and especially about convalescence; and his own observations had been very sensible. The institutional regime owed a good deal to his reasoning and his enterprise. And a few of the patients had shared this learning process. But these were not many; and even fewer had any interest in the larger world outside.

There were, however, a few who had known him more closely, and whose appraisals were not so distorted by their own concerns as to make them worthless. Some, of course, had been the sort who were inclined to assign themselves an exaggerated role in any event they recalled; and there were some, too, who fictionalized almost unconsciously, bound always to make a good story out of meager materials. Most of those who could be identified as important demonstrated the mixture to be found in most of us—part honest, part careless, part fond or critical, part hazy, part reluctant to become part of any record. Then, too, some were talkers and some were not.

Otis Moore turned out to be one of the talkers. Apart from what he had to say about the President, he was a charming and voluble fellow. It was surprising that at age sixty-three he should still have been living on his small, shabby place under Dowdell's Knob, and not have become some sort of locally prominent politician or capitalist, living in a white-columned village house dispensing influence and reeking with authority. He seemed just the type.

That, in fact, seemed to have been exactly what had happened to Ed Doyle. Ed was dead now and could not be questioned; but he was spoken of by every witness in the neighborhood. He had been a native too, and married to the daughter of a local merchant—well-to-do then, but later ruined, along with many others, by the ravages of the boll weevil in the cotton fields of his customers. This destruction of the whole rural economy was a tragic story in itself. It must be sufficient here, however, to say that Ed had owned a farm, had got himself in debt to Roosevelt, and had traded the farm in on the debt. That was not the end of it. Roosevelt, when he had got to be President, had made Ed a kind of local contact man and had appointed him a United States marshal. He would not have done this merely because he had taken a liking to him—as he undoubtedly had. The appointment was made because Ed had genuine political potency. Professionals are quite strict in their own mystery.

At some stage in Ed's translation to a higher level, Otis Moore, respectable neighborhood small farmer, had come to Ed and said that he "would like to get in on this." These words actually slipped out in the interview I am about to relate. Otis caught the phrase and stifled it half-said. But it had a meaning I understood. It was obvious from the way it came out that this was exactly what Otis did say to Ed, and that it was meant as said. There was a good thing going, and Otis wanted to share in it. What call Otis had on Ed did not appear, and I neglected to ask; but Otis did attach himself to the great man who had money and a desire to own a farm, even if he achieved it only after a couple of years of hanging about on an irregular arrangement. Ed was moving on; Otis waited for it to happen. When Ed became marshal, Otis became the farm man in Ed's place. He and his wife moved into the house provided, and he had a good enough life for some eleven years—until the Warm Springs Foundation took over ownership from the then President. At that time Otis quit, and moved to his own little place a few miles away in the valley where I went to call on him.

The parting had been amicable so far as could be told. Otis was, and continued to be, a respectable member of the community. For the eleven years of his tenure he had got his living off the farm, and had done on it what he and his principal between them had concerted to do. It had cost the President a good deal of money by the time he gave it up; and the foundation was, after all, interested in polio, not in Georgia agriculture or politics. The farm was looked on as one of the aberrations that, as everyone knew, sometimes got hold of Roosevelt. If it had some historical interest it was not apparent to the new owners.

There seems to have been some idea that the President had a weakness for Otis as well as for Ed Doyle. If he had, it is understandable. For Otis was the kind of plausible and likable fellow

11

Roosevelt appreciated. To sit and listen to him talk—as I was doing in 1956—was a pleasurable experience. He had no upper teeth and not many lower ones; but the lack of dentures did not interfere with the easy flow of words. It may be that, as one neighbor said when I was inquiring to find him, "he talked better than he worked"; but he seems to have been industrious enough on the farm to have held the President's confidence. Neither of them can have wanted the enterprise to lose money. As for the President, he may have been disappointed that it did not produce a profit; he was incorrigibly optimistic about hundreds of projects during his life, and few of them proved profitable. He may have forecast a fortune in farming on Pine Mountain. If he did, it would have been no more realistic than his usual forecasts. And that it did not succeed in that way was not Otis' fault.

Otis would certainly have liked to make a go of it. That he was philosophical about persistent reverses was because anyone had to expect failure in that country. He was a native, and so inured to disappointment; and Roosevelt, who always began optimistically, was also accustomed to the petering out of his hopes. They may have had a fellow feeling. At any rate, Roosevelt liked the lean, homespun, good-humored, smooth-talking farmer.

He enjoyed driving into the farmyard, calling for Otis, and talking things over with him. Otis humored him; he always had something to offer. If the President had no new ideas, Otis usually supplied some. His proposals frequently concerned acquisition of adjoining land, something the President had a well-known weakness for. Otis' neighbors, envying the way he had "got in on the good thing," were always imploring him to get them in on it too. All of them, apparently, wanted to "get shut of their worthless pieces" of cutover land where scrub cattle ran; but they preferred to do it, if they could, at a good price; and Otis accomplished it for a number of them. The President was hoping to do a lot of reforesting, and had some ideas about better species and methods that he wanted to experiment with. Otis gained status in the community by being a go-between in this way.

But status was something he had already acquired by not only being a friend of Ed Doyle but having direct contact with an outsider of wealth and consequence. It helped, also, that his was an old and numerous family in those parts, even though the family had never produced any remarkable members. It was the propinquity with power that really counted. When an individual with wealth turns up in an old run-down neighborhood, all of whose families have lived together for generations, and who know each other inside out, a kind of competition begins to see what benefits can be got. Otis was the potential benefactor in this contest; and he was besieged.

Struggles of this sort can become fierce. The stakes may seem small to outsiders, but to people on the margin of rural poverty they may take on a desperate quality. Once the first sharp engagement is settled by someone winning the confidence of the source of good fortune, and becoming the dispenser of its benefits, the next stage is soon entered on. The man of power becomes as hazy a figure as he had originally been. His representative—a familiar person anyway—becomes the object of solicitation. The envy may still be latent; but the position is recognized. Otis, on the farm, was able to give employment and to place orders for supplies, machinery, and livestock. Also, he could urge and guide further purchases of land.

This world that Otis ruled as the President's representative was quite separate from that of the institution and quite separate, too, from that of Warm Springs, the village. It was even a few miles removed in space. In the areas outside Otis' jurisdiction there were struggles for power too. At the institution, the victors in that struggle still ruled in the fifties—and the exiled losers were still bitter.

The individuals involved in the institution's war were of a different sort. Some were polio victims and so confined now to the constricted environment of invalidism; but they had come from a wider one, and had once been important. They had means, and they were educated and sophisticated. The weapons they used on each other were, therefore, somewhat different from those used in the rural area; but the tactics they employed were recognizably similar, and the motives were precisely the same. The fierceness of the struggle was quite as intense; the survivors were as complacent and the vanquished were as envious.

In the village, many of those who were involved in that struggle had grown old or died; but some survived in triumph or defeat. They still generally tried to exploit the source of benefits at the institution, even if with diminishing success. The number of those with reminiscences of Roosevelt to tell seemed to be rather larger with each passing year. But all in all, the community had a feeble life. The tourists were mostly intent on seeing the Little White House, Roosevelt's home at Warm Springs, up on the hill. A few of them stayed over or took a hasty meal, but most spent their hour in the environs of the memorial and hardly noticed the village itself. It was easy to miss.

This separateness accounts for Otis' unwillingness to stay on the farm when the institution became its owner. An efficient regime was about to begin. There would be restrictions and instructions. No longer would a big, affable man drive his little car into the yard and talk things over in expansive fashion, willing to listen to any of Otis' suggestions. The loss of face involved would be intolerable. Better be independent, even if poor, as he had once been, than be supervised by office bosses, and not to have disposable favors.

Otis had simply quit. He had no retirement pay. He had to scratch for a living, and his wife (a new one; the first one had died on the farm) had to work; but he had not given in to the threat of subordination. Everyone in the neighborhood was poor—not as poor by some degree as before Roosevelt had taken an interest in them, but still poor by American standards—and Otis was as poor as any. He was not able to have an automobile and this emphasized the loss he had sustained in quitting, but did not make it any way disgraceful—rather the contrary; it showed what he had been willing to sacrifice for principle. His wife's job was a respectable one. She managed the lunchroom in a nearby school. And both of them had their memories. Also they could call attention to many changes—such, for instance, as the lunchroom itself. Who had ever thought of giving school children hot lunches before Roosevelt came along?

We missed Otis on the first try. With Ed Smenner, custodian of the Little White House, guiding us, we made all the complicated turns correctly and found his house. It was only a few miles from the Springs—down the hill and around to the west until a final improbable road took us close up under the Knob. The house was dreary; like so many farm homes in the South it seemed old, but also impermanent, as though it had long outlived its depreciation period. It was set on brick piles a couple of feet from the ground and the space under it had, as most of them do, accumulated rubbish and become a refuge for animals. The yard was bare in some places, and weedy in others; but this was late fall, and although the vegetation had been frosted, it had not yet blown away.

There were some home-built sheds. Farms thereabouts do not have proper barns. Our knocking and calling did not fetch him from the house; and no one was to be found in any of the other buildings. Ed Smenner knew where Mrs. Moore's school was, so we drove the few miles there. We arrived at a busy time. The school mothers were preparing a Thanksgiving party for the children and she was somewhat harassed. Anyway, as was evident at once, she was not very outgoing. She was a thinnish woman of fifty or so, and she regarded us with slight suspicion as unexplained strangers. But she told us that Otis ought to be at home. So we went back and explored some more.

Ed tried the doors and found them unlocked, so he went inside and called; but no one was there. We looked again in each of the outbuildings. In one there were hundreds of white chickens. We could see that they were being raised on contract as was usual thereabouts. The processors furnish the baby chicks, and supplies are bought on credit. When they are the right size, they are all carried off to a processing plant where they are prepared for marketing. Many of the risks in this operation have been reduced by the addition of vitamins and antibiotics to the rations; but this so increased the supply that prices to the growers were driven down to levels inconceivable before the improvements appeared. It is the old familiar sweatshop system of home work extended to a new field. When we talked with Otis about this later, he told us there was no profit in it; but he always hoped the next batch would "bring in a little more." Besides, his time, he said, was not worth much. This was so standard a position for the small producer that his statement seemed to me to echo words from an antique phonograph record. I had been hearing them all my life.

Otis also had several hogs. He would presently be butchering them for winter meat—one of the late-fall rituals of self-sufficiency still remaining in such backwaters. There were a few cattle running in his woods; but there was no real pasture, and he was not actually in the stock business any more. At least, if he was, it must be somewhere else. We looked around pretty carefully, but did not find him; and finally we had to go away.

A couple of days later, however, we came back and he was there. This time, Ed was not with me; only the lawyer who was my colleague. There was no one around the house. But we heard the screech of a power saw out somewhere in the woods and made our way toward it through weedy trees and underbrush. It was a chilly day. The temperature had fallen below freezing, and there was a biting wind; but again the sun was bright. We came on a characteristic scene when we finally broke through the brush into a clearing, and found the working party. They were cutting up fallen timber. Otis explained at once, having to shout, that he was making firewood from the trees uprooted in last year's cyclone. He was supervising two black men.

We found it difficult to communicate with the high whine of the saw interrupting every few seconds; but we introduced ourselves as best we could. It seemed that Otis had been warned by his wife that we were looking for him; but, as it turned out, she had not understood, and he, just now, had not heard, who we were or what we wanted—only that we were interested in his recollections of the President, now more than ten years dead.

We walked some distance toward the house, clambering over logs and parting branches, and then stood to talk in a small clearing near the pigpen. He was obviously sizing us up. His way of doing it was to watch us shrewdly while he ran on about the woodcutting, the cyclone damage, the weather, the cattle and the pigs, and—in a really warm tone of voice—the pen full of hound-dog puppies he led us to. He always kept dogs, he said; he liked them; and he did some possum-hunting in the winter. I recalled a well-known photograph of the President, flashlighted as he gazed upward at a treed animal. He had been sitting in his current Ford, surrounded by the men and dogs—a half-dozen of each—that, among them, had brought one small terrified possum to bay. It was a local sport; and the President had been brought in on the kill. We spoke of the occasion and Otis recalled it in some detail.

In spite of the difficulties—the cold wind, the deafening noise, the lack of any place to sit, and his obvious uneasiness about the job going on in the woods—Otis talked easily and well. He used the west Georgia language, impossible for me to reproduce. It was rich with accents strange to my ears, yet effective in conveying what he wanted to say. There were allusions I sometimes missed because of their local reference; but it had the quality of outpoured verse.

It was not at all hard to understand how the President had been fascinated by Otis, and had often visited the farm to tap the full-flowing stream of his talk. I thought it much too entertaining to waste in such circumstances; so I maneuvered toward another meeting when my wife could be brought along with her notebook. There was not much difficulty about it. Otis was anxious to get back to the sawing, even though the impulse to talk was very strong.

When I turned away for a moment, and came back, he had begun to tell my colleague of an incident that I myself recalled. By the time he had got well into it, I realized that he had not recognized me at all. I felt that I ought to stop him, because I had been involved and I was not sure what he might say. It was the affair of the two mules that the President, in one of his moments of puckish humor, had named Hop and Tug after Harry Hopkins and myself. There were several versions of it, and I was not sure which one Otis would use; he might even have one I had not heard; and it might embarrass him to have told it in the presence of one of the principals. So I broke in.

"Mr. Moore," I said, "I think I should tell you that I am the Tug in that mule story."

"No!" he exclaimed. "Well, I be damned. I shoud've known. It's a good thing you stopped me. I might've made it worse than it was."

"Well," I said, "now go on and tell it."

He squinted at me, decided it was all right, then went ahead quickly. He ended by saying, "The thing was that a year later he [the President] asked me how they had worked out, and I had to tell him that Hop was a good mule, but that Tug was the most damned worthless animal we ever had on the place."

This was a frequently repeated story. The original incident had really happened, and I recalled it well enough—except for the last part. But Otis told it better than any reporter ever had. We all laughed together. And, having this opening, I asked if we might come back the next day when we could sit down for a longer talk. Meanwhile, he could be thinking over what he could tell us about his dealings with the President. I said I would bring my wife along to make some notes if he didn't mind. He didn't mind. So that was what we arranged.

The next day would be Thanksgiving, and I asked if that would make a difference, but it seemed not. So he went back to the woods, and we got into the car and drove away. Before we went, he shook hands with me in a way that let me know he appreciated our sharing something together.

"So you're Tug," he said. "Well, I do be damned; where you been all these years?"

I told him I had been mostly a professor.

"Oh," he said, in acknowledgment. "No business at all? Since those days? That's nearly twenty years ago."

"No," I admitted, "no business at all."

Then it obviously occurred to him that I must be well off; and he let it go. But we were still involved in recollections that had become valuable to both of us. We waved good-by with genuine warmth.

There had to be some way of accounting for the complex of agricultural programs Roosevelt had sponsored. They had been ticketed by him as emergency matters and pushed at once when he had become President.

Of course, he had done what he could for farmers when he had been governor of New York; and he had been well enough briefed about the impossibility of achieving recovery unless agriculture could be brought back to reasonable prosperity. But there had been something more, some special feeling in his expressed concern. About this one thing he had been endlessly inquiring, endlessly urgent. Where had the emotional involvement come from?

I had long thought most of it had come from west Georgia. He had always talked a good deal about his "farm" in Dutchess County, New York, but that was an estate and he could not have learned much there about farmers' problems. In Georgia he might; I thought he had.

His interest in the people of Meriwether County was, in a way, tangential. He had first come there discouraged by his inability to recover from the effects of his severe polio attack three years before. His useless legs had refused to yield to other regimens and he hoped for better luck exercising in the pools of warm mineralized water at Warm Springs.

This therapy was not actually much more successful than others he had tried, but he liked the country and came very close to some of its people. Not all of them were connected with the rehabilitation center he proceeded to build up; many were farmers he met as he tooled about the countryside in his small automobile. Even before he had a farm of his own he had driven into their yards and asked questions. He could see how hard a life they had, and how much they had lost when, on top of the depression, they had had to survive the disaster of the boll weevil.

It was old corn and cotton country. Now the cotton was gone. They kept trying; but every year the growing plants were attacked as the bolls were forming. They no longer could get their investments back. As a private citizen, or even as governor of another state, there was nothing he could do in a public way. But he generated the notion that they might find other crops and save the special way of life he admired so much.

It was for this reason that he bought the piece of land on a ridge not far from Warm Springs. It was called Pine Mountain. On it he tried a variety of experiments. It seemed possible that this might become beef-cattle country; or it might grow trees for an expanding paper industry if they could find quick-growing ones; or they might grow apples or grapes—or something else.

Everything had failed in the end; and now, as I was visiting there after two decades, the place was abandoned, and there were not many people left who could help me recall his efforts. But Otis Moore was still available as I had found; and I hoped he would talk as freely as he had seemed willing to do the day before. Today, as we traveled the complicated route into the hollow below Dowdell's Knob, it was proper Thanksgiving weather. There had been a frost and the trees rustled. Up on the ridge there was a cold wind. Down here it moved only the treetops and did not disturb the dusty weeds alongside the road.

At Otis' place there were two cars in the yard. One was Mrs.

Moore's, the other must have brought some relatives for the holiday. We realized that it had when children's shrill voices were heard.

It was Mrs. Moore who met us at the door, but Otis soon came in from tending the pigs or chickens and we took up where we had left off out in the woods. This time my wife sat in the circle with Ed Smenner, the Moores, and me. She had a notebook on her knee, but her shorthand was unobtrusive and Otis was not in the least self-conscious.

I was somewhat wary. The other day, when we had gone to see Mrs. Moore in the bustle of her school kitchen, she had seemed a capable woman, intent on work. Now, as we sat in her own parlor, she was formidable. I thought at once, and could not stop thinking, of Grant Wood's "American Gothic." She and Otis together might have been the subject of that portrait—but only when Otis was quiet, and this was almost never. His face when he talked was as mobile and expressive as his voice. Mrs. Moore was the sort who kept her lips tight. She went through the whole two hours without relaxing, except in one interlude after my wife asked her about the photographs on the table and on the old-fashioned wheezer organ. She had a boy in the air force; in fact, both she and Otis had had families before their own marriage. Otis talked easily of his former wife. It had been she who shared most of his life on the Roosevelt farm. But he often asked the present one for confirmation of events before her time. She furnished it in a reluctant, deadpan way. She was the strong one of the pair.

The lady had some records, but she was wary about admitting to having any specific ones. She did finally say that she had "a pile of stuff" she was saving for her girl to put into a scrapbook. She was unimpressed by my suggestion that, for history's sake, she might let someone put it in order.

I gradually built up a supposition, which, I realize, may have been entirely unjustified, about cartons in a closet overflowing with valuable material. This was based largely on her admission that there were "some" notes giving Otis instructions, as well as material relating to land acquisitions and finances. Otis, in fact, said there was a lot of this and was inclined to brag about the number of letters. But she looked at him, when he said this, with a grimness that said as plainly as words would have: "Be quiet; these are not people we know."

Only once, almost at the end, did she go and get something. This was a check endorsed by the President, and I was amused that she showed it first to my wife—the woman among us was less a stranger than the men. She was gone hardly a moment, so it was obvious that she had known exactly where it was. It occurred to me that she thought the material she had put away valuable and hoped some day to dispose of it to advantage. Meanwhile, it was not something to let strangers get hold of. She remained still and difficult in contrast with the voluble Otis.

The parlor was an unfriendly room anyway, and probably not very often used. It reminded me of rooms in the farmhouses I had known as a boy, only this one had that impermanent and unsubstantial look I had noticed about the whole house. It had patched woodwork, uneven plaster, worn linoleum floor, chairs with plastic upholstery brought in from the porch; but—almost everywhere in the nation now—there was electric light. A bare bulb hung from the ceiling, with open wiring leading up to it. Probably the power failed often enough so that the old kerosene lamp got some use.

There were lithographs on the wall and family photographs on the table. The fireplace had been boarded over, and in front of it there burned an open gas fire. Otis had been cutting firewood, but their heating was done by gas from the cylinders I had seen outside. What, I wondered, became of the wood? Perhaps they used it for cooking. I knew that the local women thought food was best prepared on a stove fired with wood; but I did not get around to asking. I kept to what was conceivably my business, in spite of what Mrs. Moore may have thought.

Otis could see what I wanted and he was willing to help. He had been letting recollections run through his mind. I started him off by saying that I was curious about his age. He made me guess, and I put it at sixty. This pleased him, because sixty-three was correct. When I said he did not look it, I could be convincing. He was a man with no bulges, only angles, and he still had hair, though few teeth.

Once started, he kept up a sort of stream-of-consciousness

monologue. What follows are excerpts, as my wife caught them in shorthand and afterward typed them. She missed some of the richest parts on account of the language—the west Georgia locutions were sometimes too much for her—but most of it ran along in the typescript as smoothly as Otis had produced it. It serves very well to show how the relation between the President and the farmer began, and how it developed. I quote first from his response to the question: How did President Roosevelt happen to buy the farm in the first place?

"Ed [Doyle] and his daughter was out back on the farm one evening, an' Mr. Roosevelt come along. It seemed like the Doyles walked out there and hitched a ride back to the house. They had a talk. Ed owed money. He said, finally, 'You better let me sell out to you, and work it for you.' And in the next ten days, that was what they done . . .

"I worked for Mr. Roosevelt a year and a half that time. I operated under Ed. That was all through the time when he was governor. As soon as he got to be President, he appointed Ed to be marshal, and I naturally took over. That was in thirty-three.

"But I begun to build up the cattle herd in 1926 or 1927, before I went up there to stay. I recollect when I first spoke to him, he asked me right off what was my first name. From then on, it was plain Ot [pronounced Oat], just plain Ot. He liked to call people by their first name.

"The next thing he asked was what did I know about cattle. 'Nothing,' I said, 'except that I grew up in a barnyard.' He gave me one of his big 'ha-ha's.' You could hear them all over."

I interrupted to say that I had heard various stories about the farm operation. What, for instance, had the President had in mind to do with the cattle? There was no hesitation.

"His main object? . . . I don't think he ever had any intention of makin' money. There was no beef-type cattle in the country then, and his idea was to promote them here. I asked him to buy some registered stuff; but he wanted to use the cattle the farmers had, and breed them up and show that it could be done without a lot of money.

"The first crop of calves we grew, they was only half-breeds. Right away, the farmers around wanted to buy the bulls. I asked him about it, and—that was what you could 'preciate about him, it was 'yes' or 'no'—he said, 'No. Let them bring the heifers to breed to your pure-bred bull, and don't charge them any fees.' And that is what we done."

This was a somewhat different account of farmer Roosevelt's operations from that generally accepted. Even some of his closest associates, otherwise bent toward presenting him over favorably, were inclined to admit that he had been a foolish and improvident owner of the Pine Mountain farm. Evidently there was more to be said. At least, there was further to look. It might be that Otis felt himself involved in this general charge of incompetence and was not a wholly reliable witness; it might be, but I thought not. I thought Otis had this straight and the point seemed to be established by some close questioning later on.

Presently, in his open, voluble way, Otis slid down farther in the old porch chair, swung a heavily shod foot, rocked a little, and launched into a story tangential to the matter we had been discussing, but a matter, nevertheless, with its own interest. It was a new story. I had heard most of them, but this was wholly new. He got at it in this way:

"During the 1934 drought, we got some pretty pure stuff out of them breeders who was hard hit. We got our cattle up to three-fourths, seven-eighths. It was mostly family stock we got. Some of it had no papers. We got rid of our scrubs. We got some with only a sixteenth or maybe a thirty-second scrub in them. We got one fine bull out of Tennessee, not registered, but a pure-bred white-face.

"Then Mr. Roosevelt took a trip out to the west where the worst drought was. He helped them out of their troubles. They was grateful. But a disappointing thing happend. A letter came to me from a man named Anderson. He lived out in west Texas. He wrote when he knowed that Mr. Roosevelt's party was at Warm Springs. He said Mr. Roosevelt had had Congress to appropriate money for them who was hurt, and they wanted to send him a carload of the best pure-breds they had out in that country. Each ranch was going to give one pure-bred heifer. This Anderson said they had sixty head already bred, and they was waiting to go. He said his first thought was to ship them on, but then he thought he had better contact me. I came in one day—my wife always read all those letters that came to me, I was getting quite a big mail then—and she give me this one. God Almighty, I wanted them cows.

"I told Mr. Roosevelt: 'My mail is pretty heavy and I never bothered you much; but here is one.' He spread it out and begun to read it. When he got about halfway down, he began to shake his head. He started to talk, still reading it. 'No, we can't do this. If we took gifts, we would be criticized all over the world; and we are just trying to help everybody.'

"He told me: 'If you want to accept one or two bulls for the farm, we might do that. You better go ahead, and write him a nice letter, and quote me any way you see fit, but two bulls is as far as we go.'

"So I wrote Anderson and told him the situation, but explained why we could not accept them, and told him I was glad he hadn't shipped those cows on to me.

"So them ranchers bought two bulls at an enormous price—I don't remember what it was, but it was big—and they stall-fed them and got them fat, and then they hired two cowboys to bring them here. They had ads all over that truck—Purina! Those boys told me it was more trouble getting out of the state of Texas than it was getting all the rest of the way here."

I asked him then about my own recollection of seeing Black Angus on the farm; and this elicited the story of a presidential dilemma.

"This fellow, Charlie Redwine . . . he was once in politics. You might have talked to him . . . He had a Black Angus herd, and old Charlie Harman bought it—twelve heifers and a bull—and we bought it from old Charlie. I kept them cows; but after we got them whiteface bulls from Texas, I told Mr. Roosevelt, 'We are not fixed to have two herds.'

"Show you how particular he was. I had it in my mind to confine myself to one or the other. He said: 'You put me on the spot. The whiteface people would be mad if we got rid of *them,* and the Black Angus people would be just as mad if we got rid of *them.* These cattle people are worse than the Camel folks.' [Somebody had been looking into his brand of cigaretts.] But then he looked at me, and he said, 'The old whitefaces do look pretty, don't they?' That was the only thing he said. I got rid of the Black Angus."

There was one transaction—the only one—that made a profit. It, too, involved cattle:

"That same drought year, we had sixty or seventy head of steers that should have gone to market, but the pasture had been dry and we didn't have no corn. They was skin and bones.

"Mr. Roosevelt come out, and I asked him what to do. He said: 'Here I got the whole world to look after, and you ask me what to do with some steers . . . Well, have your best buyer out here and let him make a bid.'

"I asked a man I knew at White Provision to come down to meet the President. Then he asked if he could bring *his* president. They come down. Before Mr. Roosevelt come, I said to them, 'I want you to bid on them as if you was buying from me. Don't offer any premium.' So after he looked them over, he said, 'Otis, I am ashamed to tell the man.' What he offered was two-and-three-quarter [cents a pound].

"Tap Bennett told me what to do. Tap was county agent and often give us advice. He told me to get a load of cottonseed hulls and some corn, buy it loose and grind it together. 'Then get you the best nigger you got and train him to feed them.' So we built pens and fed them 110 days. We had to buy every bit of feed. We sold them at the fat-cattle barn. They brought twelve-and-three-quarters [cents a pound] and we made money on it."

Otis told about this incident eagerly, saying at the end that it had been toward the last of November when the President had been there; that the cattle had been fed through January, February, and until the latter part of March. It was then, he said, that he had been able to remit the only check he ever sent. He recalled the amount to the dollar. He was right about the amount. But when Mrs. Moore reluctantly produced the canceled check, his story rather fell apart. He had sent it in December, not in March, and the cancellation date was February, not June. Nevertheless, the story illustrates their relationship, as well as an engaging passage between Otis and his banker.

"When I sold this herd of cattle, I was carrying a bank account, and operating the farm with it, and sometimes I went over, but they covered it for me. When I got this money, I wanted him to have it . . . it was $1,112. I deposited it, and sent him my personal check, because I wanted it to keep. I told the head cashier at the bank, Elizabeth Grant, 'You better not let that check go bad.' But it was three months before he cashed it. When he did, Elizabeth Grant called. She said, 'The big check has come in, and you can't cover it.' I said, 'How short am I?' She said, 'Four hundred dollars.' I went right over and in back to see Mr. John Peters. He told me with a straight face that they had sent the check back . . . but pretty soon I seen he was kidding me."

That was when the check was brought out for us to look at. I didn't mention the discrepancy of the dates. Things were going too well. I asked Otis why, if there was no money in it, the President kept on with the cattle. Wasn't there anything else that might do better? I had grapes in the back of my mind. There was a story about them that had been hinted at by many others. I wanted it from Otis. But he was still interested in defending the cattle project, which, he said, to his mind, "did more good than anything we did."

In five or six years after we started, there wasn't a farmer in the whole county that didn't have a whiteface bull. That was the whole idea from the start—not to make money, but to show the people . . .

"Doyle fooled around with chickens before I went up there, had a couple of thousand. He put in rabbits . . . had a couple of thousand of *them* one time . . . and we always had forty or fifty pigs."

Otis was vague about the grapes. I had been told first that Cason Calloway—every conversation in Meriwether County gets around to the Calloways, who are the owners of the largest mills thereabouts and are "into everything else" as well—had been as close to being a friend of the President as was possible in the circumstances, he being an open-shop employer on a large scale and the President being the sponsor for a new era of unionization and collective bargaining. The whole region was torn apart on this issue in the thirties. But labor was still not organized in the Calloway mills at the time I speak of, and it can be imagined what kind of fight must have been put up to prevent it.

The Roosevelt power was opposed by an equally stubborn local one. And it seems that the President had spoken softly. The two may never even have mentioned the matter between them. At any rate, I recalled a very pleasant picnic at Mr. Calloway's country place in 1934, when the struggle was at its worst. It had been an entertainment for the whole Roosevelt entourage, with Calloway as the cordial host. It was something, I was told, that happened very often.

Perhaps they had got along because they shared other interests and let the dangerous topic alone. Calloway was much interested in agriculture; he himself had done a good deal with cattle; he had had much to do with the state park; and I knew he had experimented with grapes as a possible crop. Up on the Roosevelt farm the remains of a terraced vineyard, now gone to ruin, could be seen from the road. I had been told that the vines had come from Calloway nursuries. I had been putting my pieces of knowledge together.

One of the unique projections of the Calloway energy—in its way not unlike the strain of enterprise in the Roosevelt family—was the Ida Cason Calloway Gardens. Calloway had taken a whole valley some ten miles southwest from Warm Springs, and had turned its several thousand acres into a pleasure garden. It had been planted to native flowers, bushes, and trees. It had large artificial lakes and wide lawns. Boating, swimming, water-skiing, fishing, and golf were available. There were fees, but they went to upkeep. It was a nonprofit memorial to the Calloways' mother.

All this did not exist in 1934. It had developed since, and I could imagine that Roosevelt had watched its growth with envy. It was something he himself might have done if he hadn't "had the world to look after." I imagine Calloway, who was responsible for this demonstration of rural beauty, was sometimes dismayed by the dishevelment of the Roosevelt farm. Had he made suggestions? I had heard, for instance, that he had wanted some of the acreage to be planted to muscadine grapes, the scuppernong, that vine the traveler sees so much of in the middle South, especially in the tidewater country. It grows on vast trellises, one vine sometimes covering a quarter-acre.

There was a so-called country store, also a Calloway venture, over by the gardens, where unique—and expensive—products were sold. Among them were a scuppernong jam and muscadine bread, heavy with grape flavor. These were the products of the Calloway imagination. I thought what I had heard might be so. But if it was, Otis did not know of it, and he did not satisfy my curiosity. But something else of the sort was turned up by his recollection.

"The grapes you are talking about, the ones that are there now, was put there after I left. But the old Concords was already there, I think. If they was not, we put them out in my first year. What I believe is that Ed planted them after he sold. I believe it was the first thing they done in the way of farming after Mr. Roosevelt bought the place."

This was new. I did not associate Concords with the South. That was the grape we grew so much in New York State, the one the nation's grape juice is made of. Subsequently, I learned that there was a famous Concord nursery not too far away, and that from it Concords had been widely spread over western Georgia.

Calloway still might have sponsored the scuppernongs; but Otis associated him with apples. They had not done badly with the Concords for a while, Otis said. They had trucked them in bulk to the Virginia Dare plant in Atlanta (so well known for its sweet wines). But the price got so low, it didn't pay.

"The only thing Cason done while I was there," he said, "was to furnish some apple trees." What happened to them showed that the various Roosevelt failures on the upland tract could be matched by others attributable to the best local talent. Calloway had said: "It looks to me that you ought to have more fruit, and I want to give you two or three acres of apples, and I want to put them out myself." Calloway obviously did not regard the going farm operations with favor. He would not trust Otis even to plant the apples. So Otis told him to pick out some land and go ahead, which he did. But, said Otis, with a grin, "They dried out—didn't do good. It was too high and dry for them." And it is true that no trace of an apple orchard remained.

Something over an hour had gone by now, but Otis was as fresh and eager as ever. Moreover, his wife's dourness had really moderated when my wife had asked about her boy in the air force. She spoke of him proudly. Then, to our surprise, she suggested to Otis that he tell about another project I had not yet got around to—the longleaf pine I had heard about from others. I thought it probable that most of the land the crafty natives had sold, and Roosevelt had bought, had been destined for reforestation. He was an old hand at growing trees and had always had an interest in forestry. This interest was inherited from another Roosevelt President—TR—who, whatever else could be said about him, had to be commended for his immense contributions to the cause of conservation.

Roosevelt's main legislative interest during his three years in the New York State Senate (1910 to 1913) had been forests and parks. It had continued through his governorship; altogether, he considered himself to be one of the most devoted successors of Gifford Pinchot and other pioneers. But he had done more than influence public policy; he had practiced his own preachment. Since 1912 he had been planting trees at Hyde Park. The slopes between the house and the river now had well-grown plantations.

It was not strange, then, that he should think of trees as he studied the hardscrabble uplands of the Pine Mountain ridges. It seemed to me that he may not have been so simple as the natives thought. As with cattle, so with the trees, he may have been trying to demonstrate that better stock and decent practices made the difference between success and failure. And I doubt if he ever thought seriously of anything but trees and cattle, with some feed crops to supplement the winter pasturage. The cattle would pretty much rough it and the trees, once started, would need no intensive attention.

There must have been much discussion about varieties. The whole area had been long since cutover and what remained was tangled and weedy. There had once been many hardwoods; there were some in the volunteer growth. Hickory nuts, for instance, had fallen all around us as we had walked through the woods; the porch of Charles Palmer's house, where we were staying, was thick with them. But there were many worthless jack pines and other growths that come up when cutting has been severe and no replanting is done. The characteristic desolate look of the late-fall country doubtless came from the drying out of the slopes and the erosion that follows every rain when there are no established root systems and piled detritus to stop the runoff. To bring back such a devastated countryside is not easy; it is still less easy to rehabilitate it in such a way that the forest crop can be made profitable. Otis spoke of such matters as he had known of them. He had evidently not been interested in a serious and permanent policy, but mostly in trees to be sold. He had, however, found out something about marketability.

"I would say that next to cattle, trees was the best project. People in this country didn't know you could set out a pine. We did it. But the first ones we put out was longleaf. We learned that this was not the best tree, because it took too long to grow; also there is not much sale for longleaf around here. I didn't realize that until we went to cutting it. It was seventy-five or eighty percent heart.

"I been in the sawmill business all my life. But when the lumber dealers said, 'We don't handle that stuff,' it just knocked my socks off!

"I learned it was too pitchy to work when the Baptist church burned up and they asked me to donate the lumber to make new pews. I give it to them. But when the man came to make up the benches, after it had been laying there for a year, he said, 'I can't use this stuff.' They dumped it back on me. Then they asked me to sell it and give them the money. I sold it to Jim Woodruff, who just didn't get around to paying for it. I called him a couple of times, and I finally had to go down. I said, 'Me and the President is donating this to the Baptist church, and you come on and pay up.' He finally did. And they bought some other lumber.

"We found out later that loblolly is the best; it grows faster and you can work it better."

If it seems by now that Otis had spent most of his life doing different things—raised in a cowpen, running a sawmill, and so on—the explanation is that he did them simultaneously. With the confidence of a rural jack-of-all-trades, he would tackle almost anything that interested him and promised to yield a dollar. He was not strapped when he asked Ed Doyle if he could get in on the exploitation of the northerner with so much money. It just looked like another good thing. He already had a farm and a sawmill, and was driving a school bus. He was not clear about his relationship with Roosevelt in the couple of years before he actually moved to the farm. But he had owned the land adjoining the farm, and evidently wanted to work out a simple sharing arrangement. But Roosevelt, as Otis now told it, wanted to be more generous than Otis would allow him to be.

"After we talked about a deal, he asked me if I would be interested in working on a salary. I said I didn't think so. I said, 'If you will buy me the cattle, and the wire, we will split fifty-fifty.' He said, 'I don't think that is fair. I'll give you a hundred dollars a month, and we will split the profit too.' I was running the bus, the mill, and the farm then, and I knowed I was going to go on doing what I was doing. So I said I'd take seventy-five dollars; and that is the highest salary I ever did get.

"But when I moved to the farm, I got three times that because I got everything that was growed there. That took care of the family; the little seventy-five a month didn't mean nothing.

"We had everything we wanted, living off the farm.

"Of course, the fifty-fifty split didn't mean nothin' either because there never was much profit."

The offstage noises from the kitchen area made it evident that the younger generation, gathering for Thanksgiving dinner, would not much longer be denied the run of the house. There had already been a couple of eruptions into our circle of discussion. We did go on, however, to one last incident. My wife professed never to have heard of the mules names Tug and Hop, bought for the farm and named by Roosevelt after me and Harry Hopkins. The memory started Otis on a final run and produced the most fascinating story of the whole interview. It showed Otis in a new light.

He had obviously, as time went on, seen how he was identified with the President. He had grown cautious about his talk and his behavior. He had gone further; he had sought to turn the rather sorry farm enterprise to good account. The mule deal, as he now told about it, might have originated in the mind of an Ivy Lee, and Edward Bernays—or, more likely, a Charlie Michaelson, the Democratic public relations genius, because Charlie was actually visiting Warm Springs at the time. The incident, however, had an unmistakable country flavor. No city publicity man would ever have thought of it.

It happened because Otis had begun to worry over what was being said about Roosevelt, and especially what was said about him as a kind of phony farmer. It was true that the President had rather overworked his rural status. He was always telling people he was a New York farmer, or using the Georgia place as the background of a story. This was harmless enough; he always did it merely to illustrate a point just as valid without the illustrations; but it was something easily seized on by his critics.

Otis, out of his own mind, had set up the whole show that I myself had witnessed back in 1934, and I had never realized it any more than had others. And, as far as the public relations job was concerned, it had worked perfectly. The story had been printed in nearly every newspaper in the land, both friendly and hostile. Moreover, there had been photographs to go with it. I looked at Otis when he finished telling us about it with new respect, both for his loyalty to his employer and for his unexpected but consummate skill as a creator of character. The President had been clay to his shaping. He was wrong about the year; it was actually just after the mid-term election of 1934, and not, as he recalled, just before the presidential election of 1936. But the service to Roosevelt was just as considerable, whether or not it had been appreciated as it should have been. But let him tell it from retirement in later years.

"People had been saying that Mr. Roosevelt didn't know enough about what went on . . . they had been asking him about it . . . how he handled it . . .

"We kept twelve or fourteen mules there. I asked him several times about getting a tractor, but he said, 'If you need more power, get some more mules.' Well, we had to have something. I told him one evening, 'We'll have to make a new deal here, and I think you should make a mule swap.' I told him that people had been worrying me about his not knowing about the little things on the farm.

"He asked me, 'How you want to work it?'

"I said, 'I'll have some mules brought out and you can make the deal. You have the newspaper men come, too.'

"So I went to Black, who ran the stable there and had a son.

"I told Black: 'We got to make some mule deals. Come out to the farm, you and your boy, with some mules. I want you should meet the President.'

"I picked out eight mules, and told him to have them out at the house at two o'clock. The President was coming out at three. I told the President I was ready, and to let all the newspaper men come.

"Black brought about a dozen mules, and I picked out what we needed for the farm. I think we got four or maybe six. But the President and Black made the deal with the crowd looking on.

"After him and Black made the deal, he noticed a blemish on one mule's leg. He called me: 'Ot, did you notice the knot on that hind leg?' I hadn't; but when I looked, sure enough, there was a good-sized lump on the inside hind leg. Shows you what a sharp eye he had.

"That wasn't all about the mule deal. There was one real fine pair. They was the best in the stable. He looked them over and then said he wanted to name one Hop and the other Tug."

Then he turned to my wife and said apologetically, "That is the story I was about to tell yesterday, without realizing I was talking to Tug. I was sure glad he told me. But he didn't mind, so I told him the end of it."

"What was that?" she asked.

"It was about a year later," he said, "when the President asked me. He says, 'What about those mules, Tug and Hop? How did they turn out?'

"I told him, 'Hop made one of the finest mules on the place; Tug wasn't worth a damn.' "

That was the end of our interview. We broke up with cordiality on all sides. Even Mrs. Moore said, "Come again." And we left, in a wash of grandchildren, to find a Thanksgiving dinner for ourselves.

Two weeks later I heard from Ed Smenner that Otis' wife had brought him over to the Little White House office for a special purpose. He had something on his mind and he wanted Ed to tell me about it. "I been thinking back," he said to Ed, "and checking with others that was there. I told that story wrong. It was Hop that was the worthless mule. Tug was all right—the best one we had."

2

THE FALLOW YEARS

In 1938 Franklin Roosevelt looked back to 1928, the year of his election to the governorship, and remarked on the easy optimism of the years just preceding the Great Depression. He had shared, he said, "in common with most liberals," an underestimation of "the drastic changes . . . necessary for a lasting economy." It had required the depression itself, and the experience as governor, to "bring home to me the more fundamental, underlying troubles . . . facing all civilization." He gave himself credit for having understood only two overriding social necessities. One of these was for agricultural relief; the other was for the correction of labor's disadvantages. These groups, he had known even then, received "an inadequate and unjust share of the national income."

These remarks were made in an assessing mood induced by the task of writing a foreword to the early volumes of his *Public Papers*.[1] In 1938 he had been President for five years and was as fully matured in domestic politics and economics as he ever was. But a student must suspect that he underestimated his progress before 1932, when he entered the presidential campaign as a nominated candidate. In 1932 he still did not have the knowledge

NOTE. This essay originally appeared in *Ethics*, volume 66, number 2 (January 1956). Copyright 1956 by the University of Chicago. Reprinted by permission of the University of Chicago Press.

1. The *Public Papers of Franklin D. Roosevelt* then published comprised five volumes, later added to until there were fourteen. The work of compiling and editing was done by Samuel I. Rosenman, returned to Roosevelt's service after having been for several years a justice of the Supreme Court of New York State. (Judge Rosenman's *Working with Roosevelt*, published in 1952, is an indispensable account of the campaigning in 1928, the years of the governorship, and the period of World War II. There is necessarily a gap in this account from 1933 to 1937.) They were published in three sets by Macmillan, Random House, and Harper.

As a compilation of Rooseveltiana, the Papers make a documentary record for every he needed to formulate a crisis policy with confidence, but he had discarded many of his over-simple rules-of-thumb and had begun a serious search for the explanations and remedies he needed. He had by then, in fact, a workable method best described as experimental, perhaps; and he had also a revised concept of the role of government in economic life. What still remained was to discover solutions for the particular problems vague and inexact approaches would not solve. These needed detailed and expert working out.

It has to be mentioned at once that the political and economic philosophy firmed up in 1932 did not survive intact the battering of events and the unwillingness to follow of many of those whose opinions he respected. By 1932 he had made himself a good deal of a collectivist and was reconciled to the inevitability of large-scale organization; he had a beginning of faith in economic planning and in the need for group cooperation.

This became evident in his speech at Oglethorpe University in April. Under pressure, however, in the years of his presidency he reverted to the earlier philosophy he had gradually abandoned as a result of the depression (and its lessons). By the beginning of his second term, his progressivism would be a less advanced kind than that of the then Senator LaFollette—Robert, Jr., the son of old Bob. He would be further back, indeed, than old Bob had been in 1924. How this advance and the subsequent retreat came about is involved in the history of his governorship and of his first presidential term. But the proper beginnings are to be found in the interim years, after his illness in 1921 and before the beginning of his governorship in 1929.

The years following Roosevelt's illnesses in 1921 were not easy ones. Recovery from the effects of polio was not a matter of passive convalescence. It had to be worked at daily; and it involved intervals of despair. Again and again he had to face the fact that some exercise, some regimen, some place, was not yielding the

year. They show many marks of having been worked over carefully by Roosevelt himself. This is indicated not only by the selections but also by the style of the introduction and many of the notes. Judge Rosenman was a good ghost writer; but he was not so good that a careful analyst cannot pretty accurately distinguish the material dictated or written by the President himself from that written for him and simply approved and allowed to be included without revision. This distinction is important to students of his development; they should always read his *Papers* with it in mind.

beneficial effects he had been led to expect. As he gradually became something of an expert himself, the realization grew on him that his paralysis was never likely to be more than partially overcome. He repeatedly reduced his hopes; he no longer expected complete recovery, but that there might be some improvement he was determined to believe.

Aside from the mental and physical strains involved in this repeated adjustment, there were the added ones involved in his peculiar postion. He was not, in his own estimation, just a stricken private person; however handicapped, he was destined to leadership in great affairs. He had talents. These were political; and their development allowed no withdrawal from contacts with other people and no letdown of intense concern with public affairs. A member of this profession watches with sensitivity, even when he is unconscious of it, all that goes on about him. He sees hidden meaning in events obscure to others; he watches politicians maneuver, and if he himself is not at the moment involved, he nevertheless cannot resist trying over in his mind the probable motives of the participants, the countering moves of each, and the outcome to be expected. It is a fascinating and never ending activity.

With one part of his mind Roosevelt, in these years, studied his own paralysis, assessed his chances for a partial recovery, and judged how his disability had changed the techniques he must use. With another part he went right on learning about politics from observation, adding to his knowledge and gaining in understanding. It is a mistake to think that his experience with polio revolutionized his character or his intentions; but it is equally mistaken to conclude that the changes in his life had no effect at all. The evidence is that they had considerable effect; and it is only necessary to study the changes themselves to see what the effect must have been. The emerging man who became governor of New York in 1928 had, in fact, been very deeply affected by his invalidism and the strains of his convalescence.

It was not that he was more widely experienced; it was that he was more deeply experienced. He traveled less after 1921 than he had been accustomed to do; he spent more time at Hyde Park and later at Warm Springs. He had to stop playing games—tennis and golf for instance—requiring mobility. He had to find occupations that could be carried on in bed, or in his wheelchair, and others suitable to his crutches or his later braces.[2] He needed company now, and he could not go to seek it; how much more he must have appreciated his wife and the faithful Louis Howe can easily be imagined. It can be imagined, also, how many more hours he spent reading, and how tired he must have become of light literature as a soporific. He did, in fact, turn more and more to other exercises of the mind. He had always enjoyed history; now he found it a rich resource, and he ventured in it far beyond the narrow fields he had before cared most about. He had long been familiar with local chronicles and naval history; he now studied Americans of other years; of these, the statesmen he naturally found most fascinating.

When he first came out of the hospital he went to the family house on Sixty-fifth Street, but he inclined toward country life and he was soon centered at Hyde Park. Later there were migations in search of a cure—to Farmington, in Massachusetts, to the Florida Keys, and then to Warm Springs. But he never went back—never until he was President—to Campobello, where he was first stricken. He may have felt that its peculiar northern rigors would have held back his recovery. His preference was for warmth; it seemed to give him release. Something of this he found in Florida, but more in Warm Springs where in the warm water he had more control of his body than at any other time. It seemed to support his paralyzed legs; he thought, often, that muscular control was returning. He wrote to friends that he thought soon he would be able to wriggle his toes. After 1926 Warm Springs became something of a home.

Always during these years there was a family atmosphere. Olin

2. Those who knew the younger Roosevelt agree in picturing him as having been restlessly active. He not only loved such competitive games as tennis and golf, he seemed under compulsion to keep in motion. Even when working at a desk, he kept jumping up and walking rapidly about the room.

From one who was seldom resigned to physical repose, he became one who was forced to repose most of the time. He never wholly overcame the motor impulses. His throwing back of his head, his play with cigarettes and a procession of long holders, his restlessly moving hands, even when he sat or lay immobile—all went some way to express this suppressed compulsion. Perhaps, also, his volubility increased as a result of his inability to express himself in action.

Of course his regimen included a great deal of exercise and so provided an outlet for his restlessness; but his ability to move about when not formally exercising was drastically curtailed, and when he became an official again even his therapeutic exercises were necessarily reduced.

Dows pictures the children as they were growing up.[3] Since they all had the Roosevelt energy and the freedom of affluence, overlaid already by the Groton veneer, and since their father was already famous, the five of them, when they were all home, as they were for long summer vacations and at Christmas, seemed to turn the house into a kind of adolescent bedlam. Other visitors from that time also tell of luncheon or dinner tables made riotous by high-voiced argument. The young people had the utmost scorn for each other's opinions. They regarded their mother and father as entitled to a hearing, but no more; and their grandmother was a source of clandestine gifts and funds, not otherwise to be taken seriously. They challenged their father on every issue.[4] He learned some patience; but he liked also to escape sometimes to the solace of history, to his stamp collections, to the quiet of his farm, his tree plantations, or to the solitude of his southwest bedroom whose windows looked down and across the river to the Catskills in the distance.

But the family life at this time was more cohesive than ever before or after. To be sure, in 1925 Anna was nineteen and thinking of something to do on her own; James, a year older, was at Harvard; Elliott, fifteen, much against his desire was at Groton and hating every minute of it; Franklin, Jr., was eleven and in Groton too, first form; John, the baby, who had been born in Washington in 1916, was still at home. If the stir created by this boisterous crowd at Springwood made a lasting impression on all the visitors

3. In *Franklin D. Roosevelt at Hyde Park* (New York: American Artists Group, 1949). This charming book, by a resident of nearby Rhinebeck, has a text which is merely the accompaniment of many original drawings. These reproduce scenes at Hyde Park at the various stages of Roosevelt's life. There are included pictures of the various houses he built or lived in and group assemblages of the family at its various pleasures and occupations. Olin Dows held a post in the Federal Art Program during the years 1934-39. His painting was rather objective and realistic than otherwise; there is no better way to visualize Hyde Park atmosphere than to study his book.

4. Frances Perkins, in *The Roosevelt I Knew* (New York: Viking, 1946), p. 63, speaks of this family ebullience: "In summer and holiday time the children were at home. There were boys rushing all over the place, riding ponies, practicing hurdle jumps, swinging baseball bats and tennis racquets, filling the air with their shouting. Large companies would sit down to lunch. The windows would be open, with a pleasant breeze blowing in from the Hudson River. Roosevelt would be at the head of the table, talking to everybody, bantering with his children, teasing them and they him. The youngsters would tell preposterous stories to dignified visitors to see if they could get away with them, and would burst into gales of laughter regardless of whether the visitor fell for the story or saw through it. Roosevelt played with his children as though he were one of them."

who came and went, the children themselves would unconsciously look back to it all their lives as a kind of idyllic interval.

There were many visitors. It was fortunate that Sara was comfortably off so that she was able to maintain the home with all its hospitable amplitude down to the depression—when her son would have advanced to the governorship with all its perquisites. The house, having been rebuilt to Roosevelt's plans, was reminiscent of the English country home now becoming so scarce in England itself. There was a complete staff of well-trained servants. The lawns, the gardens, the orchards, the meadows, and the woodlots were all well cared for.[5] Franklin, as part of his hold on old interests, was expanding his holdings and planting new varieties of trees under the tutelage of Dean Nelson Brown of the Syracuse University School of Forestry; he also set out in 1926 the first of the Christmas tree plantings harvested ten years later with enormous satisfaction.

Those who inquire about the life of the Roosevelts will need to understand that Franklin and Eleanor bridged in their lives such a cultural change as seldom occurs within a generation. In their youth there were recognizable American aristocrats, mostly moneyed folk, furnished with a complicated apparatus for living which was to disappear in the aftermath of the World War and the Great Depression. The places of this "four hundred" would be taken by those who made money out of previous ones. But equalitarian ideas and institutions by then would have a leveling effect. The income tax was part of the Wilson progressivism; a social security system would be part of Roosevelt's. Between them they would make a moneyed, hereditary aristocracy obsolete.

The place at Hyde Park was to Roosevelt not something bought and paid for, created for one generation's enjoyment. It was an institution which gave stability to a whole social system. It justified itself by its products; but justification was something so taken for granted as never to be claimed. What had made England great

5. The staff then consisted of cook, kitchen maid, personal maid, housemaid, waitress, butler, houseman, laundress, coachman, and a chauffeur. Eleanor Roosevelt has noted that "when we arrived with five small children there were often a tutor or governess, a nurse, and a nursemaid." She went on to remark that sometime before her death Sara had begun to reduce her staff, and "it was only because my husband could bring people from Washington that the old-fashioned type of hospitable living could go on." But before the depression the old style could be maintained; the decline did not begin until after Roosevelt became Governor.

was a culture centering in the great houses, along with the training furnished by the Etons, Harrows, Rugbys, and Winchesters. Franklin was a complete product of this culture transferred to America. He never had any other experience as a young man. From Springwood to Groton, to Harvard, to the law, and then to public life—he arrived at the New York State Senate when he was 29—was a succession quite natural to the English tradition. It must be understood as natural to the Roosevelts as well.

James, his father, loved Springwood too; but he had acquired and developed it, and he would have known that the privilege of enjoying it had to be earned. His son was schooled in noblesse; but that the enjoyment of the estate was something he might have had to earn probably never occurred to him. A whole range of emotion and endeavor likely to occupy most of others' lives was entirely absent from his.

As time went on—as he grew up—it must have occurred to him that his situation was unusual. Others of his sort saw it—Ogden Mills, for instance, Franklin's up-river contemporary. It made most of them turn almost savagely conservative. It affected Roosevelt, as we have seen, in the reverse way. Presiding over the establishment in process of coming down to him, he both understood its impermanence and exaggerated its desirability. Springwood did not, like the stately homes of England, go back hundreds of years. It went back, as a Roosevelt appendage, only one generation. No one would have thought so to look at it; and its antiquity seemed even greater after his alterations. Whether or not this was deliberately intended, it was the resulting effect. The difference between the Springwood after his reconstruction and the country houses built by his wealthy contemporaries was that his creation achieved a quiet and solid dignity lacking in most of the others. Their results seemed elaborate, lavish, and derived from Europe; no one ever used these words to describe Hyde Park, much as it owed to English origins.[6]

6. Roosevelt was responsible, years later (1939-40), for making one of these places into a museum. This was the Frederick Vanderbilt place above Hyde Park, perhaps the most extravagant and lifeless of all these mansions. He spoke to me of this project with a kind of glee. It illustrated to him the irresponsibility and selfishness of his Tory contemporaries. It would be, he said, a kind of living reproach to the moneyed, self-appointed aristocracy. The Vanderbilt place was foreign in conception and lavish in appointment. Many of the visitors who come now to Springwood and sense its solid

It is impossible to say whether Roosevelt set out to establish this kind of setting for himself and his descendants, or, if he did, what happened in his mind when the conviction of impermanence suppressed this ambition. The fact is that the Hyde Park estate as he developed it came out of his mind and heart. It was exactly what he wanted. And if what he wanted was the impression of an unreal aristocratic permanence, the impulse was very deep and characteristic. What he did to Springwood was done long before his invalidism, but not before he was the father of sons. The Warm Springs institution may have been valuable to him in convalescence, proving that he was not helpless even though his legs would not move; but it was very different from Springwood in his regard. The Hudson Valley estate was really home.

Its roots, however, were in Roosevelt, not in the estate itself. He had the impulse to heighten, to exaggerate, its institutional character. This must be interpreted as a kind of compensation. Perhaps compensation is the wrong word to use here; perhaps what should be said is that the estate became the embodiment of impulses to be understood only by looking carefully at what was created. Its qualities of dignity and solidity are obvious. What grace and beauty it had appear to have been incidental; they were not sought for. Then there were the additions he was always making. These were not merely extensions; they were a broadening and strengthening of the base supporting the institution. The significance of this, psychologically, it may be guessed, is that all of it opened out with him at its center. He was the proprietor, the pater familias.

It is even possible, without too much straining, to go further and suggest that when it became obvious to the practical sense that Springwood would certainly disappear because of changes in future years, it was made permanent as an appendage of government itself. And Roosevelt would still, in a sense, remain at its center. He does still seem to preside over it from the grave in the high-hedged rose garden. Visitors can see all the detail of his

virtues are fresh from the Vanderbilt follies or about to go there. Whether Roosevelt had in mind the continuance of these contrasting exhibits, I do not know; but I know that he was anxious for posterity to understand the moral bankruptcy of the class he had "deserted." For the formal beginning of the Vanderbilt museums see *Personal Letters*, 1928-45, II, 978. For its acceptance by the Advisory Board on National Parks, Historic Sites, Buildings and Monuments, see *ibid.*, p. 957. Both these are letters to Mrs. J. L. Van Alen, the inheritor of the estate.

existence there, even to his garments; the evidences of his work are gathered in the library; his mementoes furnish the museum; his every word and every action are preserved.

The estate may not have been the immemorial institution it appeared to be when he presided over it in life; it has become so, now that he presides over it in death. For some reason, anticipation that this would be so was a necessity. Account has to be taken of it if he is to be understood. Nevertheless it became a moving experience to go there after the building of the library and museum, and after the placing of the simple marble block over his grave, and see how exactly the whole arrangement conformed to the picture he must have had in mind.

The whole is now ruled by the ancient trees; the paths and gardens are unostentatiously set for their duties; the house quietly insists on its dignity; and every appurtenance of Roosevelt's daily life is frozen in a reverent immobility. Much the same effect is got from the Lincoln House in Springfield, for instance, or other houses of presidents, but Lincoln cannot be imagined as having planned it that way; he would, in fact, have regarded with a mixture of irony and amusement his progress toward sainthood after withstanding the unrestrained abuses of his political life, and especially its last phase when he might have expected some, at least, of the respect, even from his enemies, that a Chief of State usually commands. And surely the same can be said of crusty old General Jackson—and even of Jefferson; his intended memorial was the University of Virginia, not his home at Monticello.

Among the family parties coming to Hyde Park day by day, in hundreds, a genuine reverence does prevail. Did Roosevelt think this his due? Or was it that having been President in troubled times, he thought the whole of his Hyde Park life ought to be crystallized for later examination? At any rate he was right about one thing. The interest in the simple paraphernalia of his existence is always lively. It is as though there actually were some virtue in his old campaign hat, in the Navy cloak he wore in many a presidential progess, in the portraits of his ancestors, and in the small automobile which remobilized him after his illness.

Shortly after his first return to Hyde Park this vehicle was adapted to his use, the foot controls being transferred to his hands. He was able then to travel about his growing estate, watch the tree planting, visit his neighbors (with numbers of them he had the familiar relations it was always so easy for him to establish), and ease the monotony of his confinement. The strenuous work of trying to regain the use of his legs was never relaxed. Even when, discouraged, he had given up the journeys to Massachusetts, he kept up his training at home in Hyde Park or wherever else he might be. And as we picture him there the thoughts have to include a man going round and round a railed enclosure on the lawn, dragging his useless legs and carrying on at the same time, heartbreakingly, a conversation with those who happened to be present.

Those present might be almost any one. Even out of office, Roosevelt was an important figure. He continued to cultivate his wide political acquaintance; and he encouraged Democratic leaders from everywhere to visit him. They were sometimes disconcerted by the bumptiousness of the children; but they were invariably impressed by the sense of permanence and consequence conveyed by the solidity and homely grace of Springwood; and the man who entertained them on the lawn, while he hauled himself about, or at the luncheon table, where he presided with gay authority, charmed them to the point of uncritical approval. In spite of his invalidism, he seemed to talk practical sense. There were some historical allusions, always, and some appeal to experience. There was a good deal of laughter; and a lot of "you know and I know" appeal. There was optimism. The Democrats' day would come, he was certain of that; and when it did the faithful would be rewarded. The faithful liked to hear this; and if Springwood was an experience new to politicians, its proprietor was convincing.

The political occasions sometimes became formidable, as when, in 1924, after the acerbities of the convention in New York City, Roosevelt entertained John W. Davis, the compromise candidate, along with the loser, Alfred E. Smith, for whom Franklin himself had been preconvention manager, and in whose interest he had made his first "Happy Warrior" speech. That reconciliatory gathering of the Democratic clans seemed to be appropriately under his auspices. He was not old in years, yet he was a kind of party elder—an important politician who was interested, but who wanted nothing for himself. And of course Springwood had been the locale of a previous historic occasion—the notification ceremonies when he himself had been the vice-presidential candidate in 1920, and all the party greats had mingled on the lawn with the Hyde Park neighbors. If anyone had told those present in 1924 how many more historic occasions it would be the setting for, they might have had difficulty in accepting the prophecy; but the atmosphere of rightness for such a future must surely have occurred to them, even if only vaguely. Roosevelt was a man of destiny.

The house, as it had been redesigned, had several vantage points the reconstructive visitor can imagine Roosevelt occupying. One was the balcony (the roof of the porch) looking off down to the south reach of the river over the trees on the slope. He could be wheeled out there from the bedroom, whose windows commanded less freely the same view. Another favorite spot was the front portico, where he sat for many quiet hours with his stamp books, working over them with never failing interest.[7] He was able here, by lifting his eyes, to see the old favorites among the great trees, ones he had clambered in as a boy, and by now were coming to a great age. Then there was a favorite path, made smooth for his chair, around the short distance to "Rosy's" red house, so like his mother's before its reconstruction. Rosy, his much older half-brother, was one of the less able and less ambitious Roosevelts; but there was a fondness between them.

He often had lunch, when he was alone, or when there were no children at home and only a visitor or two, on the porch, perhaps after working inside in his cozy, dark little study at his morning's correspondence, and after having got through his designated course of exercise. Eleanor was very likely away. Her surprising personal development was just getting under way and giving her a new freedom; also, she was always conscious of not being the mistress at Springwood. The children too might be off at school or away on their own affairs. But a small and persistent shadow was

7. As a kind of guide to visitors at Hyde Park when it became a national shrine, Eleanor Roosevelt wrote a brief pamphlet, published by the Government Printing Office, telling something about the history of the house and the circumstances of its dedication to public use after Roosevelt's death. In it there is a quotation from an account written by Roosevelt himself, with characteristic attention to detail, about the estate, the house, and the library. Concerning the front porch and portico she said that it "has memories of a very particular kind, for this is where my husband always stood with his mother to greet important guests. It is where she always met him when he arrived for a visit." It was also where he stood when the neighbors came to congratulate him after each nomination and on every election night; and where he made many a graceful speech.

almost always at hand. That was Louis Howe. These were the years of his most valuable service.

Louis, leaving his work as a reporter in Albany for the New York *Herald,* had long ago become the self-appointed impresario of the Roosevelt career. As such he was by now accepted in the household. Eleanor had been won over to a kind of affection as an incident of the alliance they had formed in opposition to Sara in the early days of Roosevelt's convalescence. The older lady treated both of them, even after all these years, as inexplicable attachés of her son. Neither ever felt really welcome in her home.

Eleanor eventually found a way out of this domestic difficulty. During her husband's convalescence she began a series of enterprises on her own and they seem truly amazing in the gauche and retiring matron she had formerly been.[8] Together with two women friends, she built a kind of old-fashioned factory for making furniture by hand. It was meant to furnish part-time employment for farm workers so that they would not drift off to the city as so many were doing. This enterprise was located at some distance from the old house and directly to the east. It lay on higher ground just off a highway paralleling the Albany Post Road. Roosevelt had been buying land in this back country for his tree planting, and Eleanor had been struck with the unspoiled beauty of one site where a small stream opened out into a tree-sheltered pond and blooming weedy flowers filled several nearby fields. They had gone there many times for the picnics they both enjoyed. This was Val-Kill, the Dutch nomenclature of the region. They swam there and spread their food on the grass. The children played games and their father shouted encouragement and reproof. Then, of course, swimming was one of the few activities he could join in with gusto.

8. Edith Bonham Helm, who was social secretary at the White House during the whole Roosevelt tenancy—and the Wilson and Truman tenancies as well—was amused that anyone should think Eleanor Roosevelt's burgeoning was sudden. Mrs. Helm recalled one incident, back in war days, when the energy and initiative, later so well known, were well illustrated. This was the organization and operation of the servicemen's Union Station Canteen in Washington. It was evidently a marvel. She said, in *The Captains and the Kings* (New York: Putnam, 1954), p. 53: "I am always amused when people seem to think that Mrs. Roosevelt sprang suddenly into usefulness, either as the President's wife or as the wife of the Governor of New York. In reality she started her career of usefulness and efficiency years before those days, and added to it as time went on, enlarging her interest in things concerning women and in civic matters with the years."

Val-Kill would never have been begun if Eleanor had felt welcome in the old house. It is interesting that Franklin encouraged her. In fact, later on he built, in the same neighborhood but higher up, a house of his own. He called it "top cottage" and intended it as a retreat for his retirement years.[9] He conceived this plan after it became clear that the old estate was to be a national monument, holding not only all his state papers but his memorabilia as well. In the library there he would have a room—and he planned and furnished that room with loving care—but he would not be able to live in the old house. That would belong to visitors.

Val-Kill could be reached through country lanes; and when the small manually controlled car became available, he often motored along them to watch the work of construction. As a matter of fact he acted as contractor for the building, being dissatisfied with the bids received by the women. He claimed to have saved several thousand dollars too and was as proud of the achievement as of many another far more consequential.

Val-Kill did not prosper. It was one of the futile attempts to re-create a handicraft so many well-meaning amateurs are apt to think practical. It had a blood relationship to a far larger public enterprise of a later time—the Subsistence Homestead movement ridiculed so happily by political enemies in Roosevelt's early presidency. But the significance of the affair at this time did not lie in its practicality or lack of it. The venture represented Eleanor's emancipation and her husband's encouragement of it. He never said to her that he recognized the long injustice of her living among the Roosevelts of Hyde Park—although a Roosevelt herself—on sufferance. He never acknowledged that no home they had lived in had been hers; and that even her children had hardly been her own, what with Sara's interferences and his own tacit acceptance of them. But in these years he made some sort of, perhaps inadequate, reparation.

A historian need not be a psychologist to understand that Val-Kill, and all that went with it, was evidence of a new relationship between husband and wife. She was now in her forties and she would have no more children; she felt in herself capabilities latent until now, or, at most, sporadically used in the years of her sup-

9. He was annoyed with newspapermen who insisted on calling it his "dream house."

pression. She was at the beginning of a career as remarkable in many ways as Roosevelt's. There would be those who would say that it was parasitic, that if he had not been a public figure, she could not have succeeded as a columnist, a radio commentator, a public speaker, a big sister to millions of earnest women. This is true; but she would certainly have had a separate and useful career in any case. She could not have had the large earnings and the wide influence she accumulated if she had not been the wife of a President. But she would have been busy, independent, and self-supporting. She had both the Roosevelt ability and the vigor all of them possessed.

She arrived at Val-Kill by way of the political activities arranged by Louis Howe. She entered on them timidly, as she must, in her unaccustomedness. But presently under his critical but persistent tutelage she was also doing her share of the paper work of local and state politics. At the same time she became a schoolteacher. She was not qualified to teach at a public school of any grade. But because a friend acquired a private girls' school in New York and needed financial help, she was gradually led into not only management but teaching. She was modest about it. Her classes were largely discussion groups centering in current affairs. But for the first time at Todhunter in New York City she found herself listened to—as her own children never had consented to do—and treated, in fact, as a kind of authority.

She worked through several ranges of political service, always finding herself able to win respect and always finding something useful to do. Roosevelt, in 1924, after having failed to accomplish the nomination of Smith, and after having had a part in the reconciliation of the Democratic factions, had charge of one section of the national campaign organization. Eleanor worked in the state campaign. Smith, not running for the presidency, was re-elected to the governorship. She had had a part—if not a considerable one—in his successful campaign. She was on her way to an achievement unique in its own way; and it was even less likely from where she had begun than was her husband's achievement. It is indeed entitled to rate among the traditional success stories of America.

How much she was helped by Louis Howe she freely acknowledged. She may even have yielded him more credit than he ought to have. Still it must be acknowledged to have been gracefully done. In fact the promotion of Eleanor's career was one of Louis' real achievements. It was, at first, no more than part of his own conspiracy to attain vicarious power. Every incident in Louis' life up to a certain point has, however, to be interpreted as part of that conspiracy. He cannot be explained, as a phenomenon, in any other way. There came a change at the time of Roosevelt's illness. After that the matter was more complex. Louis was vulnerable to fondness.

The Roosevelt-Howe partnership was formed, of course, in Albany, when Roosevelt was enlarging his state senatorship into something larger, and Louis was looking on. There and then the worldy wise reporter had adopted young Roosevelt as the engine of his frustrated ambition. Few historic relationships among public figures have come to so appropriate a consummation.

He may have earned his living at that time by working for a metropolitan newspaper, but actually he was a small-town boy.[10] He was disillusioned concerning the motives of those who controlled the legislators for their own purposes. The conspiracy to exploit the common folk for the benefit of the few who knew how to get and manage the power of the state had generated in him a kind of unresting rage. He was a child of the muckrakers' era. The indignation of such investigators as Lincoln Steffens, Ida M. Tarbell, Brand Whitlock, and Ray Stannard Baker at social injustice, embodied in a remarkably evocative literature, had made radicals of many others less voluble than they; and Louis Howe was one of these. His indignation was not expressed, as Steffens' had been, for instance, in exposures of corruption. Until 1911, in fact, it had not been expressed at all. It had merely made him another completely disillusioned reporter. He had had no part in the muckrakers' campaign; but he felt all their resentment and shared their wish for retribution even when an accompanying realism told them how unlikely it was in contemporary circumstances.

Howe was older than Roosevelt by eleven years; and he was completely different in a number of ways. Those who attempt to describe him usually fall back on "gnome-like" as a descriptive

10. His father had had a newspaper in Saratoga.

phrase. If he had been one of the seven dwarfs, he would have been the one called Grumpy. He had a round head with wispy hair set on a scrawny neck. And this turkey neck rose from a bony body more appropriate to a preadolescent boy than to a mature man. It was as though progress toward adulthood had been arrested along in the early teens and a kind of withering process had set in. How this frame contrasted with the handsome and well-articulated young politician can be imagined.

He was an utterly unattractive person. It cannot honestly be said that he was a very wise person either. The advices he would have had Roosevelt follow were seldom statesmanlike, seldom conceived, that is, in the grand manner required for public policy. His usefulness was rather negative, so far as commitments were concerned. He was forever arguing vehemently against something Roosevelt intended to say or do. This, however, may have been a contribution, because Roosevelt's ebullience and energy were continually flowing toward projects of a weird or grandiose sort much better not undertaken. The picture of Louis that presents him as a Warwick, whispering wise advice into his principal's ear, is a mistaken one.

What he did do, and what he must have credit for, was to sustain Roosevelt through the most difficult years of his career with such an unwavering devotion as has to be studied to be believed. No task was too menial for him to undertake, none was too disagreeable for him to see through, none was of such consequence that he would not tackle it with complete assurance. He always was certain that he knew the best thing to do; and he was never more sure than when he was most mistaken.

It has to be recalled that Howe, by 1925, had behind him fifteen years of faithfulness to his hero's cause and that the trials of that faithfulness had been such as to confirm its strength. What would happen from here on he would share in, the share being understood between himself and Roosevelt. He would be in the background; but he would be entitled to a say. He would be First Political Representative; but the direction would be Roosevelt's own. This was a reversal of the original Howe intention. What that intention was, and how the change came about, is in itself a fascinating story. It can be only briefly outlined here.

Roosevelt had leased a house on State Street in Albany in the winter of 1911, and it became the center command post for resistance to Tammany's nomination of "Blue-eyed Billy" Sheehan for United States senator. It was during this incident that Howe took his resolution to set up Roosevelt as a contender for future preferment. He had been watching Roosevelt's behavior in the State Senate for some time with mixed amusement and amazement, and had come to the conclusion that the young man was a genuine political prodigy. His ingrained cynicism was overcome by an irrestible dream of a vicarious career. It was Howe taking the lead, with other reporters following, who created the myth that the anti-Sheehan conspiracy was conceived and directed by Roosevelt, and who consequently conferred on him a dignity of leadership he did not actually deserve.

In this sense Howe gave Roosevelt his start in political life. At least he helped greatly. And the resolution he had already taken, that Roosevelt should realize the ambitions and satisfy the urges he himself, because of personal handicaps, was incapable of achieving, was in a preliminary but convincing way confirmed. Roosevelt would punish the corrupters of political life, he would bring substantial justice into men's relations; he would reach for, and with Howe's assistance finally capture, the positions of power whose occupant could accomplish these results. The more Howe observed, the more certain he was that his instrument was fortunately chosen. Young Roosevelt was personable; he was ambitious; he had at least some political sense. His energies needed to be channeled, his mistakes needed to be warded off; but his likelihood of success seemed to Howe—an inveterate gambler—worth betting on. It was a good bet.

Roosevelt did not feel any desperate need of assistance. He gave Howe a careless but growing affection. He allowed him to do the drudgery he himself did not fancy. When Howe reproved him Roosevelt listened with an air of amused tolerance; but he allowed the familiarities Howe needed. Presently he had real cause to be grateful. That was when, in 1912, after his activities at the Baltimore Convention, where Wilson was nominated for the presidency, he was stricken with typhoid. After Howe ran and won the campaign of that fall for reelection to the State Senate, he was sealed to Roosevelt's side.

When Roosevelt became assistant secretary of the navy, Howe went to work in an adjoining office as his handyman, laboring over routines while Roosevelt occupied himself in more glamorous affairs. He assisted in, and probably originated, two of the important career decisions of the navy years—a reconciliation with Tammany, and a rapprochement with labor made possible by the navy's war work. What he thought of some other of Roosevelt's attitudes and activities can only be guessed. Whether he approved the imitating of Uncle Ted's big-navy imperialism and the generally tall talk of the prewar years is not known. Most likely he viewed them with characteristic tolerance as evidences of immaturity.

Howe was so concentrated on Roosevelt, and so jealous of anyone else who came near him, that he prevented others of first-rate ability from becoming helpers; he was responsible therefore for Roosevelt's series of inferior assistants who were kept throughout his novitiate and into the presidencey. When Roosevelt ran for vice-president Howe was somewhat neglected because he was still a Navy Department employee. There was, it seems, some feeling on his part that he was no longer wanted. The managers of that campaign did not, in fact, include Louis. Still, when he heard in 1921 that Roosevelt had been stricken, he dropped his plan to start out on his own in a new job and came hastily to Campobello.

He managed the extremely delicate public relations of the convalescence; and presently he had Roosevelt back in the running. This was the second great crisis of his life. His old association with Roosevelt had been based on the conception he had had in Albany of a surrogate for his own ambitions. His new one had its source in the love and loyalty he felt at seeing his handsome hero lying helpless and alone with his dreams crumbling about him. This had the curious and paradoxical effect of bringing Howe to accept a secondary role. Roosevelt was no longer a puppet to be manipulated; he was a loved object to be treated with tenderness. He was so strong in his weakness that Howe, from then on, accepted with meekness the impositions of the other's leadership. From pusher he became follower.

From his invalidism Roosevelt gained courage, wisdom, and strength; but the two effective allies he gained as well were immense assets. If neither Howe nor Eleanor had statesmanlike conceptions, both were quite content in secondary roles. If they had something less than first-rate analytical abilities, Howe had cunning and Eleanor had generosity. Either or both of these qualities could and did produce some fantastic mistakes; on the other hand, both could be useful—the one in political in-fighting such as went on in 1932, and the other in creating a reputation for liberalism. Howe would engage in maneuvers he would rather no one else—including Roosevelt—heard about; Eleanor would occupy positions far in advance of her husband on the reform front.

In the long run this kind of thing would gain for Roosevelt a reputation for deviousness. There would be those who would claim to have supported him mistakenly; they were politicians who should have known better. His performance was that of a professional office seeker; and professional office seekers take hard positions only on issues when there is more to gain than to lose. The approved technique is to take no position likely to lose votes and to modify this rule only in extremity—that is, when more votes are to be lost by keeping silent than by speaking.

In the twenties Roosevelt, whatever else had happened to him, had learned much about politics. He had had lessons in the classic rules. No one any more had to tell him what they were; no one could say—or can yet say—how he became so skilled in their use. The best bet is that this was his special talent. Watching and practice had developed it, but originally it had been a gift. He was the most skilled master of the political arts, perhaps, since Lincoln; but no one knew it yet—except some of the lesser professionals who worked with him. But they too were close-mouthed about the art. The only way we know how they respected him is by their judgment that he would win, when put to it, against the toughest kind of opposition.

Howe is said to have remarked, later on, when the spectacularly successful campaigning of the first nomination and election came under surprised historical scrutiny: "You don't play around with high politics without having the Presidency in mind."[11] And Roosevelt himself, when it was about all over so far as he was concerned, spoke of the presidency as having been the controlling

11. Quoted in Lela Stiles, *The Man behind Roosevelt* (New York, 1954).

guide to all his career. On occasion he had admitted as much before, but only in strict confidence.

This is said here to suggest the necessary explanation for his behavior even in these out-of-office years. He was as careful about offending any considerable constituency—even prospectively, since he was not asking now for votes—as he was in his most active days. Anything he advocated now might return to torment him when he went into action again. This was true of the hot issue of prohibition. Later on he would, to his annoyance, be forced to choose; but he avoided it as long as possible. No one knew just how far he would go in another delicate matter—the regulation of business. He let it be supposed that he followed Smith in this; but he made no commitment. Concerning the League of Nations, he was an advocate in 1920; but after that he seemed to lose interest. Even an isolationist could have voted for him in the twenties.

But if this caginess is part of the professional's stock of cultivated traits, it is also part of that stock to possess a few conspicuous identifying issues. When he was unexpectedly faced with the necessity of making a campaign for the governorship in 1928, it was clear enough that for years he had been considering what his positive fighting issues ought to be. Without hesitation he brought out the carefully selected items of this program—with public power leading. An advocate of public power must be many other things, the inference would run; he would not need to elaborate. Actually he would not spread himself very widely and so would not have many repudiations to make. There might be inferences; but not hard positions. That was the rule, and he followed it.

The fallow years allowed him to mature. The campaigner who emerged from them when the time for action came again was very different from the unseasoned vice-presidential candidate of 1920. He had developed an ease with public affairs not all evident before. It must not be forgotten that in addition to the summoning of courage to meet the problems of his crippling, there had been much enforced leisure, spent in occupations he had not previously thought agreeable. He had never been much of a reader and certainly nothing of a scholar. He had had antiquarian interests, but they had not run deep. And he had never to any extent used his hands. It was now that he began his extensive reading. The start he had made at Harvard furnished a useful background, and he even went so far on several occasions as to begin historical works of his own. He lacked any real urge, and he had no literary talent, so none of them came to anything; but fragmentary as they are, they show that he had novel notions about exposition.

His antiquarianism was a real resource. He became historian for the town of Hyde Park, and this filled many hours with pleasant activity. Olin Dows speaks of this: "His conversation was full of personal and historical reminiscences, as well as facts and stories about local history . . . He talked about Jefferson as if the third President had been one of his grandfathers. He felt the past of the United States, as well as that of Dutchess County, as if it were his own immediate past."[12] Dows notes also that in 1923 Roosevelt purchased the original Minutes of the *Council of Appointment of New York at Poughkeepsie in 1778-1779,* and that, by arrangement with the New York Historical Society, he published it in a limited edition. He also helped to publish, as part of the collection of the Dutchess County Historical Society, *The Records of the Town of Hyde Park,* edited by himself. Then, too, he edited, for the society's Year Book, *Vessels of Fishkill during the Revolution.*

It was in September of 1927 that the Historical Society met on the Springwood lawn. On that occasion, Roosevelt addressed the society on the Hyde Park patent of 1697, and the "Great Nine Partners Patent." He also spoke of the meaning, in the development of a community, of the ownership of land in fee simple. The entry in the *Record* is ambiguous. It is to be doubted, however, if his collectivist ideas extended to the ownership of land. More probably he was expatiating on the virtues of private ownership, no doubt to the thorough approval of his hearers.

Others than Mr. Dows have noticed this self-rooting in history. Archibald MacLeish thought it of first importance. It was much later, of course, that MacLeish said of him that he "approached the culture of Americans as he approached their political life and their social and economic institutions, as an historian, or, rather, as a political leader whose intellectual preoccupation was history."

12. *Franklin D. Roosevelt at Hyde Park,* p. 112. Dows also speaks of his narrower historical interests. Concerning these same fallow years, he says: "he and Miss Helen W. Reynolds, the most active member of the Dutchess County Historical Society (which he had joined on its founding in 1914) drove all over the County examining tombstones and records, locating historic sites, discovering and visiting old houses."

The significance of this to MacLeish, who certainly knew Roosevelt, as President, very well, was that "the sense of history in a political leader is a sense of the past as the past has meaning for the future. The sense of posterity is a presence in the earth. And to any man who feels it, learning and the arts are continuing realities."[13]

The evidence that Roosevelt was learning something more from his historical study than lessons from architecture and the arts is, however, ample. It was the future President speaking, with a strong voice, who said to the graduating class at Milton Academy in 1926: "Unrest in this world of ours is caused as much by those who fear changes as by those who seek revolution; and unrest in any nation or in any organization, whether it be caused by ultra-conservatism or by extreme radicalism, is in the long run a healthy sign. In government, in science, in industry, in the arts, inaction and apathy are the most potent foes."

It was in 1926 that the expanded Warm Springs investment began. Neither Eleanor nor Howe approved; and they approved less and less as Roosevelt's interest became more and more engaged. When he decided on complete reconstruction of the place as a rehabilitation center, they were aghast; but there was no stopping him. Their concern was somewhat modified by the knowledge that to be happy, he must always be engaged in some active enterprise. As it happened, the Warm Springs involvement was deepest just when the Smith forces demanded that he run for the governorship, and John J. Raskob's financial assistance for Warm Springs helped to persuade him that he was not abandoning the work there. This would later return to annoy him. It was said that the Foundation's affairs had been in doubtful shape and that Raskob's help had been a kind of bailing out—but this sort of sniping he took as one of the penalities of politics. It did not really matter.

Psychologically, aside from the satisfaction of creating something—satisfying his builder's instinct—Warm Springs fed an equally deep philanthropic urge. More than anything else in his career, except the vast social security system, Warm Springs, we can believe, gave him the satisfaction of service to the disadvantaged. Those who had the privilege never forgot the experience of joining in one of the Warm Springs occasions, once the center had

13. *The New Republic,* April 15, 1946.

attained some size. Polio's cruel crippling helplessness was, to one or another degree, at least mitigated by the Warm Springs regimen. Roosevelt himself, spending hours at his exercises, frequently worked with other patients, and played with them in the big pool such games as he could devise. In the evening he sometimes dined in the great hall—on Thanksgiving he always carved a turkey or two—and joined lustily in the boisterous singing. He made cheerfulness part of the cure. It was agonizing for outsiders to watch. They kept thinking of the solitary nights each patient must face alone with his ruined dreams. But no one could say that human experience was not made measurably more happy because Warm Springs had been created out of a dilapidated Southern resort.

How well this institutional effort accorded with his religious responsibility is easily understood. There he was able to turn his own search for health into a joint enterprise with others; he could have the satisfaction of knowing that human suffering was eased because of his effort. The student can hardly escape the obvious inference that he was following in the Master's way by ministering to the halt and the lame, the ill and the heavily burdened. The suggestion has been unkindly made that in his own regard the comparison was closer than that. I have heard psychologists invoke the rubric of identification. They suggest not only that he was doing good to others because of this identification, but that his unconscious assuming of the benign fatherly attitude in the circumstances both of Hyde Park and Warm Springs has a significance of sinister importance. But of how many others could the same thing not be said? Where does any of the kindness in this world originate?

It is of course true that the pater familias atmosphere, whether deliberate or not, was as noticeable at Warm Springs as everywhere else within the Roosevelt ambit. He dominated every company; he was the center of every circle. It was he who carved the turkey, never anyone else. He told the stories—without bothering over details, or being carefully accurate, a matter his detractors also tried to make something of. There was, at Warm Springs, no competition, as there was not at Hyde Park.

Many invalids manage to occupy the center of attention. They mostly do it by trading on their helplessness, knowing that all normal people have a tendency to submit. They are apt to become demanding and peevish, and are a nuisance to themselves and to others. Roosevelt used his crippled condition in another way. Everyone must accept it as a condition of association with him; but he asked everyone to regard him as having been merely somewhat handicapped. His life was extremely circumscribed; yet it seemed not to be. He had his home and acres at Hyde Park; he had his house in New York with a business and a law practice;[14] and he had interests in Warm Springs, including not only the work of rehabilitation but the farm and some active conservation work, supplementary to the very different sort going on at Hyde Park. For a man whose legs were completely useless and who felt compelled to spend a considerable share of every day actively trying to overcome this paralysis, his interests and activities seemed very spacious indeed.

In a way they were. They did hold his attention and fill the hours. They did, also, satisfy his urgent need to be building, to be doing something for others, and to be the center of his active circle; but all this was not his real business on this earth. There was no hour when he did not know that this was so, no hour when he did not govern himself appropriately for participation in public affairs. In his most relaxed moments—organizing miniature sailboat regattas on the Hudson, for which he carved out the hulls and contrived the rigs himself, or presiding over ceremonial occasions among the patients at Warm Springs—what he said and what he did was entirely congruous with a larger destiny.

It was not apparent in the fallow years how that destiny was to arrive. It seemed sometimes to be discouragingly remote. The years of Hoover's first term (1928-32) were those of Republicanism's most apparent success. Free enterprise was accepted; dissent was confined to a few crack-pot radicals and groups of skeptical intellectuals. It was certainly not apparent that disaster was so soon to overtake the system. Neither Roosevelt nor Howe thought it was any use to anticipate a break before 1936, when, if affairs took their normal course, Hoover would have finished his second term and a Democrat might have a chance.

14. In 1924 the firm of Roosevelt and O'Connor was formed. Roosevelt became inactive, of course, when he became Governor. Basil (Doc) O'Connor became a lifelong supporter and an extremely useful one in his work for the Red Cross and for the National Foundation for Infantile Paralysis. Progress toward the conquest of that disease must have been such a satisfaction as few human beings experience in their lifetimes.

No one loved Hoover; but everyone—or nearly everyone—respected him. He was not a toady to business as Coolidge had been; he was more its best representative, its better embodiment. He was an administrator of note as well as a humanitarian—of a cold and withdrawn sort, perhaps, but with enormous prestige. There is reason to suspect that Hoover's confidence in Republican prosperity was less than was generally known, but he certainly had no actual foreknowledge of what was about to occur. A debacle was in preparation and it would reverse the roles of Hoover and Roosevelt, but neither knew it. Hoover would be retired to the sourish unhappiness of inaction; Roosevelt would assume a responsibility greater than any President had had to assume since the crisis of Southern secession; but until it was upon them neither was aware of its approach.

All the strength resulting from the tough regimen of convalescence would be useful then; and all the study, reflection, and slow maturing would be useful in meeting the nation's need. One of the problems historians must meet—with very little chance, I think, of finding an answer—is at what time he emerged, in his own mind, from putative president into something more esoteric and difficult to define, but best described perhaps as rescuer of the American people from disaster. Speaking thusly, I am afraid of being misunderstood. There is no reason why any American should not point his career toward the presidency; and certainly many have done so—more than anyone knows about—who failed, as luck and their abilities determined, close to or far from ultimate success. Their impulses were the same as those of the successful; and their methods were not different even though less effective. So the disparagement of those who got there is inappropriate. It is especially so because we are a democracy, one professing to offer equality of opportunity even if the profession sometimes seems empty.

The qualifications for the presidency under the Constitution are simple. Nothing said there should discourage any natural born citizen from putting that office at the climax of his ambitions. But a sense of realism indicates that only a few have the qualifications, with the requisite talents, and with the luck to succeed. Only a very few come to regard themselves as in a way appointed and so required to sacrifice much else and to center their energies on this one end. We now see, I think, that Roosevelt as early as his first legal employment in the law office of Carter, Ledyard, and Milburn—before 1910—regarded himself as one of the few, not yet appointed but with an exceptional opportunity waiting to be exploited. Later on, perhaps when he began to see himself as the nation's most eligible Democrat, with his party's turn sure to come, the sense of appointment grew on him. Still later, as the economic crisis shaped up, and he began to plumb its depths and complexities, he came to feel, I believe, that not only would he become president but a national leader who must lead his countrymen out of crisis into a regime of fellowship and justice such as had been dreamed of for many centuries but never realized.

He probably was assailed by doubts. It must have occurred to him that he could be mistaken and that at some point he might be deserted by the Providence guiding his career. If he was so assailed, he met the crises of doubt alone with his God. No one was ever able to recall in him anything but confidence and serenity. He was steadily, almost gaily, going forward to his destiny. If that required of him the overcoming by almost superhuman persistence and cruel effort the trial put upon him by one of the most terrible of diseases, that was an ordeal he must come through. When he saw that he was coming through—then, I think, his sense of appointment was confirmed. About the rest, the acceptance by party leaders and his fellow citizens, he had few doubts.

3

THE SOURCES

OF ROOSEVELT'S REFORMISM

The influences affecting Roosevelt as he grew up and matured have to be found in the environment of his time as well as in his family's management of his life. That these influences would be important was guaranteed by the course of his education. It was the best that could be had and it brought to him the whole of the tradition most valued by the elite of Groton, Harvard, and the legal profession. To understand these influences it is necessary to examine cultural history; and a good place to begin is the evolution of the city.

It could be seen from L'Enfant's design for Washington that the European traditions were in his mind; it was to be a city built for a purpose, and eventually would have the same cultural accumulations. L'Enfant's was not the only urban scheme produced in eighteenth century America. "The Renaissance" as Elbert Peets has said, "still lived in the cultural air . . . Plans of Philadelphia, Reading, Savannah, and Williamsburg can be printed alongside plans of Charleroi, the town of Versailles, Bloomsbury, and Edinburgh. The average statesman or the average architect of 1790 was better prepared by education and experience to find meaning in L'Enfant's plan than were the average statesman and architect of 1890."[1]

What had happened in that century? The answer is that planning

NOTE. This essay appeared in *Ethics*, volume 64, number 4 (July 1954). Copyright 1954 by the University of Chicago. Reprinted by permission of the University of Chicago Press.

1. Werner Hegemann, *City Planning: Housing*, ed. Ruth Nanda Anshen, with a preface by Joseph Hudnut and a chapter by Elbert Peets (New York: Architectural Book Publishing Co., 1936-38), vol. II.

cannot be done without objectives and that American cities had grown with minimum provision for corporate activity. What is meant can be understood by examining the 1811 design for New York's streets. It was, in the first place, done by "the Commissioners of Streets and Roads." This in itself shows that by then the public control of civic functions had been reduced to provision for access to property. The uses of this property were not to be determined by the commissioners; and there was no assumption that there ought in future to be limits on land speculation or rules for its development. There was merely a minimum physical design to guide it; and this was extensible.

Even with so limited a scheme, however, some justification for the simple gridiron plan had to be made. So the commissioners did consider "whether they should confine themselves to rectilinear and rectangular streets or whether they should adopt some of those supposed improvements by circles, ovals and stars which certainly embellish a plan whatever may be their effect as to convenience and utility." This last was, of course, an engineer's fling at a fancy creation. But those "circles, ovals and stars" of L'Enfant in Washington did not have only to do with beauty or even only with the management of traffic. They were signs on the drawing board of civic objectives in people's minds—where there should be residences, markets, and service establishments; what their size and functions should be; how, in other words, the relations of citizens should be arranged. But the map of New York represented an abdication of public authority. L'Enfant lost out. From 1800 on the enlarging American city sprawled across the countryside completely at the mercy of its internal enemies and entirely unconfined by any design.

It is true that the New York commissioners, for instance, were unable to remain wholly uncontaminated by social responsibility. They did set aside areas for a parade ground, a reservoir, and a public market; they were even a little apologetic, saying that it might to many "be a matter of surprise that so few vacant spaces have been left and those so small." But the rivers on either side really made parks unnecessary; furthermore, the price of land was high and prudence was called for.[2] They would have felt

2. Report and map signed and sealed by Simon DeWitt, in the presence of Gouverneur Morris, March 22, 1811.

themselves justified by history, too. For city planning from then on was to be confined to routine civil engineering.[3]

Typical American progressivism—and Roosevelt was from his first public appearance a progressive—seems always to have been rooted in country soil. Why was it that during the nineteenth century the ills of the farmers bred creative discontents, but those of urban workers were so late in reaching the stage of reform? The answer must have something to do with the decline of the city. Beginning in the nineteenth century, it suffered the impact of many technical changes. Its neighborhoods were destroyed by transit lines. There was a gradual division into working, dormitory, and amusement sections, facilitated by the telephone, the automobile, and such public works as bridges and tunnels. Besides, the gross growth was overwhelming. It was not unusual for population to double itself in several successive decades. At the end of the century a number of metropolitan areas had populations as great as that of the entire continent at is beginning. All this induced hasty extension of buildings and public services, producing, finally, congested urban jungles.

By 1870 the density of population in several representative wards of New York was much greater than that of corresponding ones in London.[4] Out of those English slums came real reforms. Out of New York's, there came no corresponding movement. There were riots at widely spaced intervals, such as that desperate one during the Civil War brought on by the unequal application of the draft for military service and by the flagrant profiteering of merchants; and there were strikes—sometimes almost civil wars; but the Interstate Commerce Act, the Anti-Trust Act and its successive amendments, and other such national achievements of progressivism were put through by representatives of rural not of urban areas. There was little relief for crowded workers until the twentieth century was well under way, and then state not national legislation provided the reforms.

The cities were too preoccupied with their own ills, and the frustration of all attempts to cure them, to have much interest in national problems; but the sufferings of the workers could no

3. Compare Washington's idea in *City Planning: Housing,* vol. I.
4. *Ibid.,* p. 111.

more be settled at home than could those of the farmers. Rural folk learned this lesson earlier and more thoroughly. They tried state legislation, conspicuously in Wisconsin and the Northwest, and found but little relief. They then adjourned to Washington with at least some success. The cities, however, sank into the clutches of their boss-managed machines, and the influence of even the slum-dwellers went toward perpetuating misery rather than relieving it. Only in a few states, and then mostly in the second decade after the turn of the century, were there the beginnings of protective laws concerning conditions of living and of work.

The fact that city folk exerted so little creative influence on progressive national legislation affected its character profoundly. Reform was suited to the desires of small property holders—after the Jeffersonian ideal—rather than to the very different aspirations of the "proletariat." Those aspirations, wherever they developed, were collectivistic as corresponding American movements never were. The idea of an orderly functioning mass to which the individual owed duties of contribution and had rights of receipt adjusted to his needs was as foreign to the American mind as a Gothic tower in an Iowa cornfield. The general idea in the United States was that government activity was something quite apart from that of the individual. Its function was to protect each citizen as he went about his business. Only very reluctantly did Americans come to admit that the rights of each might possibly come into conflict and that some mediation might be necessary, such as only government could do.

This belief that citizens have many rights but few duties was in the sharpest contrast with the competing belief in many duties but few rights developed wherever Western civilization had an urban cast. The corollaries to this were laissez faire as against collectivism, and growth carried out at the will of those who expected to gain by speculating in it as against planning for civic amenity and for conservation.

The implications of the American attitude could not be seen in all their vividness until after the Civil War, when the intensified industrialism of the war years was released into the uses of peace. There were indications that Lincoln, in the midst of his troubles, had some wonder. But the act of most consequence in his time was the passage of the Homestead Act of 1862. It determined that the small landholders would be the most powerful political force in the land for many decades. This situation was reinforced by the multiplication of states. The new states, because of soil and climate, were bound to be sparsely populated and rural; yet they would have equal representation in the Senate. If the Connecticut Compromise, so called, had not been agreed on at Philadelphia in 1787 and if the Homestead Act had not been passed in 1862, Americans might possibly have developed some variety of collective government. The thousand arid miles to the east of the Rockies might have been preserved as pasture land; and the settlement of workers' problems might not have been delayed until the miseries of city life had grown intolerable.

The cult of feeble government, shaped in the eighteenth century struggles for political rights, survived into the period when the threat to liberties came rather from industrial than from political despotisms. What had been originally a check on potential invasions of rights later became a barrier to the use of the only instrument capable of defending them. It was a wide barrier too, with deep foundations in history; and the legal defenders of capitalism had only to maintain a certain vigilance—as, on the bench and at the bar, it was greatly in their interest to do. They were so successful that the last President before the great depression was moved to deprecate "federal interference" with business. Indeed the party he represented would soon become officially committed to the renewal of states' rights as a move away from government control of the business system, thus reversing its position on this issue. But as a matter of fact this was not a party issue. Neither Republicans nor Democrats believed in government interference except in their progressive interludes; and even then interference was for the purpose of restoring "free" competition.

This attitude was especially marked in municipal affairs. During the nineteenth century a junction of ideas and events was devastating in its cumulative effect. Many industries grew quite beyond the possibility of local control, since it was more and more a matter of indifference where they were located, and rigorous regulation simply led to migration. In any case, attempts to regulate were becoming more and more foreign to American ideology. Rights once belonging to individuals were now being conferred on corporations. That individuals and corporations could not simultaneously possess them was merely a disagreeable minority opinion and no attention was paid to it. What belonged to government and what to business came more and more to be defined by enterprisers. They developed the services and furnished the goods needed by people; and they took over the revenues, too. Where it was necessary they devoted some of this to the systematic corruption of officials or to the installation of puppets. There ensued that period in city life documented so thoroughly just at the beginning of the twentieth century by the muckrakers.

These were individuals who, like the elder La Follette, believed in the system of business enterprise but saw it as having been corrupted. They were indignant when aldermen sold a franchise for a street railway or when the police accepted fees for permitting gambling houses to operate. They traced the history of treasury-looting from the outright stealing of the early and middle years, when methods were crude, to the later hidden manipulation of contracts and the merely biased management of city finance difficult for even the most ardent reformer to uncover. The most thoughtful of this group missed the conclusions obvious to later students—that business and government had become in many aspects indistinguishable; that it was false to set up dividing lines between the two and to call one function private and the other public; and that this was mostly done to secure immunity from inspection and regulation.

Industry grew so rapidly that such a distinction came to have less and less meaning in municipal settings, yet the cities were grossly affected when their legislatures or their executives were subverted. Transit, gas, and electric services were plundered, however, without much dispute, except as to who should get the yield. This was because they had their fastest growth at the apogee of bossism. Exposures of corruption caused momentary indignation and even led, in some cases, to formidable movements for public ownership, sometimes faked for blackmail purposes, but sometimes also really reformist.

The city reformers were not men of their own time at all. They belonged back in the Middle Ages or forward in some new regionalized era. They still considered that the city had objectives, whereas actually it had become merely the creature of entities without public objectives.[5] Business was running industry. Nothing could be more natural than that it should run government too. The appearance of Mark Hanna, a businessman-politician, on the national scene was not more smoothly accomplished than that of Charles (Boss) Murphy in New York, William (Fingy) Connors in Buffalo, and others of their sort. There came a time when city government was almost reduced to a ceremonial survival. In some places, like New York, even the police functions had had to be taken away by the state. Reformers were confused by an apparent functioning much like the physical life of a mentally ill individual. They always looked for the giant to throw off its chains; but the trouble was in the giant's blood; the time for reform had passed. Only reconstruction could be of any use. And the barriers to this in American ideology remained firmly fixed.

The city reformers who tried to revive a distinction between the sphere of government and that of business were attempting the impossible. The causes of the merging were not, as the reformers supposed at first, merely surface phenomena.

It was not the fault of the reformers that they took contemporary standards too literally. They assumed that the talk of preachers and teachers was a guide to conduct. This was devastating. The going conventions required that one sort of morality should be professed but that another should be followed. There are particularly good openings for reformers at such moments in history as the beginning of the twentieth century. Throughout Lincoln Steffens' reporting, he kept coming upon corrupt relations between government and what he called "Big Business." This monster bought franchises, bribed officials, swung elections, supported racketeers, and made alliances with bosses and their machines. The total effect was a change in the locus of power over economic matters from the electorate and its representatives to businessmen. Legislators submitted to an un-

5. Said F. C. Howe, *Confessions of a Reformer* (New York: Scribner, 1925), p. 113: "The possibility of a free, orderly, and beautiful city became to me an absorbing passion." Howe was starry-eyed; so was his mayor, Tom Johnson. How quickly the city of Cleveland reverted to type after Howe and Johnson were gone shows the strength of the competing forces.

official and hidden direction. This, to the reformers, was the perversion of an ideal; and they made it the center of their attack.

Such occurrences in democracies respond slowly to the impact of outside changes. But, recognized or not, the change happens. The tides cannot be kept back with a broom—or with a stubborn wish. They can at best be ignored for the time being. The American electorate no doubt wished business to remain small and uncoordinated; people wanted to believe that prices were adequately controlled by competition; they wanted enterprise— and even speculation—to be free because they expected, even if only in a small way, to join in and to profit by such ventures. If they had been asked, they would doubtless have said also that the cities were getting too big and that people lived better in the country. The bright lights were symbols of sin; and corruption was natural to such an environment. People not only respected rural values; they professed still to have them.[6] They pretended that the

6. Roosevelt felt very strongly that this was so—a feeling which was to have more serious consequences than most men's feelings have. In February 1911, when he was a state senator in New York, he journeyed to New York City to address the Columbia County Society and was interviewed by Virginia Tyler Hudson of the New York *Globe* (the interview was published in that paper on February 6, 1911). Part of what he said was the following:

"I fully believe we will have direct nomination before long and I would like to see us have the recall too; but I do not believe New York is ready for that yet . . .

"I believe a new spirit is abroad in the land today—at least we call it new; but it is really nothing more than a return to the old idea of representative government. It is up to every man who thinks and reasons, who holds the good of his country and his fellow countrymen, at least to see that this spirit is fostered; that the law shall stand for social progress. Education has done much and the enlightening processes which are going forward today, especially in the country districts, will do more. In fact, I might almost say that the political salvation of the country lies with the country men and boys. Not because they are more honest or more patriotic than their brothers in the cities, but because they have more time to think and study for themselves, to know what the country needs, and have the courage to stand for what they know is right in the face of organized opposition with the precedent of years behind it. Of our little band of twenty insurgents, eighteen are from the country. [This refers to the famous insurgency led by young Senator Roosevelt against Tammany's effort to elect "Blue-eyed Billy" Sheehan to the United States Senate which was in process at that time.]

"Another reason that the man from the country makes a better and more honest politician . . . is that people in the country not only have time to think but are willing to think; and their fathers and mothers were thinkers, though they had not the advantages of education and enlightenment . . . possible today . . . The lives of you city people are artificial. You don't breed exactly the same kind of people we breed in the country . . . and no matter how many jokes may be made about the countrymen who sit around the stove in the village post office and settle the affairs of the country, they are not jokes. From just such men who think and argue over national and political matters in their state comes the material that makes our best lawmakers and who in time will see that only the men that will serve the people wholeheartedly and unreservedly will be elected to office."

neighborliness of village life still governed human relations, or if it did not, it ought to, and their list of immoralities was cast in the mold of this pretense. This refusal to recognize reality was an asset to the practical pirates about whom the muckrakers wrote. They knew what was happening. Reformers would always fail until they went to the root of the matter and that, they saw, was impossible in the prevailing ethical system. Meantime, the pickings were easy.

The result of this general devotion to unreality was the delivery to private interests of virtually all economic functions—that is, all the profitable ones. The cities lay supine, yielding themselves to the looters while their leaders preached and taught the old moralities, usually with subsidies from the exploiters.

Until the cataclysm of 1929 the looting of the cities was amazingly successful; it survived one reform wave after another, and the insiders were seldom embarrassed. Steffens, before he finished, knew that he was dealing with something beyond a reporter's power to explain. He knew, too, that Big Business was only a slipshod name for the enemy. La Follette never succeeded either. To the end he believed that regeneration lay in the freeing of small businessmen and farmers. Steffens was not thus fooled. But he was confused and wholly at a loss. Until just before he finished with critical appraisal, he believed that public functions lay on one side of a line and private ones on the other and that different rules applied to each.

The success of the confusion-makers in piling propaganda on prejudice can be measured by their success in keeping the reformers, until 1929, completely away from the issue they feared most of all. Communist hunts and red-baitings had to be resorted to more frequently than was desirable or genuinely effective in the later years; but still the success was tolerable. The vast mass of people regarded city government as an ineffective—when not inevitably debauched—instrument for serving them. It had usually to be trusted with fire protection and the maintenance of streets. Such functions had never been reached for seriously by private interests for reasons of their own;[7] but beyond these duties city government was not to be trusted.

7. Even here reservation must be made. Police had been made blind to wrongdoing by graft; fire departments had been paid for favors in the way of easy inspection of dangerous premises; and even the streets were the prey of contractors. Nothing the city

On the other hand the myth concerning the efficiency of private business survived even the depression. This myth had not the slightest substantiation in fact; but the significant thing was precisely that it needed none. The discordant note in the symphony of exploitation came from the country. There was insistence on an antitrust program with mild approval among small businessmen, trade unionists, and, of course, all those who called themselves economists; but this was not sufficiently effective to stifle continuing praise for free enterprise or to modify the alternate hymn of dispraise for government joined in so unanimously by those who profited, those who hoped to, or those who, for moral reasons, believed that others should.

When the income tax became effective this gulling of the public remained a deductible expense by way of institutional advertising. Those who were exploited were thus made to pay for their own exploitation.

These attitudes, as attitudes do, had ways of becoming institutionalized. The orthodox revenue system of the cities sought to avoid burdens on business, and settled on realty taxes. Municipal income therefore had its source in a system of values based on perpetual private property in land; and city officials became the most ardent defenders of real estate speculation. No one who considered the problems associated with planning for city life was blind enough to miss the fact that low values meant better living for citizens; yet mayors and their tax departments felt compelled to combat any change looking to lower prices for the use of property because their taxes might be jeopardized. This particular fixation had more important results than some others. Of all the possible choices between private and public activity—not excepting utilities—the ownership and management of land and the manipulation of its values had perhaps the most disastrous consequences. Yet from the first it was in the United States, in contrast with European cities, reserved rigidly for private exploitation.

What the reformers called corruption was only one result of the

---

possessed was really immune from sale. These safety functions were maintained in public possession largely because no one was willing to trust competitors to manage them, and because it was not, after all, too difficult to arrange matters comfortably with officials.

maladjustments inherent in the changes sweeping over the whole Western world. The beginnings lay far back in scientific and technological discoveries. Social organizations were affected when inventions emerged, as, for instance, electric motors, new materials, scientifically arranged processes, and greatly increased output in agriculture and industry. Ultimately the leaders of business had to manage government to protect their own organizations. They felt no proprietary interest in it; to them it was only a nuisance, being made up of demagogues with their hands out asking to be bribed. If government had been running the railroads, making electric motors, and so on, all this technical change would have forced organizational changes there, just as it did in the United States Steel Corporation or the Standard Oil Company. It is true that city governments, and even state governments, changed somewhat, but belatedly and not greatly, and not in such ways as to make them much more effective. Why should they? They possessed no economic functions. The cities might conceivably have owned and managed at least their land, their utilities, and many of their service industries. If that course had been taken, as it was in Europe, the corruption would not have arisen, since there would have been no need to push contentious officials out of the way, and since government would then have evolved toward service to its citizens.

This possibility was suggested over and over again; but the suggestions fell on deaf ears. Once the concession had been made that everything capable of yielding a profit should be private, the psychological and institutional reinforcements of the system began to enlarge irresistibly. Accepted American principles prevented people from seeing that transit, power, water, and other such services were public and that prices and rates they paid for them were indistinguishable from taxes. They always resented paying for police and fire protection; they formed taxpayers' leagues to keep such charges down, and they supported citizens' committees to enforce economies; but no one thought it necessary to force the electric light company to economize, for no one doubted it was being run as efficiently as possible.

It is true that a "quasi-public" category was set up and commissions appointed to regulate the "utilities." This was done on the ground that they were "natural monopolies" whose prices the market could not be expected to fix. But the most significant end of regulation was not better service and lower rates but more obstruction, more bribery, more corruption. By the time of the great depression, the disillusion of the informed was fairly complete. Industries could not be controlled from outside. Only recognition of their essentially governmental function, laying aside the false distinction between public, quasi-public, and private, would have brought results.

There was one more experiment to be tried—the mixed management device whose national manifestation was the National Recovery Administration (NRA). The idea of mixing government and business was not strictly new, but it was still novel in 1933. The concept had grown directly out of the kind of relations the bosses and businessmen had set up in the cities, the kind that had been so thoroughly exposed by the muckrakers. It would violate all the traditions so usefully brought together in the Federal Trade Commission Act and in the various regulatory commissions of the states and cities. There would be no alternative short of almost universal public ownership if this device failed. But such lessons the reformers had not taught Americans to understand.

Lincoln Steffens was a thoughtful and honest man. His *Autobiography* is the odyssey of a conscience much like those of all good citizens. He was confused and indignant at first, coming gradually in age to tolerance and the certainty of permanent evil. No man did more to reveal Americans to themselves, with all their hypocritical acceptances of necessary corruptions so long as those corruptions were hidden. One time, as he sojourned in Boston, muckraking with E. A. Filene's support, he went to President Eliot of Harvard and asked permission to "give a short course to seniors on 'the forms in which the first steps to bribery and corruption come to young men in all walks of life' " (for one of the things Steffens had discovered was that there was less honesty and more corruption among the good and respectable folk than there was among the reputed crooks). Says Steffens, "he was almost moved to a consideration of my proposition till he happened to ask me what my course would lead up to. 'You would teach those things to stop the doing of them?' he asked. 'Oh, no,' I blurted. 'I don't mean to keep the boys from succeeding in their professions. All I want to do is to make it impossible for them to be crooks and not know it.' That ended me with Mr. Eliot."[8] That was a puzzling experience. Eliot was interested primarily in reform, Steffens in knowledge of evil. But he knew it for evil. And he must have known that identifying it was only the beginning of eradication. Far from wanting to draw industry and government together again, he was still unable to conceive of anything but separation.

Yet close to this passage in his *Autobiography,* another equally characteristic one told of a businessman's inability to escape. It was the president of the New Haven Railroad, who called him in and asked him how he could get himself and his railroad "out of politics."

That is about as far as Steffens got—at least until he had long been done with muckraking. In these passages there is perhaps more of the typical journalist's hatred of humbug than there is of wisdom for the governance of society. But that was all the wisdom he had. Or was it? There were glimpses here and there in his observations of something more profound, nothing connected or systematic, nothing clearly illustrated, a chance phrase or an isolated sentence. But they were fugitive, half exposed.

Would it have been reading something into the reflections of Steffens, Frederick C. Howe, Ray Stannard Baker, Brand Whitlock, and the others whose recollections issued in memoirs to suggest that almost unconsciously they were on the track of something else, and that that something else was an understanding of the phenomena they were preoccupied with throughout their lives? It happened that most of them spent their active younger years either in city reform movements or in close professional observation of them; and that all had later years of leisure for meditation and for writing. It was Howe who made the observation, growing out of his experience with city government, that he believed it to be corrupt because neglected, neglected because unimportant, and unimportant because shut out of those economic affairs closest to people's concern. The logic of this he never pursued; but a formidable later movement toward the public ownership and operation of utilities would indicate that a reestablishment of the city's importance might come by that route,

8. *Autobiography* (New York: Harcourt, Brace, 1931), p. 608.

though not, perhaps, because of a conscious development of reasoned action from his premises.

That movement toward public ownership evolved out of necessity. Traction companies, electric concerns, and other utilities had the best of reasons for growing to be citywide in extent. Those reasons were technical. But the economic advantage from this process was usually dissipated in graft paid for the necessary franchises and for protection. Consumers gained little or nothing. The need for protection where they were most vulnerable forced these organizations to perfect wider and wider combinations with no technical reasons for existence and with overhead organizations of immense size. These city monopolies would ultimately return to the city; Howe's suggestion would in the end resemble prophecy. The good effects of civic care about utility management would spread to other city services as well; but this would be when all the reformers had passed from the scene.

Not only Howe but most others of that early-century group discovered that in struggling with the problems of the city they were at grips with one tentacle—or perhaps two or three—of an octopus whose vitals they could not reach. Sooner or later all of them were led into state or national politics or into consideration of national problems where, they came to feel, the solutions lay. Because the higher-ups kept getting higher up, the real control more remote, the system of holding companies became more and more complex. Stock issues without assets necessitated by overpayment to reluctant members of a potential combine, or by payment to underwriters for the slick work of creating several shares of stock where before there had been only one, were in the end held by innocent investors—the "widows and orphans" for whom so many crocodile tears were shed. The face of elaborate innocence these combines turned to the public, and the protection given them by the press, made it difficult to separate the technical and honest from the financial and dishonest reasons for their expansion.

As time went on these problems were by way of being solved; and who could say that the worrying attacks of reformers had not helped? There were moves toward city ownership of consumer services; but they were not easy moves, accompanied as they were by wails of anguish and hymns of hate for the agents of the evolution. If public ownership always turned up as the long-run solution, it was for reasons Steffens, particularly, seemed to glimpse time after time but never could see wholly and clearly. It was for similar reasons that the NRA would be stopped by the Supreme Court, in the early years of the New Deal, from experimenting with halfway measures. Americans were bound by conventions in these matters and were not willing to believe, even in the midst of depression, that new approaches were necessary.

Roosevelt grew up, of course, without much exposure to such movements for reform. His father, in fact, was one of the participants in the railroad building after the Civil War, and his fortune was based on speculation. Insulated as he was, however, he was taught noblesse by his parents and responsible citizenship at Groton, so that when at Harvard he did read widely, during an added year, under the tutelage of professors who were sufficiently sophisticated, he was quite ready for the lessons. Just at that time too (1904), he was much stirred by the campaign of Theodore Roosevelt for the presidency and understood that progressivism was a reformist movement. Knowing this it seems less strange that a few years later, on becoming a New York state senator, he should at once engage Tammany Hall in a fight and soon after that join Josephus Daniels and Wilson in Washington. From them he absorbed the progressivism being taught by Brandeis in succession to the reformers of the muckraking period.

At Harvard Roosevelt read Steffens and the others of his sort, as well as some more scholarly literature about economic affairs. No more than any of them, however, did he learn the hard lesson that reformism was not enough.

The danger in generalizing about the widespread lodgment of democracy and individual dignity in the minds of Americans was strongly felt by the reformers, but none, because of some fear of this sort, centered on the fact that what had begun as the personal liberty of little enterprisers had ended up as the absolute despotism of the financiers and businessmen who controlled the great combines. The struggle was to be between despotic industry and democratic government. They could not exist peacefully side by side—one or the other had to give way. Roosevelt was slow to discover what others—like Steffens—never discovered. Steffens, for instance, traced the trouble out of the cities through the state capitals to Washington; and he had some bitter words to say about what he found there.[9] Then he was drawn back to business and there discovered a parallel whose fascination was fatal. Big business, he found, was bureaucratic; it was corrupt; its managers were grafters who sold out their stockholders and profited from inside information. From this he came to the sad but tolerant conclusion that he had simply been tracing through all the manifestations of human organization something generated by human nature whenever its power expanded.

He never came to see that government in his time had had its functions emasculated or stolen; that it was corrupted because it had no positive, only obstructive, functions. Business would infiltrate government in some other nations with an ease the muckrakers would all live long enough to see. Their recoil would be instinctive rather than analytical. Their contributions were finished before the Nazis and Fascists had come to power; and before Roosevelt began to struggle with the accumulation of problems in the United States.

Both Whitlock and Howe had been members of reform administrations. Tom Johnson, with whom Howe had worked as a young man in Cleveland, had called his vision of a Cleveland remade the "City on a Hill."[10] This was, perhaps, a sentimental and high-flown idealization. Yet those were days, as we can see now, when a kind of civic romanticism was at work within the sprawling, blowsy, municipal body. There were many signs of it. Lord Bryce had said that if what was fine in America was to survive, there would have to be a revival of city life; he made specific reference to democracy. Tom Johnson, so little understood because he had in his nature a directness disconcerting to those whose conduct was guided by a devious smugness permitting sin without approving it, had made a fortune by corrupting municipal governments. He had then had a kind of conversion from reading Henry George—whose influence was, indeed, immense on all that generation but especially on city reformers,

9. Compare John Chamberlain, *The American Stakes* (New York: Carrick and Evans, 1940), pp. 30.
10. See Howe, *Confessions of a Reformer*, chap. xiii.

because his remedy, the single tax, could so obviously be applied there. Johnson turned on his class, and with this knowledge of business methods and an administrative genius enabling him to provide effective city services even while he seemed to devote all his time to politics and propaganda, had transformed the sodden shame of Cleveland into what for the moment seemed like a movement for regeneration. Jones of Toledo and Pingres of Detroit had preceded him by a little; and even after the defeat and death of these old champions, there still remained in Ohio "the three boy mayors," all reformers: Whitlock of Toledo, Baker of Cleveland, and Hunt of Cincinnati. From the time of Golden Rule Jones on, there was hardly an interval when, in some city, there was not at work one of these evangelistic groups.

They would not have liked to think that posterity would consider them evangels. None of them had many illusions, either about human nature or about the permanence of their reforms. Whitlock, who had two other careers after his experience as mayor—he became ambassador to Belgium during the war, and never gave up being a novelist and biographer—closed the city-service phase of his life with a book called *Forty Years of It*. It was the history of a romantic wrestling with all the ugly problems of those years. "I did not know much about municipal government in those days," he said, "except what I learned in Jones' campaigns . . . But . . . nobody knew much about it except that Bryce had said that it was the most conspicuous failure of the American commonwealth." He went on in this same passage to speak of the contrast between American cities and those of Europe. And on the same page he marveled that Steffens should have seen so clearly what most others had not even the sensitivity to feel: "He went at his task quite in the scientific spirit, isolating first that elementary germ or microbe, the partisan, the man who always voted the straight ticket in municipal elections . . . Then he discovered the foul culture this organism blindly breeds—the political machine, with its boss. But he went on and his quest led him to the public service corporation, the street railway company, the gas company, the electric company, and then his trail led him out into the state, and he produced a series of studies of politics in the American cities which has never been equalled and so had a noble and splendid part in the great awakening of our time."[11]

The members of this group all knew about each other; they were extraordinarily conscious of what they were doing and literate about it too. Being well-read and urbane, they had a remarkable sense of their own unimportance. In this they differed from the preceding generation. Of those older leaders Whitlock said that it was a "peculiar instance of the whimsical and profligate generosity of the fates that the three cities grouped at the end of Lake Erie, like those cities Walt Whitman saw, or thought he saw, 'as sisters with their arms around each other's necks,' should have had at about the same time, such mayors . . . the three men were different in everything but their democracy."

The mayors of Cleveland, Toledo, and Detroit were alike in more than that, as Whitlock would have seen if he had had less interest in literature and more in economics. But economics bored

11. Brand Whitlock, *Forty Years of It* (New York: Appleton, 1914), pp. 162-163. Whitlock furnishes one of the most interesting character studies to be found among American progressives. In the early Toledo days, under the influence of Jones and more remotely of Johnson, he tried to be a man of the people, sharing the luck of the poor, working with and for them, laboring for their political education, sweating over injustices and civic crime. It was a direct and honest man too, who wrote *Forty Years of It.* But when at last there came about a progressive national administration and his friend Baker got him appointed to the Belgian ambassadorship, he became a literary dilettante who distrusted democracy. In the old days Steffens had been an admired friend and adviser. On the Riviera, when he read the *Autobiography,* he dismissed it in a letter with no more than a comment on the "poor writing." Allan Nevins, Whitlock's editor, quoted the observations of one who visited Whitlock after he had been a few years in Europe: "In default of an economic philosophy he was apparently devoting himself to living, in a very debonair way. He had some beautiful dogs. His house was filled with honors from the Belgian government. About his tables were members of the aristocarcy . . . I saw him next some years later at an hotel on the Riviera. He was scrupulously dressed; careful in his habits; detached in his emotions . . . Living was a thing to be finished off in a refined, artistic . . . way, possibly unsoiled by what was going on without."

It was perhaps ironical that the great depression should have shaken his detachment by threatening his inherited income. There was, as Nevins remarked, much truth in what Eugene Wood wrote Whitlock just after the election of 1909. "My dear friend—I wish I could say comrade—the axe must be laid at the foot of the tree, not at offending limbs." And Nevins went on to say: "The progressive movement, of which Whitlock was a part, was never really a radical movement; it never got at the root of the matter." (*Letters and Journals of Brand Whitlock,* ed. Allan Nevins, New York: D. Appleton-Century, 1936, Introduction, p. xlvi.)

Whitlock died in the English hospital at Cannes, in May of 1934. The Provençal spring he loved was in full rush, the nightingales he wrote of so often to Albert Bigelow Paine were mating; he was a long way from the cold, unfriendly wind which comes across Lake Erie and seems to intensify all the problems the reformers (even the reformers who scorned reformers) left unsolved in Toledo.

the reformers, and because it did, they oversimplified it for themselves and for their constituents. Yet they knew that an economic problem lay at the heart of the evil they faced. They realized sadly, sometimes, that at best with their equipment they could do little in their time.

When Golden Rule Jones died, Whitlock himself observed that the best tribute his friend's memory received was not the lamentations of those he had befriended; it was that the stock of the street railway company went up twenty-four points next morning. So great was the dependence of the reform movement on the appearance of a strong personality from time to time! This was, of course, only partly because it required a strong-minded man to resist the moral reformers and center attention on more fundamental needs.[12] It was more because the system was weighted against government and in favor of business. Even a strong-minded man could not prevail in such circumstances.

The corporations, whose lawyers perverted the Fourteenth Amendment as well as the Fifth, and gained virtual immunity from national as well as state regulation, were not likely to be checked by so small an annoyance as a city. Nevertheless, because the city was a natural unit for some industries—such as utilities— and because the exploitation of consumers somehow seemed more

12. The division in the city would be as close as we would come—at least down to the depression—to division into classes. Both Whitlock and Howe spoke of that. The following is from Howe: "Before the expiration of the first two years of Mr. Johnson's term of mayoralty the city was divided into two camps along clearly defined economic lines. There was bitterness, hatred, abuse. Also social ostracism and business boycott. The press was unscrupulous in its attacks. On the one side were men of property and influence; on the other politicians, immigrants, workers, and persons of small means. This line of cleavage continued to the end. And I was not on the side where I would have chosen to be. The struggle brought me into conflict with friends, clients, my class . . . I suffered from the gibes of men with whom I had once been intimate. I could not see why my opinions on municipal ownership should make me any less desirable socially than I had been while living at the settlement engaged in uplift work" (*Confessions of a Reformer,* pp. 115-116). There was much more in this same vein.

In Whitlock's *Letters* there is one to Steffens in 1909 as he entered on a campaign for reelection with the machine and all the "good people" allied against him, especially the "respectable big businessmen." After telling at some length the incidents of the previous weeks, he cries: "What a bitter, wicked thing this class fight is . . . and these are but skirmishes to what is coming later."

It was no accident indeed that Roosevelt would inherit this same hatred multiplied a thousandfold. No attempt to recapture for government its lost powers could escape this division. No reformer who sought to reform "conditions" rather than people could remain respectable.

wicked when what was being sold was electricity or water than when it was shoes or building materials or drugs, it was in the city that serious inroads on business power were first made.

The movement started by the Ohio group would eventually hunt profit-making out of city business. Home rule would drive utilities into the holding company swindle, whose strength would at last be matched with that of the federal government itself in famous battles. But meanwhile there were many obstacles; of these the worst, perhaps, was the rural domination of state legislatures. The cities grew more rapidly than country districts and were for that reason constantly falling behind in representation.

The muckrakers, early in the century, had discovered that the links between what was considered legitimate business and what was criminal were very intimate indeed. In the city it was hard to determine just where one left off and the other began. These relationships did not end as a result of the muckrakers' exposures. It is probable that reform efforts had no retarding effect on them at all. Certainly during Roosevelt's maturing years more exposures would reveal the same kind of relationship, reaching into the highest circles of both business and government—the only new development was the tendency for city gangs to link up into nationwide organizations, more powerful than ever and more immune to attack. Reformers could still appeal to a latent conscience. Occasionally a newspaper went on crusade; occasionally the "racketeers," as they came to be called, became overbold, and some public prosecutor made a reputation by indicting and convicting the more repulsive characters among them.

Roosevelt, as governor, had to act on the corruption exposed by the Seabury investigation. He risked a good deal in driving Mayor Walker into exile and making Sheriff Farley's "little black box" famous. These were Tammany Hall insiders, and he was running for president. He gained more than he lost by these proceedings but he could not know it then. He was face to face in 1932 with what the reformers had been pointing out since 1906.

Exposures of corruption and scandals such as Roosevelt acted on, however, merely taught the bosses and racketeers to hire better lawyers, operate more carefully, subvert the most powerful politicians, and protect themselves with fewer flagrant offenses against public order.

The ineffectiveness of early reforms, even after many exposures and after several examples of decent city government, indicated that the time had not yet come for any permanent change. The firm basis had not yet been established. Corruption was too natural an extension of what was approved in business; it was, in fact, too closely connected with business. So long as business remained what it was, there existed no fertile ground in which the seeds of virtue could grow.

The seeds had sprouted and they were being cultivated against the future. Outside of business, competition was not acknowledged to be the chief end of man. Getting the best of one another was not seriously defended as a definition of human relationships. The community, enlarged into the city, was quite capable of engaging the loyalty of good citizens. In the universities the study of local government had become realistic. In the Wharton school, at the University of Pennsylvania, the first of the schools for administration, not only the methods of business but the methods of government had been seriously studied and taught since before the beginning of the century.

About the same time such teachers as J. W. Burgess and Frank W. Goodnow had begun, mostly in graduate schools, to explore government problems in the careful German way they had been trained to follow. Roosevelt had some introduction to this at Harvard. It was not until 1926, however, that the first systematic study of public administration appeared. It was the work of Leonard D. White of the University of Chicago. It was Professor White also who proposed to the Social Science Research Council the formation of a committee to survey public administration at work and to make recommendations for its improvement. He became the chairman of this group, being succeeded by Luther Gulick in 1930. This did not directly result in any change, but the various discussions led to many subsequent developments—such, for instance, as the immensely useful Public Administration Clearing House. An earlier movement had resulted in the establishment of a federal budget in 1921, against the bitter opposition of the Congress, but it was ineffective, at first, because behind it there was no public awareness of the necessity for order and responsibility.

The educated younger generation was aware of the possibilities of betterment. In Philadelphia the university circle widened out into a devoted city club; and soon there were citizens' clubs and unions in New York, in Chicago, and in other cities as well. Harold Ickes, in Chicago, was an old hand at reform when he was discovered by Roosevelt, defeated but not reconciled. Charles E. Merriam, a professor of political science at the University of Chicago, had served as alderman in that city and had made a powerful bid for the mayorality. He too would be a Roosevelt appointee.

But in New York there had grown up the most effective group of all—perhaps naturally, since New York was most noted for its corruption. The work of the City Club and of other associations of first citizens would eventually (in 1936) issue in a new charter for the city, giving it the most effective institutional setting for government yet devised in America. This particular reform would be led by Fiorello H. La Guardia whose administration had been prepared for long before. There existed a Municipal Government Association of New York State. When Roosevelt was a state senator (from 1910 to 1913), this Association persuaded him to introduce legislation at Albany looking toward home rule and better government in the state's cities.[13]

It would be significant if it could be shown that young Senator Roosevelt had had a real interest in this city movement; but it does not appear to be true. There would be many others in his administration who were reformers—not only Harold Ickes, but Frances Perkins, Harry Hopkins, Louis Brownlow, and many others of lesser prominence. Of these, Professor William Fielding Ogburn, also of the University of Chicago, would be typical. The impulse leading him to serve in various New Deal capacities—the most important being his Consumer Counselship in NRA—had begun long before in that extraordinary center of governmental invention, the Pacific Northwest. During a professorship at Reed College, he had, in fact, been one of the founders of the Oregon

13. The names on the letterhead of the Municipal Government Association correspondence with the future president show the respectability of its membership. They included John K. Sague of Poughkeepsie, one of young Roosevelt's mentors; William H. Crosby, Dr. F. Park Lewis, and Charles Rohlis of Buffalo; Arthur Schoellkopf and George W. Knox of Niagara Falls; and from New York City, Charles A. Beard, J. W. Grubs, Dr. Albert Shaw, Sam A. Lewisohn, Richard S. Childs, and John Finley. These letters, concerning the Roosevelt connection with city reform, are among the unpublished papers at Hyde Park.

Civil League. "I recall," he has said, "that in the last autumn I spent in Oregon (1916), I made 45 speeches off the campus in addition to my teaching."[14] A similar service was being performed at the same time in Philadelphia by Simon Nelson Patten, Scott Nearing, Clyde King, and other University of Pennsylvania professors.

There seems to have been somewhat less active concern in Boston for civic reform; but Harvard professors were equally active in their own way. Roosevelt had been an undergraduate at the height of the muckraking fervor. Unless he had done a good deal of outside reading, it probably would not have been presented to him as an interesting field of exploration by A. Lawrence Lowell or A. Piatt Andrew, for instance. But others would have introduced him to reformist literature; and even before his presidential campaign the earlier Roosevelt had been a heroic figure to the younger Roosevelt. One of TR's most adventurous periods had been in New York City as police commissioner. What a police commissioner knew of corruption, Franklin must at least have heard about.

Roosevelt's transition from elite indifference to active progressivism has given students of his career some trouble. They are inclined, in despair, to conclude that a kind of conversion occurred at the time of his illness; and they put the date at about 1921. But he had graduated from Harvard seventeen years earlier; he had practiced in New York's municipal courts for Carter, Ledyard, and Milburn; he had been a state senator and had had his historic tangle with the Tammany bosses; he had been Assistant Secretary of the Navy under Josephus Daniels and Wilson; and he had run for vice president in 1920.

In all this experience Roosevelt must have come both directly and tangentially into contact with city problems more times than are recorded. He certainly knew all about bosses and had consistently opposed them whenever he could. It cannot be said that, like his uncle Frederick Delano, who was so prominent in both the Chicago and New York reform movements, he had a vision of the city as a high expression of human aspiration. He always did, and always would, think people better off in the country and would

14. "Reminiscences" on the occasion of his retirement as Avery Distinguished Professor of Sociology at the University of Chicago in 1951.

regard the cities as poor places to live; but that did not imply that he was ignorant of their problems and unsympathetic to reform.[15] Quite the contrary. Still he was not a city progressive but a rural one. He understood farmers and trusted them. When he went to the White House, he took with him much the same intellectual freight as Harold Ickes, Charles Merriam, his uncle Fred Delano, or William Ogburn. But all the old neglected ideas went into the New Deal potpourri. Their origins were not required to be examined, only their usefulness in a crisis threatening to make reforms irrelevant and total reconstruction necessary.

Herbert Hoover had had more notion of the city's essence, its organic possibilities, than had Roosevelt, and this may have been important. The Hoovers belonged to the same social circle as the Roosevelts in the years between 1913 and 1920 when both were serving with Wilson. It would be interesting to know what they talked about—whether they helped to educate each other. Hoover then might have been a Democrat, and he was thought to be a progressive. He served in Wilson's administration as part of the war apparatus; and there was a time when the 1920 ticket might well have been Hoover and Roosevelt instead of Cox and Roosevelt. It is entirely possible that the older man's sense of organization and efficiency was a good example for the Assistant Secretary of the wartime Navy. When Hoover became Secretary of Commerce in 1921, there isssued from his department the first model city planning law as a guide to local governments; and he generally had a high regard for the possibilities of reconstruction in the cities—too high a regard in the circumstances of nationwide depression.

It ought to be recalled that Hoover's program for curing the depression, correct in principle but insufficient in volume, did include several devices that would be simply enlarged and reactivated by Roosevelt. Hoover's superior sense of form and order, even if not touched by the reformers' revelations, would have led

15. Cities, however, in his early regard, could be made tolerable by institutionalized links with the country. He said this, as a matter of fact, in an address to members of the Chamber of Commerce in Washington on November 11, 1913. Suburban farms ought to be provided for city dwellers, he suggested; and this would make the city a place "where people will be pretty proud to hail from." This, of course, is an interesting anticipation of the subsistence homesteads program of the New Deal. The reference here is to a manuscript still unclassified in the archives at Hyde Park.

him to think of the efficiency to be gained by better organization. It is not hard to imagine him among those groups of better citizens who supported the city manager movement and the establishment of various institutions for planning. His Stabilization Board was the product of a sense of balance (although it got its impetus from the unemployment crisis), just as the model city planning law of 1928 had been.

It would be easy to make too much in this connection of the city planning movement. In practice it was usually blunted and distorted by the real estate interests who very early saw that they could make use of it for their own purposes. The movement is usually said to have begun officially in New York in 1916 when the first zoning ordinance was passed to prevent a repetition of the conditions resulting from a particularly annoying incident: the vast Equitable Insurance Building, by stealing light and air from surrounding properties, had seriously reduced their values. Zoning by itself was not planning; it was a kind of mutual protection granted by the city to property owners whose competition in bulding had become chaotic; but until there existed a view, a design, for the city of the future, there could hardly be any intelligent use of the means—such as zoning—to achieve better order.

The designing was here and there undertaken too, not by the cities themselves, at first, unable as they were to struggle free from realty interests, but by groups of good citizens. The most notable of these was that in New York, sponsored and largely paid for by the Russell Sage Foundation. A study was begun in 1911; by the thirties it had emerged in big handsome volumes. These gave a first view to an American city of what it could and ought to become. It was a purely physical overview. There was included an estimate of the cost; but not of the resources likely to be available.[16] It was, however, not a long jump to the conclusion that such a design would be useless if no devices should be adopted to achieve it. The

16. *The Regional Plan of New York and Its Environs:* Volume I, *The Graphic Regional Plan* (New York, 1929); Volume II, *The Building of the City* (New York, 1931). The committee responsible for these reports consisted of Frederick A. Delano, Chairman, Robert W. de Forest, John H. Finley, John M. Glenn, Henry James, George McAneny, Dwight W. Morrow, Frank L. Polk, Frederick B. Pratt, and Lawson Purdy. The general director of Plans and Surveys was Thomas Adams.

One of my more precious possessions is these volumes, inscribed to me by the then chairman, George McAneny, on the occasion of my becoming the chairman of the New York City Planning Commission in 1938.

result of that conclusion could be found in the revised Charter of 1936. It provided for a City Planning Commission with the duty not only of continuing to work out the design of the future—called a Master Plan—but also of making from year to year the city's capital (or improvement) budget. For the first time in the United States a vision of the organic city was given the governmental means for working year by year toward its realization.

The issuance into legal definition and the shaping of institutions for city planning had been, as in so many other instances, preceded by a long period of gestation. Transformation of the cities and elimination of their worst weaknesses seemed hopelessly slow, nevertheless, generation by generation, it proceeded. As early as 1909 the movement had progressed to the point of national conference. This first meeting was held in Washington; among its participants were many who are now honored as pioneers: Henry Morgenthau, Frederick Law Olmsted, Frederick R. Ford, John Nolan, and many others, some of whom were actually practicing city planners and some, merely concerned citizens. The meetings were presided over by cabinet members. It was noticeable that many participants appeared as chairmen or secretaries of civic associations; and praise was heard for the work of the American Civic Association and the National Municipal League. It was obvious that the planning movement was not only respectable but already formidable. There were suitably pious references to even earlier beginnings.

It would not be realistic to link this movement too closely with institutional change in New York, and with ideas for creating and realizing a vision of the future for the nation; but they were at least parallel. The Burnham Plan for Chicago, following the inspiration of the Columbian Exposition, was the prototype for later fashionable ones, even that of New York. And when Chicago progressive reformer Harold Ickes became not only Roosevelt's Secretary of the Interior but his Administrator of Public Works, it was natural for him to think of planning in connection with it. One of his first acts was to establish a Public Works Planning Board. The identification of Charles E. Merriam and of Frederick Delano with this board carried over the associations of a city movement both had worked for all their lives. Another member, Wesley C. Mitchell, had been chief of the price section of the War

Industries Board during World War I and was an authority on the financial implications of planning. It seemed in that moment of enthusiasm as though the concept of an organic nation, part linked intelligibly with part, advancing to the fullest extent of its capabilities, might be realized; but such a hope was premature. The special interests battening on divisiveness were too strong to be merged involuntarily in such a scheme. The United States was not yet a nation, except in crisis and great distress, and the New Dealers' hopes would soon enough fade.

There would, however, be a residue in the cities. And, indeed, even in the circumstances of 1933, the cities could be seen to have a working approximation of that organicism so lacking in national life. A new generation of administrators would do a good deal to foster this self-conscious development, with the consent, if not the active leadership, of President Roosevelt.

It seems something of an anomaly that the muckraking episode should have originated and run its course in the first decade of the twentieth century, for by that time there had been substantial progress toward municipal reform. This progress consisted more in the exploration of possibilities than in actual changes in municipal government; nevertheless the preliminaries for basic reform had been established. They had originated in severe reaction to the scandals in the post-Civil War period. The Tweed Ring in New York had been overthrown in 1871, and there had been several investigations of municipal affairs whose chief permanent result had been the setting-up of citizens' organizations to combat franchise grabs or to correct peculiarly corrupt situations. These groups usually developed no definite long-run program for betterment; but some groups were bent on eliminating the "spoils system" and did have such programs.

Henry Adams had written an article in 1869[17] that was afterward designated by John Gaus as "the first example of public recognition and consciousness of administrative problems."[18] Adams was followed by others—for instance, Woodrow Wilson, in his academic phase. In New York a Civil Service Reform Associa-

17. "Civil Service Reform," *North American Review,* 109 (1869): 443-465.
18. In "A Study of Research in Public Administration" prepared for the Advisory Committee on Public Administration of the Social Science Research Council. Mimeographed, New York, 1930, p. 1.

tion was organized in 1877; and in 1881 this and twelve similar associations had a first meeting at Newport. The result of this meeting was a National Civil Service Reform League. From then on, a merit system was fought for consistently by an active and influential group who knew what they wanted. They were responsible in large part not only for municipal progress in this direction but for the passage of the Pendleton Act by the Congress in 1883. So far as this reform was concerned, it now remained only to extend coverage and enforce effective administration. The city machines found numerous and ingenious ways of circumventing enforcement; but improvement, under sporadic citizen pressure, did take place.

At the time of the muckrakers, this movement, like several others of a similar sort, was about ready to pass into the more positive stage of administrative reorganization. Philadelphia's Municipal League was founded in 1892, the City Club of New York in 1892, and the Municipal League of Boston in 1894. Out of these there came the first Conference for Good City Government in Philadelphia in 1894. Eleven cities sent delegates. There the National Municipal League was founded; and within a year there were 180 branches. By 1899 this group had reached a set of guiding principles considerably more comprehensive than that of the Civil Service Reform League. These included widened home rule for cities, unicameralism, the strong-mayor plan—with all department heads except the controller appointed by the mayor— the separation of municipal from state and national elections, the merit system of appointment and promotion, and effective auditing of municipal accounts.

It was ironic that the funds for administrative improvement should have been furnished by those same big businessmen who had been pointed to by Steffens and his co-workers as the corrupters of the cities. There is an analogy to be drawn here with the devotion to philanthropy of many of the large fortunes put together in pre-income tax times—an attempt, as the more radically minded like to point out, to salve consciences grown tender in age. It is fact that the great foundations, to whose keeping so much of the Rockefeller, Carnegie, and other fortunes were entrusted, were the principal support of the movements for civic reform and the improvement of city management.

There were members of that generation who knew exactly what the results would be and who would have welcomed them. Joseph Fels, for instance, who was won over in his later years to Henry George's argument for the single tax, said openly that he meant to devote his fortune to "tearing down the damnable system" which had enabled him to build that fortune. But he was a notable exception. Much more often the movement for reform was camouflaged as "good business." The businessmen were loading a gun that they somehow believed would not be fired, or at least not in their direction.

It did seem a simple proposition that city business—and eventually the business of the federal government—ought to be efficiently run. And it seemed an even simpler conclusion that tax burdens might be reduced by the economies of honest administration. One of the most notable achievements of the century would be the introduction of budget systems presented by their advocates as money-saving measures. This happened first in the cities; but it was obvious that once planted there the idea of simultaneously visualizing income and expenditure would quickly be seen to be appropriate for the federal government. The instinct of the politicians was to oppose this as they had the other reforms. How, they asked, could they maintain the freedom to grant those favors, concessions, and privileges the businessmen demanded unless they were able to proceed without the interference of experts equipped with rational plans? Plans laid out a complete organization, part related to part; and any departure would put a heavy burden of proof on a politician who would manipulate public improvements as his supporters demanded.

Budgeting was an indispensable device of planners. And once accepted it accumulated its own momentum. Congressmen, like the city politicians, were very reluctant to accept any such addition to the executive establishment; but no one else was against it; and when it became clear that the business community was for it, they gradually, even if protestingly, with mutterings and misgivings, gave way.

Actually, the federal budget resulted from the work of a Commission on Economy and Efficiency appointed by President Taft. Frederick A. Cleveland, director of the New York Bureau of Municipal Research, was made chairman of the commission at the instance of Taft's secretary, Charles D. Norton.[19] Thus city reform moved on to Washington. The other members of that commission were William F. Willoughby and Frank J. Goodnow, honored names in political science. In 1912, the commission's report, entitled "The Need for a National Budget," was transmitted to the Congress by the President.[20] The Congress was moved to condemn the President for permitting officials to waste their time working on "this new and unauthorized plan of a so-called national budget."[21] And the commission went out of existence. But what had been begun could not be stopped.

In 1916, Norton organized a continuation of the commission's work. There was established an Institute for Government Research, with Willoughby as its director. It was financed by Rockefeller funds—a connection noted by those opposed to the effort. But between 1916 and 1918 the institute published five volumes on budgeting and fiscal administration; and these left the opposition with very few arguments.

A Bureau of the Budget did actually come into existence in 1921—not that the congressmen were tamed; far from it; they went on making budgets of their own with very little reference to executive proposals, and would continue to do so for years to come. Yet whimsical expenditure began to be limited. It was far from having been ended in 1933; but Roosevelt was a confirmed believer, and his appointment of Lewis W. Douglas to be its head was notice that he intended to make full use of the Bureau. Douglas had been a congressman, and the Congress was on notice that the old ways were ending.

The relationship between the fight for the administrative budget and the New Deal consisted in Roosevelt's interest. One of his most obsessive preoccupations as President was with detail and arrangement. This characteristic had appeared in Albany when he was a legislator trying to make government more effective; and it had much to do with his success in improving construction and operational activities when assistant secretary of the navy. When the executive budget had been under discussion in the Congress,

19. Norton and his son were to have a notable role in the fixing of planning in New York City's government and in protecting it from subversive attacks.
20. House Document No. 854, Sixty-second Congress, second session.
21. Cited by G. A. Weber, *Organized Efforts for the Improvement of Methods of Administration in the United States* (New York: Appleton, 1919), p. 89.

he had been one of those who appeared to testify. He not only argued for the budget but went on to argue for other principles of better management, principles he had learned from his navy experiences.

This furnishes something of a preview of his sophistication in such matters as he entered the presidency. One of his first acts, it will be recalled, was to ask for blanket reorganizing powers; and it was he who moved the Bureau of the Budget from the Treasury into the executive office directly under himself.[22]

I have spoken before of the weakening of government.[23] That was with reference to the emasculation of the presidency during the regimes of Harding, Coolidge, and Hoover, to the overly effective operation of the Constitution's system of checks, and to the consequent escape of very powerful interests from regulation. But it will be seen, even from the brief résumé here, that when the proper time arrived there did emerge the devices necessary to arrest that decline. Energetic leadership from the White House also might be expected to rejuvenate the presidency and overcome the imbalance resulting from the Senate's attritions on the executive. Such leadership would be likely to result from any national crisis causing widespread distress; and that is what happened with startling rapidity as the depression of 1929 ran on into 1932, and Roosevelt emerged as a presidential candidate with alternatives to offer.

It is a notable fact that most of the preliminary work necessary to such an expansion of government as would presently be undertaken had been done in the cities. The agricultural distresses of preceding years had not caused many governmental changes. The farmers had looked to Washington rather than to local government for relief. Even the Non-Partisan League, although it had for a time dominated several state governments, had left almost no residue of permanent reforms; and there were no contributions from

22. These matters are discussed in Frank Freidel, *Franklin D. Roosevelt: The Ordeal* (Boston: Little, Brown, 1954). In fact Freidel gives a whole chapter to the subject at this point in Roosevelt's career: chapter ii in the second volume of his *Life,* called "Toward More Efficient Government." References to the various documents mentioned above will be found in this chapter.

23. In "The Decline of Government," *Western Political Quarterly,* June and Setpember 1951, pp. 295-312, 469-486.

any of the agricultural agitations. Clearly good government as a movement had its beginnings in the cities. The merit system came from there; so did the budget; and city planning was already an old movement before it began to be thought of as a national possibility.

Not all the administrators assembling in Washington in 1933 had city backgrounds, but most of them did. There was urgent need for agricultural relief, and it would require the services of Henry A. Wallace, Mordecai Ezekiel, Louis Bean, and others who were to devise the Agricultural Adjustment Administration. But there were numerically many more who had had urban experience and had been engaged in the long struggle against municipal corruption. Among these were Harold Ickes, Harry Hopkins, Raymond Moley, Frances Perkins, Jerome Frank, Frederick Delano, Charles E. Merriam, Wesley Mitchell, Louis Brownlow, Leonard D. White, Frederick C. Howe, Henry Hunt, Morris Cooke, and many others. Harold Ickes carried many scars from old battles. Frances Perkins embodied the tradition of government intervention on behalf of the weak and unprotected in New York City; Harry Hopkins brought the whole paraphernalia of urban social work. Some others, not destined for great public notice but very influential in their places, were the very ones who had been responsible for the establishment of institutions to secure the permanence of reform. Indeed, the whole apparatus of municipal improvement came to Washington in 1933. It would have enormous effect there before the New Deal had run its course. The muckrakers and reformers had not lived in vain; neither had those other heroes who had borne the burden of battle. Tom Johnson, Brand Whitlock, John Puroy Mitchel, and Blankenburgh had not been permanently defeated, and the patient advocates of better administration had started an evolution essential to the burdens of a welfare state. Their spirits lived in successors who were now to have a belated success.

4

ROOSEVELT'S

PROGRESSIVE ORTHODOXY

The disappointments of some of us during the campaign of 1932 were doubtless by reference to an impossible standard, but recollection of its incidents still causes some discomfort. The force of it is best recaptured in the surviving notes or memoranda for speeches compared with the speeches themselves. We were unhappy.

In spite of this frustration, as I read over the *Public Papers* and consider their tortured origins, the original labors, the controversies, and the compromises they represent, the feeling comes uppermost that we made a good start—the Brains Trust did—but that it had an ending. In our group, Raymond Moley, Adolf Berle, and I had a well-shaped economic and social philosophy roughly to be described as "concentration and control"—to use Charles W. Van Hise's phrase—as opposed to "enforced atomism," to use a deprecatory phrase of Moley's, who was a Van Hise disciple.

In the early stages of the campaign, it seems to me, though I recognize the possibility of prejudice, there was a clear indication in all our candidate's public pronouncements of this philosophy. I say "early" because the departure from it can be dated at August 20, 1932, when the old progressivism came uppermost in an address at Columbus, Ohio, and it began to appear that reform was to center in the regulation of banks, exchanges, and holding companies, not in changes reaching the system itself. On that day trust-busting was returned to and any hope for holism was aban-

NOTE. This essay appeared in *Ethics*, volume 64, number 1 (October 1953). Copyright 1953 by the University of Chicago. Reprinted by permission of the University of Chicago Press.

doned. This was only the third speech after the nomination, with many more to come.

As I study this reversion to the old individualism now, after the tentative expositions of collectivism, it seems more and more striking; and there is about it an element—perhaps imaginary, though I do not think so—of departure from a genuine preference. Sophistication was abandoned and Roosevelt reached for the approbation politicians all are so eager for, in a common-sense statement of what he thought people preferred to believe.

As the campaign progressed, from Columbus on, our candidate constantly widened his appeal, and this meant making it more simple and more traditional. This, we continued to feel, was not more but less practical. This in the long run would cause trouble for a president. We—and everyone by then—knew he would be elected; and we thought he could afford to put forward the later solutions he would have to adopt. He had a chance to move with history; he rejected it for safety far beyond political necessity. We were no politicians, but looking back, I, at least, cannot be convinced that we were wrong.

Systems analysis, the elements of costing, the manner of chromosome pairings, or the establishment of critical mass—to refer to a few various but consequential intellectual devices—are not matters of common sense; and neither are the strategic elements of public policy. None of the subject matter we were dealing with lent itself to simple apprehension. That was precisely the attitude lately proved to be so insufficient; it was, we thought, discredited by events. It was because Hoover and his helpers had refused to use an economics comparable to the higher mathematics engineers use in building bridges or tunnels or skyscrapers that they were now in trouble. A bridge, it is generally recognized, cannot be built if only elementary arithmetic is used; yet it is expected quite commonly that the more complicated social processes may be provided for without the use of devices for measurement, of institutions for coordination, or reference to the relevant devices of social science. It is puzzling to know whether that is what really is expected, or whether the controlling emotion is a preference for individual profit-making even at social cost.

This is not a pleasant imputation; and it is probably too baldly stated; for people can fool themselves with amazing effectiveness.

Protecting profits, for instance, becomes very easily a struggle for "liberty" or some equally well-recognized ideal. Still, in baring the Hoover philosophy we were almost forced to say that he was, in an almost impossible sense, unaware of the great current setting in toward social integration. It did not seem to me that we could put forward an alternative program with any seriousness at all unless it had its premises in coordination or collectivism as over against individualism and atomism. Yet there was no precedent for collectivism. In its adherence to a common sense approach, the traditional progressive philosophy was as individualistic as that of Hoover; and the progressives were our people, not his. If we based ourselves on a literal progressivism, we had no right to any complaint other than that he had made bad judgments—that he had permitted private monopolies to interfere with the automatic functioning necessary in a free competitive order.

Such a campaign was not impossible. For Hoover, no less than his predecessor, Coolidge, had a curious theory of the state, and especially of the presidency. Each devoted a good deal of energy to maintaining feebleness in Washington, apparently on the theory that the true government lay elsewhere and that the federal government ought not to interfere, in any serious way, with the really significant operations of society and especially its economy.

It would be apparent in later study of these documents that our candidate had had attitudes more typically American than we had appreciated at the time. It is possible to cull passages from his speeches representing the most advanced holistic position; indeed this preference predominates. Yet, as I have said, there always came a reversion to older ways of thinking; and finally the change from the beginning was striking. It was in this sense that he was typical in edging away from difficult reality. The nation was advancing into a future no more than half understood; it was also resented, and yet it produced goods and services people would no longer consent to do without.

Roosevelt's New Deal lingered at an arrested stage for years, unwilling to name the sacrifices of private privilege necessary to a general security achieved by social management rather than by the accidental concurrence of individual schemes. This lingering between two worlds was reflected throughout American life. It dominated public polity. It was evident in the cautious and halfhearted approaches made to any guaranties of common security as well as to the behavior of industrialists and financiers. Roosevelt either came very slowly to understand the deep contrast in these two positions, or he compromised. It is my belief that the contriving traits of his mind did take hold of suggestions for better organization, and that in his thoughtful moments he understood the momentum of collectivism; but that he pulled back from the implications of acceptance. He judged them to be generally unacceptable.

Adolf Berle and I—I more than he—were, in the subsequent years, called some harsh names: Reds, Communists, Socialists, Anarchists, and even, on occasion, Fascists. Perhaps the only approximately accurate label would have been Collectivists, although if we were to accept it, we should have had to insist on its dictionary definition rather than the one intended by those who flung it at us. It represented an approach to economic and government problems in complete contrast with that of the atomizers, just as it did, also, with the approach of those who, like the later Moley, seemed to think that business confidence was all-important. But Moley had had other views in 1932, and they had seemed to be the same as ours.

That this campaign represented a crisis in American attitudes I fully believed; it seemed quite possible—as turned out to be the fact—that we should linger long at the fork in that road without decision as to which route to take. Because of this confusion it is revealing to examine the pronouncements of that campaign. There is a copious record. Not counting the numerous extemporaneous talks and considering only prepared addresses, it required 220 pages in the first volume of the *Public Papers*; the dates range from the Forgotten Man speech of April 7, 1932, to the last address at Madison Square Garden of November 5.

My general conclusion is that until this campaign Roosevelt had not wrestled with the tormenting habit intellectual difficulties have of becoming paradoxical. Like moralities, they come into conflict with each other, and choices among them are of more or less, not satisfying absolutes. He had not had, for instance, to reconsider the maxims of his own progressive tradition. He had not had to find a reconciliation between collectivism and individualism, to see how they interpenetrated and were evolving together in perpetual conflict. He instinctively wanted a new interpretation; he felt rather than understood the insufficiency of the old. Yet he had not reached a conclusion, and in his public addresses he tended more and more to appeal to the simpler minds before him.

A great deal of creaking humor was expended on the Brains Trust. We were college professors, and there was a journalistic stereotype for academicians. No one had taken the trouble to reexamine it for some time. The freshwater college professor of Greek was the model—as much a stock character as the stage Englishman. Also journalists, being employees of publishers, had one standard plea to put forward when situations threatened to get out of hand. "What we need," they said, "is a businessman for president," "a practical man for mayor," or for whatever office was in question.

There was a short period when editorial columns were remarkably free of this cant; that was when business was thoroughly discredited after 1929. Who but businessmen had created the mess we were in? Others, it would seem in the circumstances, might now be allowed a hearing; and Roosevelt sometimes spoke with a sophistication we made available. There is no pride in this. The creation was not ours. We were merely the middlemen of collectivism in the sense that we saw in prospect an economy capable of feeding, clothing, and making secure, in some of the amenities, a whole people; and we did not think this could possibly result from any accidental concatenation of events. We believed that integration was a principle of civilization's advance. We believed in direction. We believed it was the function of government to establish and maintain the necessary conjunctural institutions.

There was a good deal said by Roosevelt about such matters in the campaign speeches, especially the early ones in the spring of 1932. For one who wishes to understand the intellectual background of the campaign and of the program of legislation to be worked out in the special session following immediately on the inauguration, it may be informative to examine certain previous writings of Adolf's and mine. To take one instance, in 1927 I had called attention to the conclusions of visiting industrialists from other nations; and I had found a useful point of departure in the search for the secret of American productivity they so much admired.[1] It could easily enough be demonstrated that real wages in the United States were at least twice as high as those in Britain and perhaps three or four times as high as those anywhere on the continent. This was a startling contrast; it provided a challenge to the pride of Englishmen and Germans.

I had two Englishmen especially in mind who had concluded that the secret lay in the habit here of producing a large volume of goods at low prices, thus securing wide distribution. This in turn insured the continuance of the kind of mass production resulting from the use of natural power and aggregations of machinery to take the place of men. That has since become a commonplace; it seemed novel in 1926 when Bertram Austin and W. Francis Lloyd published *The Secret of High Wages.* We, in America, had been riding high in those days. The Englishmen, in conducting their investigation, had been taken about by industrialists and experts with some pride, and had come to what seemed to them a conclusion overriding paradox. It seemed that the secret of perpetual prosperity had been discovered, and there was no intention to hide the light of it under any bushel.

As I considered this, I generated a desire to persuade my fellow economists that production had changed so greatly as to invalidate many of their theories concerning it; but also I thought the industrialists and leaders in scientific management had been guilty of some unjustified boasting. High wages, I said, were relative; workers' pay was high enough only if it provided sufficient purchasing power to carry off continuously the volume of goods our highly efficient productive system was prepared to offer. In my judgment, it was not sufficient. While industrialists were patting themselves on the back because wage levels were above those in Europe, the whole system was in danger of collapsing because purchasing power was actually and chronically deficient.

I put in a demurrer, furthermore, to sole emphasis on wages. The one necessity for sustained prosperity, I said, was a purchasing power whose values equaled the values of all the goods the system could produce. Wage earners did not constitute the whole com-

1. In *Industry's Coming of Age* (New York: Harcourt, Brace, 1927).

munity; there were other income receivers to be considered. If all consumers were to be effective, a balanced relationship had to be maintained between costs and prices, so that everyone could buy, not only workers but all income receivers. The fact was that costs were being reduced so sharply that a lowered level of prices was possible; it was more than possible, it was essential if consumers were to purchase all the goods we could produce. If they were not bought, production would slow or perhaps stop and unemployment would rise.

I went on to express the belief that an unmanaged system would never produce this concurrence. Not enough of any market was under sufficient control to keep its prices in accord with its costs. There were speculators who, as a matter of business, *created* price fluctuations. The production of goods in large quantities was often deliberately prevented. Worse, consumers were unable to buy because their incomes did not match the prices demanded by suppliers.

Somewhat later,[2] I examined the notion of some of my more optimistic colleagues that the improved processes of scientific management and the more effective machinery rapidly being installed did not increase unemployment because an enlarged product resulted. Their theory was that this, when sold, was turned into funds for the hire of an increased labor force. There seemed, I said, to be a contradiction in this. Economists had always assumed, merely from reasoning, that this adjustment was the result of free market operations. This classical conception had been set out a good many years before by Francis Amasa Walker, among other American economists; Walker's widely used textbook had represented the apotheosis of laissez faire thinking. The theory depended, I said, upon the continuous working of a process that took place nowhere but in economists' imaginations. Their assumption that yields from the sale of goods and services were automatically turned into purchasing power was illusory; it simply did not happen. To show that this was so I traced the way surpluses were actually accumulated and disposed of. I left out of account for the moment individual savings and considered the

2. In "The Theory of Occupational Obsolescence," *The Political Science Quarterly*, June 1931, pp. 171-227.

more important corporate accumulations. Practically all American enterprise was corporate in form. Most of the funds, therefore, from the disposal of goods came first into the control of corporate directors.

Here I would have been bolstered, had I known of it, by the work of Adolf Berle and Gardiner Means were doing, which eventuated in their study of corporate interrelations and concentrations.[3] But even without this support I had felt safe in saying that as funds became available for disposal by corporate directors, they had only a few alternatives. They could keep a large cash balance in the bank as individuals do against a rainy day; they could invest in other corporations' securities; or they could allow their funds to be loaned in the open money market. If they chose not to distribute their profits to stockholders they might enlarge their own plants. Still another alternative might be spending for distribution costs or for business luxuries what they saved by more efficient production. The savings of the engineers, in other words, could be—obviously they often were—spent on enlarged advertising appropriations to build up what was called "good will," or in other extravagances of a similar sort, even elaborate surroundings and inflated salaries for executives.

The significant thing about all the alternatives open to the disposers of corporate incomes was that none of them enlarged very much ultimate purchasing power. It might be said that money put in the bank would be loaned to some other enterprise; or it might be said that investment made in other corporations' securities would set up a demand for labor to carry on whatever activity that investment made possible; but these were enlargements of the productive plant rather than of ultimate purchasing power; and in the long run they tended to make the situation worse by providing even more productive capacity for even fewer customers.

My conclusion was that our much-praised system would break down because of overinvestment and underconsumption. This would always be so unless some discipline was imposed on enterprisers. As for the theory that technological advance had not increased unemployment, that simply was not true, because the free flow of funds assumed to take place was actually interrupted

3. *The Modern Corporation and Private Property* (New York, 1932).

by judgments exercised in favor of individuals and against society. Income would run off into sterile pools and these would threaten the whole system as a malarial swamp might threaten a city.

I had got that far before the depression came upon us. Berle, working with Means and others, had come to the conclusion that the real control of American industrial activity was concentrated in some two hundred corporations. This, they pointed out, had a significance far beyond the sinister aspect it presented to the orthodox economist. The American system was ready for social management; actually it *was* managed, but for private benefits rather than for a public one. Moreover, the role of financiers had been an excessively influential one, and was more and more centered on the profits to be made from the flotation of securities or industrial loans, and less and less on those to be made by providing goods. An arrangement of prices such that the goods could be disposed of in large quantities was no longer a rule.

They also pointed out incidentally that the "profit motive" so often talked about had practically disappeared from the lives of most Americans. Its operation was confined to a very few, and those not usually producers; the rest were a kind of helot class, living on sufferance.

I should be guilty of gross exaggeration if the conclusion should be drawn, from what I have said, that Berle and I were responsible for the genesis or even for the main development of this theorizing. A body of unorthodox economics was being built up throughout this period, especially in the United States by such people as W. C. Mitchell, who was analyzing the business cycle, and in Britain by J. A. Hobson. I simply call attention to the activities of Adolf and myself because, largely by accident, our material was used in Roosevelt's campaign arguments. We took to him the generalizations available in our profession that were more congenial to our own bent than the preindustrial theories of a past generation.

After the depression had gone on for some time, and it had become apparent that Hoover had no intention of sponsoring any sufficient remedies, my indignation got the better of me and I prepared a brochure[4] collating Hoover's writings and speeches. I

4. Published as a pamphlet by John Day Company under the title *Mr. Hoover's Economic Policy* (New York, 1932).

set out as clearly as I could the theory behind them. The pamphlet had a considerable distribution. It disclosed Hoover not only as a determined defender of free competition but also as an equally determined opponent of a sufficiently implemented public program for the cure of the ills brought upon us by the existing system.

Not satisfied with that, I went on to discuss, in a *Current History* article in January 1932, the economic attitude represented by his refusal to provide adequate relief at the same time that energetic measures were being used for the rescue of business. Eugene Meyer, then governor of the Federal Reserve Board and chairman of the Reconstruction Finance Corporation, had said in advocacy of the corporation: "The present situation is peculiar, in that instead of the weak being afraid of the strong, the strong are afraid of the weak and the main object aimed at is the removal of that fear from strong institutions, so that they may go ahead." This, of course, was another statement of the Mellon "trickle theory" frequently used to justify shifting taxes from the rich to the poor. The idea was that if the rich were relieved, their prosperity would find its way downward to poorer dependents.

Neither Meyer nor Mellon originated these views. Lord Brougham had held them early in the nineteenth century. His sorrow that nothing direct could be done for the workers had rested on the dictum of the economists that if Capital were frightened it would cease to employ Labor. It is suspected now that the whole wages-fund doctrine of the English economists was shaped to this apology for avoidance. Meyer would not be the last—any more than he was the first—to express this view. It would crop up still later as "business confidence," and be presented all over again as sanctimoniously as though it had not been refuted a hundred times in theory and practice. Not least of my own future regrets would center in a long passage to this effect in Moley's *After Seven Years*. I would say to myself that he knew better than this. Why should he say it?

It was about this time that Hoover began to put forward his theory, or perhaps I should say alibi, for our economic sickness. It was this: the depression was an aftereffect of the dislocations remaining from the war; it had begun in Europe and spread to America; it was not a particularly serious matter because foreigners bought only a small percentage of American production in any case; it would soon be over; minor precautions would be needed but no federal unemployment relief, for instance, was necessary. Having convinced himself that this was sufficient he, and others in his administration, had taken to pooh-poohing the statistics of decline and issuing the fairytale statements that became so preposterous a part of public discussion in those days. Prosperity, they said, was "just around the corner." In an unguarded moment, Hoover offered the suggestion that a way out might be found in repeating the maneuver of financing exports "by means of loans to backward nations." We were to make a good deal of that during the campaign. As though we had not troubles enough with foreign debts!

It was in view of these official attitudes, and with this background of analysis, that I had made, early in the spring of 1932, an address at Teachers College, Columbia, called "Discourse in Depression," the most important, as it turned out, I had ever made.

> The problem is one of overcoming a kind of paralysis extending throughout the economic system . . . It is . . . a time for emergency measures. Our paralysis is not only one which affects the usual working mechanisms but which also affects our judgments and our wills. This last may well be the clue to recovery since it prevents the formulation of an effective policy for setting things in motion . . .
>
> It is relatively easy to trace the support for this attitude to those who are favored by our present arrangements, who do well in prosperity, and who escape the worst effects of depression . . . The ugliest feature of our system is illustrated by an unsporting refusal to share, running all through the present emergency action, regardless of ability to help and regardless of the favors of the past. It is quite true to say in general that those who are asked to make the greatest sacrifices are those who have benefited least from our institutions. The workers, having lived poorly in prosperity, are asked to insure society as a whole by bearing the burden of hard times. Insurance, on principle, is only possible as a consequence of an accumulation of surpluses; but now that we have depression the possessors of surplus are relatively immune; and those who have none at

all are asked to assume the risks. It is not too much to say that the whole program in this emergency has been framed for protecting privilege rather than any analysis of cause and cure.

This attitude of business and political leaders might, of course, see them through, however much others might lose. But, I went on to point out, this would be unlikely, since this depression had by now spread everywhere. In the years 1930 and 1931 there were losses of wages reaching to at least twelve and perhaps fifteen billions of dollars. In these same years the dividend payments of corporations had actually risen by some two or three hundreds of millions. Why should not some of the surpluses have been used, I asked, to meet these wage losses and to re-create a purchasing power that would have done something at least to prevent further unemployement? Obviously because it was preferred to stake everything on a gamble that the depression would end as suddenly as it appeared to have begun. What might have saved us, and what was still necessary to be done if we were to make any impression, was in direct contrast with all that had been done.

The energy and the initiative we are now expending on our financial institutions ought to be turned toward the repairing of a nationally damaged purchasing power—*not confidence; but actual power to buy.* Even the objectives it has been hoped to attain by the various financial measures undertaken with such romantic éclat really depend on such a restoration. For the values of property are built on the income derived from their use and these incomes will fall as long as paralysis continues. To attempt to support values for property among an idle and. impoverished people is a futile gesture. To attempt to save the country by insuring the status quo of its banks is like attempting to revive a dying tree by applying fertilizer to its branches instead of to its roots ... Purchasing power in the hands of those who ultimately buy and use goods is the one indispensable need; lacking this we lack everything; possessing it we have everything. It cannot be brought into being by magic, as many people seem to believe. Neither is its creation so mysterious as to be beyond possibility. In a stable productive system this purchasing power is a function of production. Factories and machines run. People are paid for building them and running them. With this pay they purchase the goods ensuing from the process. This on-going process gets out of balance at times. In such a situation there is just one remedial thing to do: take incomes from where they are and place them where they are needed . . . This is a hard doctrine to accept. For those who have to consent are those who will be required to make the sacrifices. In fact it never has been accepted.

Any ameliorative action at all has been undertaken with extreme reluctance and only when disasters seemed immediate among institutions it was desired to protect. Any attempt to remedy the disaster to individuals and families was met by the argument that we ought not to resort to doles lest the liberties of our citizens be threatened. Subsidy was resorted to only for the protection of banks, railroads, and insurance companies whose commitments had been made on the basis of values now so eroded as to leave them insolvent. This program could not possibly accomplish more than temporary support. The level of values must ultimately rest on a capitalized income from property. Income from property depends on the prices consumers will pay for the goods and services property furnishes. The prices they will pay depend on their power to earn. The support of earning power is the point of attack. Whatever got us into these difficulties, the one principle we can cling to is that purchasing power must be protected and, where it is lost, restored. Instead of distributing fertilizer up among the branches we must dig it in around the roots.

There was a great deal more to this address. It laid out a program consisting of six points derived from its arguments. It went on to insist, in a final section, that the general cause of our insecurity and political stagnation lay in the nature of laissez faire and that the logical antithesis of this was a managed system with private initiative subordinated to a charted scheme of production. In the rare instances, I said, when economists had allowed their imaginations to wander toward a more desirable arrangement, certain aspects of Utopia had been clear enough. There was always a bias toward a substantial sharing of tasks and pleasures; toward cooperative rather than competitive enterprise; toward considered stability rather than irresponsible speculation. These biases doubtless represented revulsion from the praise of piracy, of miserliness, and of cunning, forced, as things were, on the sycophants and apologists they supported so generously.

This was perhaps more than a simple aversion to the degradations of the time. It may have been that the consistencies running through orthodox literature represented a severely logical recognition of the conditions necessary to change. Equality, cooperation, and stability were consistent with the other dream we had all cherished: that of progress in easing the conditions of work and in widening the access to a growing store of goods. They were really the conditions of any such progress. It was the hope of getting a little of each that lay behind the search for a new direction in current discussion. That discussion, I suggested, might be the thing remembered about the 1930s long after the sufferings they had imposed had been forgot.

How much did Roosevelt owe to the school of thought represented, however inadequately, by Adolf and myself? This is a question best answered by examining what he said publicly.[5] The Forgotten Man speech was made on April 7. This was an unusual opportunity: under the auspices of the Democratic National Committee, a candidate for the party's nomination was given a chance to present his case more than two months before the Convention; and it drew wide attention.[6]

He began by saying that no one, in such times, could talk merely as a Democrat. The depression had become too serious to be viewed "through partisan eyes for partisan purposes." He went on, in the next paragraph, to call attention to his earlier service during the war. That effort necessarily "conceived of a whole Nation

5. Stanley High (who was an NBC lecturer and one of President Roosevelt's speech writers in 1935-37) seemed to think that the influence of Adolf and myself was considerable and that it was exercised for the "benefit of America's depressed classes . . . In this, as in other matters, he did not reach his conclusions from reading but rather from his contacts. It is probable that the two men who helped him most to sharpen his thinking and give it definite outline in this regard were Adolf Berle and Rexford Guy Tugwell. Both of them were members of the 1932 Brains Trust. They shared Mr. Roosevelt's social enthusiasms. They had come to their conclusions by dint of wide reading and hard thinking. Their operations had been almost entirely in the intellectual realm. But in that realm they had a plausible, definite, and, in general, sound knowledge . . . They did not change his opinions but they helped to strengthen the intellectual foundations under them."

6. This important address owed much to Moley's talent for this sort of thing.

mobilized . . . into a vast unit." "It was a great plan," he said, "because it was built from bottom to top and not from top to bottom." The relevance of this recollection he made clear in curt, short sentences: "In my calm judgment, the Nation faces today a more grave emergency than in 1917. It is said that Napoleon lost the battle of Waterloo because he forgot his infantry . . . These unhappy times call for the building of plans . . . that put their faith once more in the forgotten man at the bottom of the economic pyramid."

Aware that he had no more than a few minutes to make his appeal for the presidency, he admitted that he could not "lay down the ten or a dozen closely related objectives of a plan to meet our present emergency"; he could, however, set out "a few essentials, a beginning, in fact, of a planned program." He proceeded to the troubles of agriculture: approximately half the population, the farmers, had lost their purchasing power; in consequence, the other half in the cities could not "sell industrial products to the farming half of the Nation." There were to be considered also the home owner and the farm owner, who were in danger of dispossession. These were distant from the great financial institutions of Chicago and New York, but "the two billion dollar fund" of the Reconstruction Finance Corporation "at the disposal of the big banks, the railroads and the Corporations" was not for them. The Administration offered nothing even for small enterprisers, to say nothing of individuals. He mentioned the tariff, saying that small people had no interest in high tariffs. In all these matters the Administration had "sought temporary relief from top down rather than permanent relief from the bottom up." It had "totally failed to plan ahead in a comprehensive way . . . We are in the midst of an emergency at least equal to that of war. Let us mobilize to meet it."

This speech was our first success. Perhaps I should more modestly say it was Moley's success: it was he who readapted the "forgotten man" expression from William Graham Sumner; and it was he who drafted and redrafted its paragraphs. The forgotten man allusion, rather than the holistic commitment, was most noticed at the time; but I felt that the other point had been gained as well. This had been mine; and between then and the Jefferson Day speech on April 18 at St. Paul, I lost no chance in our counsels to argue for my notion of economic parity among the groups making up the whole. Given equality, I argued, these groups would be able to exchange products with each other and so keep each other employed. This resulted in the use of a phrase only less well advertised than the "forgotten man." This was "concert of interests." We tried to crowd into this what we believed to be not only our own but Jefferson's conception of interdependence. It appeared not in one speech but in several.

There was a touch of Moley in the introduction of planning; in the St. Paul speech a remark of Chesterton's was quoted. The citizens of the British Commonwealth, he had said, got to know each other only in case of accidents. So it was, Roosevelt said, that only in a crisis did we appreciate our common American concerns.

> Then ... we look to a larger measure of cooperation, a more exact measuring of our resources, and, what is most important, a more imaginative and purposeful planning ... I am not speaking of an economic life completely planned and regimented. I am speaking of the necessity ... in those imperative interferences with the economic life of the Nation, that there be a real community of interest, not only among the sections of this great country, but among its economic units and the various groups in these units; that there be common participation ... planned on the basis of a shared common life, the low as well as the high.
>
> The plans we make for this emergency ... may show the way to a more permanent safeguarding of our social and economic life to the end that we may ... avoid the terrible cycle of prosperity crumbling into depression. In this sense I favor economic planning, not for this period alone but for our needs for a long time to come.[7]

There followed next in this speech a long passage summarizing the conclusion reached in my own study of business regulation, the subject, in fact, of my doctoral dissertation, ten years before. Immemorial usage, I had concluded, indicated that the services supplied must be adequate to public needs, that the prices charged must be reasonable, and that all customers must be treated alike.

7. The quoted excerpts from these speeches are from the *Public Papers,* vol. I, *The Genesis of the New Deal.*

In the next section he developed the germ of what was to be our view of the tariff, and I recognize a passage I must have furnished, but one I should have been more cautious about using if I had foreseen the attitude of practically all economists toward later monetary policy: "Just before the Hawley-Smoot bill had been presented to President Hoover for his signature, a thousand American economists told President Hoover that he should not sign the law. I am told that never before in history have so many economists been able to agree upon anything. But the faults of this bill were so open and palpable that they found easy agreement. Hoover ignored their warning. Would he have ignored a warning by a thousand engineers that a bridge that the National Government was building was unsafe?"

A moving passage described Jefferson watching from Monticello, in the twilight of his life, the rise of manufacturing and the growth of cities. Roosevelt quoted from Woodrow Wilson to the effect that Jefferson's principles were sources of light because they were not made up of pure reason but had sprung out of aspiration, impulse, vision, and sympathy. He ended by saying: "Jefferson labored for a widespread concert of thought, capable of a concert of action, based on a fair and just concert of interests."

A month later at Oglethorpe University, on May 22, he pursued this same theme. "As you have viewed this world," he said, "of which you are about to become a more active part, I have no doubt that you have been impressed by its chaos, its lack of plan." He spoke then of this lack in higher education itself, of overcrowded professions and closed opportunities for many of those who sat before him. Then he went on to apply the lesson in industry:

> We cannot review carefully the history of our industrial advance without being struck with its haphazardness, the gigantic waste with which it has been accomplished, the superfluous duplication of productive facilities, the continual scrapping of still useful equipment, the tremendous mortality in industrial and commercial undertakings, the thousands of dead-end trails into which enterprise has been lured, the profligate waste of natural resources. Much of this waste is the inevitable by-product of progress in a society which values

individual endeavor and which is susceptible to the changing tastes and customs of the people of which it is composed. But much of it, I believe, could have been prevented by greater foresight and by planning. Such controlling and directive forces as have been developed in recent years reside to a dangerous degree in groups having special interests in our economic order, interests which do not coincide with the interests of the Nation as a whole.

I had nothing to do with the writing of this passage. There are sentences I might well have written; but I believe the original drafting was done by Ernest Lindley.[8] Any well-read American will recognize it as derived from Thorstein Veblen and W. C. Mitchell—the revisionist school of American economists. Much of the language does have the typical Rooseveltian inexactness of expression. It was certainly redundant to speak of a *chief* outlook which was *tinctured* by the hope of profits; no newspaperman would let such an expression stand. That sentence must originally have read: "whose outlook is controlled by profit-making." The draft was undoubtedly modified extensively. Later he went a long way further than any public man had ever gone toward commitment to collective action. It must have been deliberate. "We are

8. Ernest Lindley ought of right to be included in the list of those who are meant to be included when the Brains Trust is spoken of. His was an intimately informed knowledge. Incidentally his books about Roosevelt are still valuable. He was not only a reporter; he was a highly educated observer and he wanted desperately to see Roosevelt's political career made useful in establishing a stronger and better integrated nation.

It is my recollection about this speech that Lindley wrote the first draft because he had said frankly to Roosevelt that what was being produced was neither forthright enough nor as bold as people demanded. He was told in a challenging way by the Governor to produce a speech himself if he didn't like ours. And he did.

It may be of interest to note that Judge Rosenman's recollection of the Oglethorpe speech, which was such a significant one, agrees with mine. In *Working with Roosevelt* (New York: Harper, 1952), he said of it:

"One day the small group of New York newspapermen in Warm Springs with the Governor—Walter Brown of the Associated Press, the late James Kieran of the *New York Times,* Louis Rappel of the *New York Daily News,* and Ernest K. Lindley, now of *Newsweek*—were off on a picnic with the Governor and Missy. They were all having a good time. After a while the newspapermen began ribbing Roosevelt about some of his recent speeches. He said, good-naturedly:

" 'Well, if you boys don't like my speeches, why don't you take a hand at drafting one yourselves.'

"Lindley said, 'I will'—and he did.

"The other newspapermen did some prompting and editing, but it was chiefly Lindley's draft. The Governor made very few changes in the language; a reading will show a style quite different from his usual style" (p. 65).

presented," he said, "with a multitude of views as to how we may again set into motion that economic machine. Some hold to the theory that the periodic slowing down . . . is . . . a peculiarity which we must grin, if we can, and bear . . . This attitude . . . requires not only greater stoicism, but greater faith in immutable economic law and less faith in the ability of man to control what he has created than I, for one, have." "That which seems most important to me in the long run is the problem of controlling by social planning the creation and distribution of those products which our vast economic machine is capable of yielding. It is true that capital, whether public or private, is needed in the creation of new enterprise and that such capital gives employment . . . Our basic trouble is not an insufficiency of capital. It is an insufficient distribution of buying power coupled with an oversufficient speculation in production. While wages rose in many of our industries, they did not as a whole rise proportionately to the reward to capital, and at the same time the purchasing power of other great groups of our population was permitted to shrink."

He went on to indicate his belief that it was well within the inventive capacity of man, who had built up so great a productive machine, to insure that all should receive from it at least the necessities of life. It would be necessary, of course, to raise wages and reduce profits, especially the profits of speculation. Too many leaders, he said, "fail to recognize the vital necessity of planning for definite objectives. True leadership calls for the setting forth of the objectives and the rallying of public opinion in support of these objectives . . . When the Nation becomes substantially united in favor of planning the broad objectives of civilization, then leadership must unite thought behind definite methods. The country needs and, unless I mistake its temper, the country demands, bold, persistent experimentation . . . The millions who are in want will not stand by silently forever while the things to satisfy their needs are within easy reach."

This was his last speech before the acceptance on July 22. It is quite evident that our conversations concerning the causes and cure of depression had been working in his mind as he rested and exercised at Warm Springs. They had also been working, to even better effect, in Ernest Lindley's. He was by now, if he had not been before, a partisan of those of us in the Rooseveltian counsels who pressed for economic integration.

Roosevelt was expounding the causes of American progress. To suggest bold experimentation and planning was something entirely new from an American statesman.

He intended, however, to go even further than that, as one passage indicates. In it there was a clear call for the rallying of public opinion in support of his objectives. He meant to appeal for a mandate. On the whole it appears still to have been not only a direct expression of his intention, but the most courageous of his public addresses; but this, of course, was before the nomination, before the party elders had counseled caution, and before he himself had concluded that nothing need to be said to insure victory and that the less said the less there might be to retract later.

I was disappointed in the references to farmers' troubles in the acceptance speech made in Chicago at the close of the Convention; but there was another equally disappointing compromise. I had suggested that he might go further in advocating the planning institutions promised in the Oglethorpe University statement. He had said then that the Democratic party must be one of "liberal thought, of planned action, of enlightened international outlook, and of the greatest good for the greatest number of our citizens." It was not his choice, he had said, but the choice of the times that the depression should be the overshadowing issue of the campaign. And he had gone on to analyze some of its causes.

This, of course, was before the campaign was well begun, but he had announced a theory of depression, and he had indicated that the remedy lay in public management rather than in mere reform. He was now avoiding further commitment of this sort. Indeed there was a retreat almost at once. When his attack was made on Hoover's economic policy at Columbus on August 20, he offered quite a different program after an identical analysis. What he proposed seemed to me a non sequitur. I was puzzled and depressed by its implications. He began by saying: "Both platforms and the speeches of acceptance . . . have agreed upon one thing: the major issue in this campaign is the economic situation." He then went on to describe how the Republicans' platform had claimed credit for American prosperity in 1928 and had shown how the expansion of export trade had been furthered. It was not chance, Hoover had said; things like this do not just happen. Now Hoover was attacked for interfering with business and for claiming that prosperity of the 1920s was owed to Republican policies: "Apart from the futility and danger of such interference, the President's thought is a wide departure from the Republican tradition as voiced by President Harding's slogan of less government in business. Republicans everywhere should understand and see this in this year, 1933. It is completely alien to the traditions of their party. The coincidence of the two policies is as dangerous a mixture as fire and powder. This is the tragic folly of the past four years."

Here was Roosevelt, who up to now had been making speeches in praise of planning and public management, attacking Hoover, not because he was a bad planner, but because he did any planning at all.[9] He then appraised the situation "in the bitter dawn of a cold morning after":

> We find two-thirds of American industry concentrated in a few hundred Corporations, and actually managed by not more than five human individuals.
>
> We find more than half of the savings of the country invested in corporate stocks and bonds, and made the sport of the American stock market.
>
> We find fewer than three dozen private banking houses, and stock-selling adjuncts of commercial banks directing the flow of American capital.
>
> In other words we find concentrated economic power in a few hands, the precise opposite of the individualism of which the President speaks.

9. Concerning the main point here—that Roosevelt exhibited a kind of theoretical schizophrenia about planning—Roy Peel and Thomas Donnelly in their standard account of the battle, *The 1932 Campaign, an Analysis* (New York: Farrar and Rinehart, 1935), completely overlook the earlier commitments and the gradual regression to orthodoxy. It seemed to them: "The issue which was conspicuously avoided by the major parties was national planning. In the face of an overwhelming public sentiment for planning, which had begun to sweep the country in 1929, and which was clearly recognized by such official agencies as the Federal Trade Commission [the FTC release of October 26, 1931, for example, clearly foreshadowed the NRA], the chief advocates of Republican and Democratic success were strangely silent . . . Diligent examination of the records reveals a sentence here and there in Roosevelt's speeches to show that he was familiar with the concept of planning, not in the European sense, but in its more limited aspects of coordinating international and national movements, public and private action, consumption and distribution" (p. 140).

We find the Republican leaders proposing no solution except more debts, more conferences under the same bewildered leadership, more Government money in business, but no Government attempt to wrestle with basic problems. And we have stirring appeal to the intrepid soul of the American people.

Now I believe in the intrepid soul of the American people; but I believe also in its horse sense. I am going on now to outline my own economic creed, and a substantial part of the constructive program that I hope to initiate.

I, too, believe in individualism; but I mean it in everything that the word implies.

I believe that our industrial system is made for individual men and women, and not individual men and women for the benefit of the system.

I believe that the individual should have full liberty of action to make the most of himself, but I do not believe that in the name of that sacred word a few powerful interests should be permitted to make industrial cannon fodder of the lives of half the population of the United States.

I believe in the sacredness of private property, which means that I do not believe that it should be subjected to the ruthless manipulation of professional gamblers in the stock markets and in the corporate system.

I share the President's complaint agains regimentation; but unlike him, I dislike it not only when it is carried on by an informal group, an unofficial group, amounting to an economic Government of the United States, but also when it is done by the Government of the United States itself.

Basing himself upon this reversion to Adam Smith, Roosevelt, with what seemed to me a kind of mock-heroic eloquence, proposed "an orderly, explicit and practical group of fundamental remedies . . . measures, like my whole theory of the conduct of Government . . . Based on what? Based on telling the truth." And he went on to a seven-point program, including security and exchange regulations, more rigid supervision of commercial or investment banking, and the withdrawal of Federal Reserve Banks from the rediscounting of speculative securities.

I do not need to say that I had no part in the writing of this speech. I must say, however, that I had my chance to argue against it in several of our Albany seminars and that I failed to make any impression at all. It was quite obvious that if Roosevelt had not changed his mind, he had determined to change his tune. He was going back to catch up on the old progressivism; but he was not going further with the experimentalism that had seemed to be emerging so clearly at Oglethorpe University a month or two before. That was to be dropped.

The changeover from the philosophy Adolf, Ernest Lindley, and I—with Ray consenting—had so ardently championed to a different one was owed to the availability of an alternative argued for quite as ardently by those he had admired and revered before our association with him.

It will be recognized that this last excursion into the relations of government and business was the forerunner of that series of regulatory acts which had to do with the repression of holding companies and the setting up of the Securities and Exchange Commission. It was Frankfurter—surrogate for Brandeis—in his visits to Albany and Hyde Park who had argued, day in and day out, for this approach to business regulation. It was one way of "making little ones out of big ones."

This approach appealed to Johnson, perhaps because it was high-sounding but also innocuous. And Howe favored it because his guiding animosity was an irradicable suspicion of investment bankers. It would not be true to say that Adolf or I opposed reforms. We too thought they were necessary; but we did not consider that the proposed measures had anything to do with recovery. It was in the tradition of Populism, of La Follette progressivism. It was what Brandeis had schemed out for Wilson.

It is true that once or twice more during the campaign Roosevelt spoke of public management. He said in his address on the farm problem that he would "reorganize the Department of Agriculture, looking to the planned use of the land." He went even further to say that this kind of planning, designed primarily to gain a better and less wasteful distribution of agricultural productive effort, "inevitably will point the way to readjustments in the distribution of the population in general." And later, in the Commonwealth Club speech in San Francisco on September 23, he foreshadowed not only reform of holding companies and investment banks but also industrial self-planning.

Without further analysis of the commitments during the campaign, it can be seen, I think, that Roosevelt began by rather enthusiastically presenting to the young people at Oglethorpe a view of economic society at once challenging and optimisitic, saying to them, in effect, that what man had created he could control if only he would undertake the task with forthrightness and courage; but later on, the same analysis was followed by the assertion that no more was necessary than such as would result in "truth telling"? Was the Commonwealth Club speech in any sense a reconciliation of these attitudes?

I am quite certain Roosevelt understood the implications of the design worked out with Moley, Berle, Lindley, and myself. I am quite certain he felt that something like it was necessary; but as he explained to me in a later conversation, "that kind of thing has to grow rather than be campaigned for." Also he had evidently been unable, as he thought about it, to visualize its practical embodiment in acceptable institutions. We protested that no institution could begin to evolve until it had come into being, and also that people frequently learn the wrong lessons from trying events. "Could a political campaign be educative in the true sense?"[10] In two of his speeches he said it could. But, as he said privately to us, a political leader had first to assure his election. He was now running for office.

It was on the day of this conversation that luncheon was interrupted by a telephone call taken at the table. Putting his hand over the transmitter, Roosevelt turned to the rest of us with a broad grin and said, "It's Huey," and he held the receiver so that a crackling voice carried out into the room. The Louisiana dema-

10. Afterward, in *Looking Forward* (New York, 1933), a book compiled by Earle Looker from past speeches and other public papers, and published before inauguration, Roosevelt would do greater honor to the educative function of a statesman than I should think warranted by the campaign, and at the same time rebuke our impatience for results: "The achievement of good government is . . . a long, slow task. Nothing is more striking than the simple innocence of the men who insist, whenever an objective is present, on the prompt production of a patent scheme guaranteed to produce results. Human endeavor is not so simple as that. Government includes the art of formulating policies and using the political technique to attain so much of them as will receive general support; persuading, leading, sacrificing, teaching always, because perhaps the greatest duty of statesmanship is to educate."

gogue had read on the news ticker that Owen D. Young had visited the Governor that day. He was calling, he said, to warn his candidate against such contacts. He said: "If I hadn't stood by you in Chicago you couldn't have been nominated"; and with profanity just short of obscene, he went on to indicate what he would do if there was any more consorting with these party conservatives like Owen Young, Norman Davis, Newton Baker, and the rest. The torrent of language went on for some time. When he finally replaced the receiver, Roosevelt said to us, no longer amused: "It has its funny side but actually Huey is one of the two most dangerous men in the United States today. We shall have to do something about him."

Clearly there was much in what he said; but to tell why would be to probe deeper into American life than we were to penetrate in the campaign, or, as Long himself tirelessly reiterated afterward, than Roosevelt would attempt when he became President. Long would furnish a voluble if distorted picture of alternatives to the policy being developed. His slogan, "Every Man a King," was an appeal, demagogic it is true, and impossible in a practical sense, just as others later on would be—for instance, the Townsend and Bigelow schemes for guaranteed incomes—but one that offered a continuous invitation to Populist extremism. It was a call to insurrection.

Eventually Roosevelt responded to this thunder on the left in his own way; but at the time I write of, competing ideas were tossing about in his mind. This was evident from the appearance of first one, then another, in his public addresses. These were sometimes such typical key expressions of commitment that it was difficult to escape the generalization that he was devoted to the whole line of thought they implied and that he might be expected to develop the action it called for. If he praised planning, Adolf and I concluded too quickly that our hopes might soon find legislative embodiment; if he spoke of regulating the security exchanges and eliminating selfish monopolies, the ghost of Populism seemed to have entered into him; and again, if he talked of confidence, economy, and the protection of profits, it was assumed that he believed in the reestablishment of the predepression business regime in all its essentials.

These were the three warring systems successively represented in his speeches. I was often in despair as inconsistency appeared again and again. Doesn't the man know, I asked myself, what he is really saying? Or does he enjoy the discomfiture first of the progressives, then of the businessmen, and so on? The truth was, of course, that, although his sense of humor was active, and although his Dutch stubbornness played a certain part, he had a genuine indifference to systems of all sorts. He was determined to reach certain objectives but was not committed to any methods for their attainment. He was appealing first to one, then to another, group of voters.

I wondered frequently whether he realized that patterns, symbolized by such words as "planning," "regulation," and "law of supply and demand," come to be stereotypes; and in their channeling of individuals' motor impulses, they could be dominant. Sometimes the most inventive people in one kind of endeavor were the most stubbornly reactionary in others. Indeed they were apt to be. The famous Yankee ingenuity in production and technology was often accompanied by the most stolid refusal to improve social devices. These attitudes seemed, in fact, to be normal associates; and it might account for our relative technical excellence in a framework of obsolete institutions. For a long time I failed to see that Roosevelt was most unusual in having escaped much of the grooving so characteristic of other Americans.

He often seemed to be impatient with the kind of patterning others' minds fell into without reasoning—for the protection of their practical interests—and he was unwilling to be counted on as belonging to any system or committed to any philosophy. This was especially true about government-industrial relations. He wanted to be known as a devoted conservationist, or as a believer in specific reforms, but in areas of controversy he refused commitment. I should later conclude that he had objectives and schemes of his own, deeper and wider than we knew;[11] but at this time I could not understand his contradictory sympathy with the under-privileged and his frequent excursions into policies favorable to their exploiters. Nor could Long; and his disaffection was at once more understandable and less dangerous than Roosevelt thought it to be. He was concerned about Long because he offered an alter-

11. They are stated best, perhaps, in the Introduction to volume I of the *Public Papers*.

native, even if a specious one, of attaining the very objectives Roosevelt hoped to reach by quite different methods; but there would be times when I should wonder whether Long did not have the right of it. He seemed wiser to me—mad as he was—than Lewis Douglas, who would be present at the President's morning bedside briefings almost daily during the first months in the White House and would seem to be listened to with approval.

It is a kindness of time that we are unable to recall the worst of our besetting fears. There was, as fall came on in 1932, a kind of hysteria in the air no one could escape; even the buoyant optimism of Roosevelt was diminished by its prevalence. Thrifty families in every locality of rural America were being torn from the acres they had cultivated and turned loose in communities where they had no place. Those who were able to remain on their farms awoke each morning to a little more rust on their machinery, a little more flaking of the paint on their barns, and a little less credit with merchants. In the cities, with winter not yet begun, the bread lines were lengthening. The streets were crowded with idle men. Businessmen had seen their occupations disappear; and vanishing values had reduced everyone's savings by half or more. No wonder Long's seductive voice was listened to.

It was in such circumstances that Roosevelt had gone out to talk about the national condition. Never had our people been so conscious that their arrangements for producing and distributing goods were matters for government concern. Never, I thought again and again, had there been such an opportunity to call for drastic changes. Still it had been quite clear, as the politicians saw, that nothing of the sort need be said to win the election. Almost from the first, no one, except possibly Hoover and a few of his officials, had believed that the Republicans might win.

Roosevelt had adopted the policy suited to the circumstances as the party elders understood them. He had to make the customary speeches, and they had to be carefully written; but although they dealt with economic subjects, their intent had been to convey, without much specification, a sense of new possibilities growing out of disaster, of a prosperous future replacing a dismal present.[12]

12. "The election was primarily a vote of lack of confidence in the Republican party and Mr. Hoover. Mr. Roosevelt had yet to win the confidence of the country . . . To assert that Mr. Roosevelt, as a candidate, had brought about such a realization and thus

His natural buoyancy and his apparent optimism had served this purpose well. Everywhere he went the people, at first in thousands and finally in millions, had responded to his personality. I will not say that the work our group did was wasted, but certainly it had little to do with his approach to the voters. Our memoranda were just the instruments he had used to shape an appeal of his own composing. Its theme was in fact trivial; but it seemed to lift the deflated spirits of Americans.

Moley, in the latter part of the campaign, was away from New York much of the time traveling on the long swings around the country. We talked with him often, from our Roosevelt Hotel headquarters at night when some speech was successfully past and the next one had to be thought of immediately. We sent him the material he wanted if we could get it together. As time went on, the local politicians, senators, congressmen, or state bosses began to be asked to sit in as the speeches were written. Some of these speeches, toward the last, were weird productions indeed. Still, they revealed somehow the Roosevelt temper.

By September, victory seemed so certain, and the need for the kind of material we were supplying became so diminished, that I even found it possible to spend two weeks in Mexico escaping hay fever before my work at the university should begin. Neither I nor any of the others except Ray, Sam, and Doc O'Connor were ever taken on a campaign trip. I myself never heard a speech except over the radio, and none of us were ever commended or, for that matter, reproved by Roosevelt. I learned afterward, when I knew him better, that this was characteristic; but certainly it did not occur to me at the time, though I have often been asked about it. I cast my vote along with other citizens on Morningside Heights in New York without as much sense of participation as might have been expected.

Some of us did listen to the early election returns together at the hotel, but from the first their trend was so obvious that there was no excitement in that. A little later in the evening the others went over to the Biltmore, where the political command had its

inspired the millions to follow him would be an exaggeration. His campaign was one of extreme caution. To a large extent he dealt with generalities in his speeches." Cleveland Rodgers, *The Roosevelt Program* (New York: G. P. Putnam, 1933), p. 12.

headquarters, and stood in a big crowded room while Roosevelt appeared on a balcony with one arm around Jim Farley and the other around Louis Howe, as was fitting enough. I went early to bed with a sense of a job completed—and if not well done, then done as well as had been expected.

A few years later the speeches I have been discussing appeared in the collection edited by Judge Samuel I. Rosenman. My greatest curiosity, as they were published, centered in the introductory notes Roosevelt himself was to write. How would he classify this effort? What label would he find to cover the compromises he made and the line he had chosen to follow? "Consistently I have sought," he said, "to help our people gain a larger social justice." Evasive again? I think not. Planning seemed to me to involve disciplines and controls so difficult that their attainment ought to be our main effort. For him it was one instrument in the "functioning of the representative form of democratic government in its modern sense." He meant to arrive at that "larger social justice."

When, long after his administration was over, I looked back on those spring and summer days of 1932, I thought he had always kept to that course, though I did not understand this at the time. At any rate I was at peace with him. He had taken something from me, something from others. As time had passed, our Albany group was repeatedly enlarged, usually with orthodox business-minded people—like Johnson. He had found their ideas more approved by the professionals and he had heard from the old Justice who knew what he wanted. Holistic ideas were ditched for the campaign. But I had done what I could.

The succeeding decades have shown that in the 1930s we should have used any opportunity to escape the old confines. We should have responded to the technological imperatives. That, I still believe; and I believe Roosevelt missed the best opportunity we would ever have in our lifetimes to recast the economy and redefine the objectives of our people.

5

PREPARATION

FOR THE PRESIDENCY

To follow the learning processes of a man like Roosevelt, to trace the sources of those actions which, when he reaches full maturity, give him character, is obviously difficult; but make such a man President, adding to the complexities of his nature those attitudinizings and distortions apparently required by that office, and the search promises nothing but defeat. It will be undertaken, for all that, many times in the years ahead. We are still too close for perspective but not, I think, for exploration. The Roosevelt shadow will grow longer, at least while any of us now alive remain to record our accounts as witnesses, in one way or another. Any contribution may have some value. At least none ought to be withheld without good reason.

Raymond Moley in his *After Seven Years* tells of leaving the old Congress Hotel in Chicago on a day in June of 1932. He was on his way to the convention hall where Roosevelt was shortly to be nominated—a fact not yet known, far from it, indeed, since that was the day of fright for all Rooseveltians. Ray picked up a paper from a newsstand, he recalls, and read an attack on Roosevelt by Heywood Broun. He does not say so, but I was with him, and looked over his shoulder. We read that piece of Broun's together. There was early summer heat in Chicago, the street was noisy, and the fumes of motors was thick. And we could have jerked off Mr. Broun's toenails with pincers if we had had him well tied down. For he had written that our man was "the corkscrew candidate of

NOTE. This essay appeared in the *Western Political Quarterly*, volume 1, number 2 (June 1948). Reprinted by permission of the University of Utah, Copyright holder.

a convoluting convention," meaning that he agreed with what was then a common appraisal of weakness, of anything-for-advantage willingness to be all things to all people. Had not Ray and I—along with others—just put in three of the most gruelling months of our lives having part of that candidate's education dug out of our entrails? For we did not bring him much that he wanted; he had to mine for it in us and send us out to get more ore. "Corkscrew candidate!" Ray says he boiled with indignation, but that is a poor description. He erupted, he stamped and cursed, and he swore that we'd show them. I think we can say that we did.

As a matter of strict fact my attendance at the political convention was the by-product of a directed exploration. I had been sent West to discover more about the latest plan for the relief of farmers. I had already explained it, I thought; but not, evidently, with enough clarity. To show how close a margin we were working on, I may recall that what I learned from M. L. Wilson, later Undersecretary of Agriculture Henry Wallace, later Secretary Mordecai Ezekiel, his adviser, and several others had only been gathered together in the preceding week. It had gone to Albany by wire; and had come back to Chicago by plane—incorporated in the Roosevelt acceptance speech. Our candidate was quick enough; he did not have to be briefed repeatedly if the first briefing was lucid. Much, however, depended on the pattern he was working out—and that was what made life miserable for those of us who had patterns of our own. He knew what ours were. He should have known: we had not yet ceased to be pedagogues; when we left the Columbia campus and, a few hours later, climbed the long hill at Albany toward the old executive mansion, we shed no teacher-like responsibility. We told him too much, all rounded out and trimmed down, when he gave us that kind of opportunity. He had to rummage a good deal, I can see now, to get what he wanted. He never told us anything—anything much, that is, useful for guiding us. He said a good deal; but all his words were for his own use. He was thinking out loud. The tying up, the systematizing, went on somewhere below—or above—the levels we moved on together. He was working out accommodations calculated for political effect. These we were not prepared to understand.

The Governor—as he was then—did however illuminate for me the art of politics he practiced, by leading me, figuratively speaking, out into the open fields as soon as he discovered my upstate origin. I recall how when we were alone, one evening, we began to talk about forests, wildlife, and their conservation, and he hinted at what afterwards became the Civilian Conservation Corps. From this we went on, even that early, to the difficulties of American farmers. I differed sharply with him about remedies. Up to this time his policies had been those needed by a governor. The experiment in the hills near Cornell of removing submarginal land from production, and returning it to grass and trees, we both thought a significant intimation of regeneration; but obviously if it succeeded, a lot of rural people would be displaced, just as millions in the cities had been excluded from increasingly mechanized factories. He thought they might be taken care of on subsistence farms in nearby valleys where more intensified practices were possible.

I followed him that far; but when he suggested that this might also be done for many idle city folk too, I balked. We argued back and forth and I thought I had made my point that if they made a living they would add to the already troublesome surpluses of stable crops, and even if they raised only produce for home consumption they were by that much reducing the market for commercial farm products. As to his argument that small industries could be induced to move to such colonies, I contended that people had always had to move to industries in the interest of efficiency and that less efficient operations would not attract private enterprise.

We abandoned the argument then, but several times later returned to it. I know now that he was reinforced by his wife and by Louis Howe. They finally would have their way, too, and when he became President a brave trial would be made at Arthurdale, Pine Mountain, Westmoreland, and several other places. But what is of interest here is that he suggested in the course of the argument, speaking with unconscious nostalgia, that country life had been a favorite center of interest for another Roosevelt— "Uncle Ted" he called him. By the way he spoke I realized that I had been shown a persistent pattern within his mind. I followed it up rather shamelessly as an opening. True, his penchant was congenial to all I believed and hoped. But its usefulness was in the entree it furnished. Again and again we talked of the amenities furnished by country life, and detailed the possibilities of improvement. This led to conversations about conservation. He thought of himself as being in a direct line of descent in this and recalled with obvious pride his many services to the cause. I had, myself, a slight acquaintance with Gifford Pinchot and with other old-time forestry and wildlife people who had been through the early discouraging struggles against the timber cutters and those nearsighted reclamationists who would have drained all the marshes and dammed all the streams. I was thus able to meet him on ground foreign to the others of our group. Hugh Johnson's interest in farm relief came by way of pioneering experience in Oklahoma, in cavalry life on the Texas plains, and in running a farm implement business; Adolf Berle was a world citizen without obvious feel for the rough texture of common country living; Ray Moley was an artist whose senses responded better to words than to the sights and sounds of October mornings afield; Sam Rosenman and Doc O'Connor were incorrigibly citified. In our group only the Governor and I were interested in such speculations—and on occasion we left the others silent as we indulged in talk only we understood.

It is surprising how many subjects open out from beginnings of this sort. It was not difficult to advance into a discussion of public works in this way: we could improve small town post offices, wildlife refuges could be constructed, any amount of work could be done in reforesting land retired from production because it had simply been worn out. This last I had long thought was one element of a program for agricultural relief with real possibilities; another related one involved the resettlement, under carefully determined individual plans, of the displaced families. I think now that these discussions not only helped lead Roosevelt to the most unlikely judgment, if considered politically, that I should be useful in the Department of Agriculture; it later led me to think, in setting up the Resettlement Administration, that I might have backing for a program which—together with the Agricultural Adjustment Administration—would set us far ahead in the rehabilitation of country life so plainly slipping into shabby circumstances.

I remembered also, and used equally unscrupulously, I am afraid, Roosevelt's sense of continuity from Theodore Roosevelt.

That ebullient leader had touched at one time or another nearly every phase of American life. In my private opinion he had neither settled anything nor advanced his causes much; but he had opened many subjects for discussion. It was Lincoln Steffens' observation that TR "thought with his hips," meaning that his intellectual processes had something visceral about them. The later Roosevelt was, in a way, subtler; he had more resources of charm and yet more directness of thought. He used his head, all right, and not his hips, but it was a kind of thinking I was often unable to follow because he had pictures for reference I could not always visualize. It was sheer luck that I caught the significance to him of country life; I suppose the TR business was more obvious. Perhaps he grinned to himself when, much later, I reminded him in conversation about the Food and Drugs bills (he was not giving me the support I felt entitled to) that the existing act had been a product of TR's progressivism in 1906, and that no president since had dared tighten its restrictions on the patent medicine men or the purveyors of poisoned cosmetics. The comment had the desired effect—until it collided with political interests.

These matters would not be less mysterious to all of us in after years than they were then—something not chargeable to deficiency in Roosevelt, as is sometimes suggested, but rather to a lack in us. Gradually we learned, some of us more successfully than others, the trick of moving with his mind and supplying its needs. But we had to learn what it meant to desystematize. We could venture pieces of theory; and perhaps they would find a place in his scheme. We could suggest relations; and the inventiveness of suggestion might attract his notice. But the tapestry of policy he was weaving was guided by a conception not made known to us. Perhaps it never could be. In any event, did it have to be? We were the journeymen, he the master craftsman. Some of us at times forgot our places; but he did not let that affect his conclusions, and he was gentle—too gentle to reprimand us in any harsh way.

My own association with the Roosevelt education began accidentally, of course, even though it may have continued out of mutual respect, even liking. It was chance that the furious resentment eating me in that third depression spring should, for an instant, have appealed to the dramatist in Ray Moley, organizer of the Brains Trust, and that it should have survived the scrutiny of

Rosenman and O'Connor, trusted helpers, who had to agree that I might be an addition to the Roosevelt group. It was equally a matter of chance that the Governor should have found useful the energies generated by that resentment. Whatever the probabilities, however, the spring and summer of 1932 did turn into a time of intensive work, educational in a more than academic sense. The pressures were intensifying visibly from week to week as unemployment grew and as deflation bore down harder. The old policies were more and more discredited and new ones correspondingly being looked for.

Activity throughout the whole economy seemed to proceed with protesting noises. There was sand in the gearbox; the oil cups were empty; a dismal clanking emerged from the centers of commerce. High above these sounds there had begun to rise frightened wails from the self-appointed chiefs of industry and finance. It was no longer a theoretical depression, a problem in management, of scheduling production and arranging finances. Reserves were being exhausted; and corrosion was striking in toward the strongboxes of the mighty. Depression had become a personal matter to those whose raised voices counted. The immunities of superior place were giving way; the crisis was at last affecting more than workers, more than the poor in their miserable homes. The wave of liquidation had swept up through the middle class institutions—insurance, banking, investment—and was now threatening to break into the most luxurious executive offices of the tallest skyscrapers.

Pleasantly, I imagine, Roosevelt had somewhat earlier contemplated his possibilities. It is to be remembered that he was fully committed to a progressive tradition, by now arrested. Wilson's foreshadowing of a reformist program back in 1916—The New Freedom—had been the last leafing of a tree whose roots ran back to pioneering and populism. And a Roosevelt could scarcely be unaware that his name was identified with the general course of action once projected under the symbol of the bull moose. He had served his apprenticeship with Wilson—eight years of it—in Washington. It had familiarized him with the implications of sea power and the uses of diplomacy; even, to an extent, with congressional vagaries. Then, after a long interval, with the trial of sickness midway, he had had the experience of governorship in trying times. But neither an assistant secretary of the navy nor a governor of New York learns in the course of his duty how to be a useful president of the United States. He picks up a good deal about foreign relations and about political difficulties. But adeptness at diplomacy equally with superior political technique is a matter of method rather than of policy. A leader must know what to do as well as how to do it. Roosevelt was doing a good deal of filling in that spring. He was far from sure that he knew what must be done although he was sure he would know how to do whatever it turned out to be.

He had a difficult problem. It was not merely that the policy he had to oppose politically—the one whose ruins lay all around us as we talked—was discredited; it was that the alternate he was at least half prepared with, and, in the minds of many, was committed to, was equally useless in such a holocaust. Quite evidently, there were new untamed forces at large whose behavior was not contemplated by the obsolete progressive doctrines. They might have been sufficient for their time; but this was another, and far more complex one. Now there was need not for the treatment of symptoms but for the surgery precedent to rebeginning. No one could tell him how to conduct that operation or even how to acquire the technique. We could give assistance but it was only that.

Historians will doubtless want to know, and will try to find out, how much truth there was in the contemporary picture of a wishy-washy candidate who never could make up his mind and refused to take positions on important issues. It is not hard to see how such myths are created; it is sometimes harder to see how they persist. The Albany newspapermen, either because they were told to do it or because, as is so often true, it "seemed like a good story," gave the country a picture of an amiable and ambitious but incompetent and wobbly governor who was dangerous because a shrewd campaign for delegates had made him the most serious contender for the Democratic nomination and because he was wholly unfitted for the presidency. A significance gradually attached itself to this fable because of the growing likelihood that a Democrat this time might well be elected. A country repeatedly urged to accept this picture of Roosevelt, and perhaps encouraged by the character of the subsequent cautious campaign for election, would later on have to reconcile the stereotype with a boldness and assurance such as had not been associated with the White House since the other Roosevelt had moved out. The same editorial deplorers of weakness would have an embarrassing turnaround to make before their boldface type could be employed to shout "Dictator!" But, of course, none of it was anywhere near the truth. If Roosevelt could be represented in such primary colors his education would not be a matter of interest. Even his detractors were to discover sometimes that they had to deal with a persistent and practical idealist equipped with subtle intelligence, immune to shallow emotion but moved intolerably by apprehensions of national weaknesses; they never learned to discount his surface amiability and to value correctly a Dutch stubbornness which brought him back again and again to the items of a program carried concealed in his mind, if nowhere else.

A president—or a man who may become president—is difficult for the public to understand because almost no one approaches him except on a selfish mission. No one regards him as a potential friend for whom small services can be done and who may make return in the affectionate way of usual intercourse. Everyone who seeks him out or is sought out begins at once to size up the consequences of the association—not always a matter of personal advantage, sometimes one of fancied good for a cause—and this makes the development of a satisfactory assessment impossible. The aura of consequence was already upon Roosevelt when I first met him in April of 1932. And I, no less than others, regarded him more as a possible instrument chosen by fate to stay the bleeding of the country's wounds than as a man who might become a friend. Only later did I discover in myself another feeling—that affection come by so late in such circumstances. It was only when friendship was recognized that I became involved in a struggle for better understanding. But that was not really so much later. At least it was well before we knew that the presidency lay down a straight road clearly revealed.

I could see, even before that, something of what he had to do if he was to become competent for a great part in public life. Facts stuck to his mind like insects to old-fashioned flypaper. We were not often able to tell him much in that way. But he was weak on relations, on the conjunctural, the joining together of forces and processes, especially in the national economy. A governor does not have use for such knowledge. And Roosevelt knew only a little about the competing ideas seething then in the less formal literature of the social sciences. My specialty, if I had one, was the study of social invention—especially, of course, in economic life. I had always been enormously interested in the creative intelligence—how things were made and ideas shaped, how novelty was possible and where it came from. And I had a good deal of work behind me; but not more than Adolf Berle, who was my junior by several years but had been a prodigy of early learning.

The intensities of those days made us familiar with one another. Doc O'Connor and Sam Rosenman never pretended to know anything. And, in the pre-Convention days, Adolf and I certainly had our chance. For Ray was by preference, as he himself has indicated, perfectly Baconian. He served as good water serves a thirsty man: with satisfaction, even with sparkle, but without substance. Adolf, so slight, so brilliant, and so contentious, and I, so determined and hopeful, carried the briefing burden alone, except for a little piecework, so to say, on the part of Joseph McGoldrick, Lindsay Rogers, Charles Taussig, and a few others.[1] Picture us then, after a Rooseveltian meal of some weight, settled in what must have been the ugliest room in any luxurious home in the State of New York—as was perhaps fitting in a governor's mansion —probably with a fire, and with Roosevelt very likely talking full volume. Ray, looking for an opening, would find it finally, and hand out a memorandum or give one of us a chance to state a thesis from notes. Then there would be reading or a monologue. But those memoranda, and expansions on them, were not accidental; their contents were planned, and often asked for. Before long, also, we, even if we could never get Roosevelt to do so, began to have a sense of passing time; there was not too much between where we were and the Democratic Convention. It had to be well used. Our calculations had little result, perhaps; we thought so then; yet there were many indirect consequences of those evenings. If we had thought more of him and less of ourselves and our clever schemes, Adolf and I, we might have been much more useful. But much as I should regret that early selfishness of purpose, it was tempered by the certainty that not much more could have

1. Joseph D. McGoldrick and Lindsay Rogers were members of the Political Science Department at Columbia; Charles Taussig was a New York businessman.

been done anyway. Roosevelt was getting what he thought he wanted. None of us could foresee that the deepening crisis would precipitate action quite so rapidly as it did.

The discussions centered, of course, upon the depression and what to do about it. And the conversations went on ceaselessly all spring and continued into early summer. But the pieces began to make a picture when the campaign began. It was a picture I did not like; and I failed if my purpose was to influence policy. I had my vindication later on, but that was no consolation for a lost year of opportunities. Roosevelt's mind was struggling all those months, evidently, to crystallize some program beyond the reestablishment of old institutions or of their reform. We did not supply it for him convincingly; and he did not put it together from what he had available or what anyone else supplied. This was what he most needed, and he could not dig it out of us. If he came to March 4, 1933, with what was generally regarded as the nation's worst crisis to meet and had to fall back on "the reestablishment of confidence"—on building up trust again in the old institutions—that was our failure and his together. That it has a *succès d'estime* for the moment was seized on for too much justification. Americans would have followed him in any proposal for change on that day, and he had nothing much to offer them. He would have to try to hammer out new devices in the years when legislators would no longer bend to his will, when business had recovered from its fright, when the people were no longer grateful for renewed faith in themselves. And not much would ever be done. It is true that more of the Wilsonian reforms were finally, with much recrimination, put through; but that these were not essential in any vital sense was gradually learned as the chronic frictions of economic life inevitably became again the center of concern. Depression, driven off repeatedly, was always waiting, a gaunt wolf on the threshold of the future.

Roosevelt had a weakness for alluding to experiences in his past, as governor or as practicing farmer in New York and Georgia, as though these were contributions to his education. Everyone does this on occasion; but the fallacy in it is almost too obvious to require pointing out—except that it underlines, in Roosevelt's case, the truth that, after having a relatively rich experience, he still had ahead of him all the essential education for the presidency.

Nothing that a man has done or gone through, only what he has specifically learned, is of much use to him in the White House, really, although it seems more popular to testify that the reverse is true. Nicholas Murray Butler records a conversation with President Harding in which a frank admission of incompetence was made. I can understand how Harding can have convicted himself in this way; and what it means to me is that he might have achieved a certain effectiveness if he had lived. For humility in the assumption of great responsibility is certainly the indispensable beginning. The dangerous man is he who is intellectually arrogant and who consequently sheds his worries and neglects to study.

Whatever Roosevelt may have said about the contributions of his previous experience, and however confident he may always have appeared, he did not feel adequately prepared in 1932. He often got down in the scholar's dirt with the rest of us and worked, worked hard at the specific task of knowing what government at Washington had to be and to do in the challenging circumstances of depression. This work was by no means always relevant to campaigning. The knowledge never seemed to him easy to come by, nor did the solutions he examined appear to have the satisfactory simplicity of common sense. The whole process was quite like that undergone by every searcher when he finally reaches the boundaries of what is known. To push out further he may have to invent a new methodology, or at the very least call up all his reserves of learning, before his mind can take hold of the problem and conceive the instrument needed to pry back the next stone across his path. Roosevelt did not have enough to go on. That is the truth. But he had the advantage of knowing this in advance rather than belatedly discovering it in the midst of mounting responsibilities.

In 1933 a good deal of senatorial and newspaper talk arose about having a "dirt farmer" in the Department of Agriculture; this had to do especially with my appointment. One of the more humiliating phases of the inquisition leading to my eventual confirmation as Undersecretary had to do with the uncovering of a past for me with experience in field and stable as well as on campus. That was phony, just as Roosevelt's farm experience was for the tasks he had begun to see ahead. It contributed exactly nothing to the invention and the workmanship embodied in AAA, in Resettlement, or in the conservation of soil, forest, and wildlife. Those were technical jobs, furthered by acquired craftsmanship in administration, not cultivating crops or breeding animals. Roosevelt's rural experience had no more relevance than mine did—except that, having it, he was able to recognize the utility, for instance, of our domestic allotment scheme and that for the retirement of submarginal land. Putting all this together he recognized as his own task. No one could help him to be the Chief Executive of our Constitution. I think we held him to essentials, sometimes, when he might have found it easier to slip off into seductive schemes for reform; but actually he would not abandon these even when recovery was what the nation most needed, so perhaps we were not so effective after all.

Whatever else can be said about him, Roosevelt was not, when he reached the presidency, one of those who regard the fortunes of the nation as the simple sum of its individuals' or its groups' fortunes. We may have helped in this. I like to think so, since that lesson is the first necessity for the shaping of national policy; but, in spite of his frequent insistence that states' rights were important, and his repetition of the old progressive fallacies about the virtues of little business and the reestablishment of competition, I recall many other occasions in that fusty Albany room or on the broad porch in summer when we went on from memoranda on railroads, banks, insurance companies, farmers, or unemployed workers, to genuinely conjunctural problems: taxes, budgets, credit, planning devices. I am certain that he did not think it sufficient to leave control of the economic system to the free-for-all struggle of the market. The contrast here, I think, was made as obvious then to him as it has since become to others. And although a politician has to convey to many groups the feeling of solicitude, the truth is that a president has to struggle constantly against such seductions. Specific group interests, if furthered, may upset the necessary balance among them all. I think Roosevelt knew that. His administrations were to be one long struggle for a policy including, and ordering properly, all the economic forces, and harnessing them to one national purpose.

This sense of complexity, of tenuousness, of continuous trying for balance, we may have helped him to begin seeing as the central necessity. There went with it a realization that the national interest would never emerge from unrelated individual actions. He was inclined to exaggerate goodwill and to be optimistic about melioration. He was a little loose in expectation, and somewhat soft in granting favors. Certainly the greatest efforts he made as president were not intended for the relief of classes or groups or individuals, but centered rather in a national policy to which all efforts were contributory: the National Recovery Administration, the Agricultural Adjustment Administration, money and budget manipulation, the distribution of relief, and the laying of taxes. But most people were even less sophisticated in such matters than he himself. The Congress had not advanced far enough in sophistication even to legislate nationally; or perhaps the existing institutions offered them no motive for supporting integrative as against divisive policies. Roosevelt was not able to supplant the old with the new. However much he might try, his successes were few, limited, and temporary.

What I have been trying to say is that, with his flypaper mind, he had an enormous fund of that information likely to be handy anywhere in public life, but that he was almost grossly lacking in knowledge of the theory and practice of manipulating economic forces. I am quite certain that by revealing much material, we made some contribution to his preparation; but I feel too that we may have helped to lift him into the strict realm of the presidency by forecasting with him, one by one, and quite precisely, the instruments he would need. I doubt if even he was aware of all the political difficulties, and certainly we were not. I would at first be surprised by his acquiescence and then despairing of any accomplishment at all, which shows, I suppose, my own amateurishness. I did hope for a more willing march toward what I regarded as a future we had committed ourselves to but, curiously enough, had not yet accepted. This indeed was the source of our troubles.

We all knew that although government is expected to cure economic disease, it is not expected to interfere with private economic activities; and that each group and region expects favors and is unwilling to moderate its demands to achieve balance. But no one foresaw the bitterness of later years. If he had had intimations of the divisiveness of the nation as it emerged from self-made disaster, it is possible that he might have adopted a different scheme of timing and perhaps other and more drastic devices. But, like all of us, he had a weakness for what was familiar and trusted and this led him to overestimate the sufficiency of the tried methods and to underestimate the rapid onset of obsolescence.

On these matters we were of no use. But what he foresaw of these difficulties, he expected to meet anyway with the "persistent, bold experimentation" he mentioned that spring in his revealing speech at Oglethorpe University, so that our uselessness was unimportant. It was naive to assume either that experiment would be tolerated or that it could be carried out, with any familiar techniques, on the scale necessary for genuinely national planning. But our candidate was a big man in whom the tides of vigor ran full; and with this vigor there went an irrepressible optimism. Difficulties were never to him anything more than challenges; they seldom even affected his purposes except in matters of timing. And if we were of no use—nor was anyone else—in this, he felt no lack. Napoleon once remarked that two good generals were worse than one poor one. There was no question in anyone's mind of sharing Roosevelt's generalship, though Ray Moley's later theory would seem to involve some resentment because of change in that respect. Moley's was a superior status and the rest of us shared some, but not all, of the delegations made to him; still I am sure that it was merely delegation, just as, for educational purposes, it was a really joint exploration only on occasion. I, for one, never thought I had shared any confidences as of right; and if occasionally my eagerness got the better of me so that I offered advice, and it was not taken, I did not judge myself aggrieved, although I might not like what was finally done.

If Roosevelt seemed to assume that his experience up to then had an exaggerated value, this was the mistake of observers. He may well have felt that he had evoked a Frankenstein's monster as the pledged delegates piled up. It was not in panic, or anything like it, but nevertheless in genuine need that he turned to us. If what he got was hammered out by himself more than extracted from us that was bound to be true in the circumstances; and any other result would have had consequences far worse than those by now recorded in history. He could have taken worse counsel; in fact, he did, before the time came to act. We never confirmed his most naive views; we sharpened his intellectual rather than his emotional processes; with us he had no pretensions and no ambitions to discount. Others who came later were often yes men, soothers, confirmers. That we never were. They held up to him what he wanted to believe, not what he must believe if he were to effect what he must effect; we insisted on the plain, if unpleasant, tasks necessary to recovery from what had become a national sinking spell.

He was busy enough even then, but the atmosphere was academic by comparison with what came later. We never had the seminar air of free exchange after the convention. The purpose narrowed. We became not inquirers but devisers then. If after the convention the atmosphere in which they took place was quite changed, so was the personnel. For General Johnson was now in our midst, and he proceeded from quite a different base and came out at quite a different end than Adolf Berle and myself. His policy had a curious consistency of contradiction: he was inclined to feel that government's true function was reassurance to business; but he also felt that it had a responsibility for ending, as it had for having begun, the crisis. He put these together by holding that reassurance to business—to be achieved by conservative finance, lowered government expense, reduced taxes, and so on— would end the depression. With one motion government could reduce its importance and discharge its most pressing responsibility. This was doctrine as seductive as the facts Roosevelt liked too well. And it has to be recorded that immediate presidential action was to be more consistent with this view than with our own. Ours implied a harsh, relentless discipline. Johnson's implied a harshness only to those who were widely considered to have it coming to them. For nobody liked the unemployed except the unemployed themselves, and nobody at all liked government employees, even others such as themselves. Nobody minded if the confidence of business required such people to have their incomes shut off or reduced. If what had to happen was mostly directed at such people, the remedy was relatively easy. But if, as I, at least, felt, a heavy hand had to be laid on the very citadel of faith— business—and if it had rigorously to be directed and disciplined, that was a hard solution to accept.

We gathered during the campaign to discuss not a memorandum, but a speech to be made by a candidate for the presidency who was obviously leading. Hugh Johnson was, on the whole, hostile to us and we to him. I appreciated his color and his real genius for invective. But I suspected his associations. I distrusted his principal, Bernard Baruch, and I resented his coming among us after what we believed to be service with the stop-Roosevelt movement all spring. So did Ray, though he was inclined not to recall it very vividly when he was writing his later books. Adolf's contentiousness met its match in Johnson's belligerence; there was plenty of interesting friction between them, although there existed a lawyer-client relationship between Adolf and Baruch. But I have not been revealing if I have neglected to convey the mutual acceptance among us all which made life tolerable among the tensions.

The perception, in the stress of campaigning, was dim, necessarily, but I nevertheless felt that Roosevelt's development was taking a turn toward what was easy and meretricious and away from the discipline Adolf and I felt he must in all honesty adopt. The turn toward orthodox views set him in the way he was to follow for some time. The only modification of essentially reactionary finance policies in his first year was represented by the public works title of the National Industrial Recovery Act, the initiation of the Civilian Conservation Corps, and, in another way, the establishment of the Tennessee Valley Authority. The expenditures involved in these "spending bills," as they would later come to be called, were expected to be saved by reducing veterans' allowances, pinching unemployment relief, and discharging vast numbers of employees in the regular establishments of government and lowering the pay of those who remained. This process would not enlarge activity or assist in reducing unemployment; quite the contrary; but there was a Johnsonian scheme for that—known as the Reemployment Agreement. It was an afterthought; in any case, its limits were soon reached, and within six months it was abandoned.

Roosevelt began very early to look for another easy escape in monetary measures. Currency manipulation, particularly through changing the price of gold, came to have the fascination of all simple solutions for difficult problems fruitlessly labored over. The establishment of balance among economic sectors and its maintenance by controlling their elements, involving a certain amount of discipline, was one way—the hard way—to ensure that everyone could buy everyone else's products. He could because his own sold at "parity." Roosevelt probably did not expect to achieve the same results with monetary measures. He expected to raise the price level and arrest deflation, thus rescuing those who had made investments—insurance policies, securities, homes, farms, and the like. He felt that with these grinding pressures relieved, activity might be resumed; but if he believed that anything of this sort would prevent the recurrence of depressions, he must have judged that all our reasoning was nonsense.

Taking the easy way was, from the first, the very thing we had feared; the institutions of balance and continuity must be managed. They are not automatic. Some of the forces in a high-energy economy—big business and finance—had upset the balance among groups and would resist its reestablishment. Restoring the situation once would be like the early socialist suggestions for redistributing wealth; it would last such a short time as not to be worthwhile. Power would return to its former possessors. What was needed was a control of income, not of wealth; a control of prices and of investment. If expedients were to be used, benefits for the unemployed, public works, and the like were the ones with the most promise.

Ultimately, what those of us said who took this view would be proved to have been sound; but I, at least, am ready to believe that for some reason our lessons were unworthy of professional teachers. Certainly when we had to compete with General Johnson and Professor Warren we were unsuccessful.[2] Only the more drastic educative lessons of experience were sufficiently effective. But I should like to point out not only that Roosevelt learned but that—whether by careful design I do not know—he provided himself with our line of defense in case it should be needed; he was at one time equipped with a revised Federal Reserve capable of influencing the volume of credit and, to a certain extent, prices; with an NRA capable of effecting control over production and prices; with an AAA to manage farm surpluses and raise prices; with a Reconstruction Finance Corporation to stimulate business through direct loans; with relief and public works funds for expanding purchasing power; and with flexible control over tariffs

2. George E. Warren, Professor at the Cornell School of Agriculture, who advocated the manipulation of gold as a recovery measure. It would, he thought, make unnecessary all the bureaucratic machinery of such devices as the Agricultural Adjustment Administration.

and so over international trade—all this in addition to what I regarded as an ill-advised economy act and manipulation of the price of gold.

In view of what was to happen, it was certainly ironic to have called our group a "Brains Trust." And I have no doubt that James Kieran, Albany reporter for the New York *Times,* meant to be ironic when he first used the words. It is pretty obvious that the man we worked for was, all the time, getting a good deal of that conjunctural education. We may have stimulated him to feel the need of other advice from those who were not much noticed at the time—George Warren and others at Cornell, Felix Frankfurter, Lewis Douglas, businessmen galore, the old war horses of politics, Swager Sherley, Key Pittman, Homer Cummings, James F. Byrnes, and others, all of whom had decided views on the questions at issue, however sound or otherwise they might be according to our criteria.

I can see now that this matter of orthodox preferences must have run heavily against us then, just as it did later. Soundness is measured only by customary approaches, by familiarity of doctrine, not by its realism or its utility. Moley has recorded the policy outlined for the crisis of March: it included not only the restoration of confidence, the rapid reopening of banks, and the immediate initiation of an economy program, but also the suppression of Adolf Berle and myself as administration associates. That was not difficult then. Adolf had only a nominal office and I was buried in departmental work. The reactionary policy had a full chance to show its possibilities. Sounder men than we were put to operating the conjunctural machinery.

Put to the test, the Reemployment Agreement helped some, and public expenditures—when they finally got started—helped more, but nothing, finally, served to conceal the need for more drastic changes. Roosevelt really learned by doing. Ultimately he would resort to the devices for control; but most of them had by then been eroded. Congress would no longer consent to expanding expenditures; NRA and AAA had been killed by the Court. So when not only Roosevelt but the requisite number of others knew what to do, it was too late to do it.

It is, however, important to note that holding back from many of these necessary measures was not only a matter of Roosevelt's choice. He seldom felt he could act when he himself was convinced of the need, only when others had also been persuaded. Compulsory delay or the warping of policy might result from anticipation of opposition; or it might result from the sudden development of such circumstances as, for instance, the closing of all the banks, precipitating action before it could be well thought out. There is possible a wide difference of opinion about the strength of opposition, but when it comes right down to it one man has to make the estimates; and the common judgment was that Roosevelt usually, though with important exceptions, went as far as a backward Congress and an annoyed Court allowed—in some instances farther. Crisis action has to be decisive, but it also has to be acceptable. Roosevelt certainly knew he was doing less than was necessary; but he had become convinced of the need to allay rising panic. It was his decision to make and it was as competently done as his education permitted and as circumstances allowed.

This is to say that, although I deplored much that he did, I still, along with the others, must share whatever fault there was. My mistakes were made day by day; so were those of others; and none of us could go back, nor could we engage in tours de force. A teacher is often faced with the results of his incompetence; but I have never known how to repair old mistakes. Do better in the future, yes; but how about a case like this? There is no future in helping presidents educate themselves.

If there was a decisive change when the nomination was won and a flood of new influences and pressures swept in upon the candidate, this was even more true after the election. The first flood consisted largely of Democrats who either pretended they had been for him all along or who frankly said that hatchets might better be buried in Republicans than in each other, and that adjournment of differences was in order. The second flood, however, included the real power and might of finance and industry. Considering their responsibilities, the generals of our economy permitted their wishes to influence their judgment to an amazing degree. Most of them supported Hoover to the last, though there was some changing of sides late in the campaign. But once the election was over, their desire to become the confidential advisers of the new President-elect led to much unseemly gate crashing and even to assumed humilities. They were willing to take charge of his education now; and they appeared to feel not only that most of it remained to be done but that the President-elect was still a kind of *tabula rasa* to be written on at will; and the fact is that it was not altogether too late for their purposes. He accepted a good deal from them.

For instance, they showed him how to handle the banking crisis; or, rather, they handled it for him. True, their approach fitted Baruch's constant leaning toward retrenchment and the restoration of business confidence; but it was their technique that was used. Ogden L. Mills, Arthur A. Ballantine, and Francis G. Awalt, all members of the Hoover entourage, stayed on for weeks to operate the machinery. As Moley, converted to their views, said in *After Seven Years:* "We were just a bunch of men trying to *save the banking system.*" This was probably accurate; he doubtless identifies the banking system with the general welfare now, and perhaps he did then. I must, however, except myself from such a conversion. I thought the panic of depositors could have been allayed in other ways. In any case, the men and women—millions of them in the past year or two—who had faced day after day with no food in the house could have told bank depositors the true meaning of panic; and there had been no sudden hysterical stir over their plight.

I did not recognize, removed as I was from the councils of the financial rescuers, the man who in Albany had sat with us night after night, not depressed certainly—for he was never that—but concerned, deeply concerned to discover ways of doing something directly for those most deeply injured by depression. I am ready to concede that I may have been wrong, that this was another instance of his unfailing instinct for public consent. The middle class might have revolted and torn up the streets or invaded stores. Perhaps, as Moley says, if other advice had been taken, it would have "wreaked incalculable damage upon our whole economic order." However, I cannot agree. I believe he confuses, just as Roosevelt did in that crisis, the interests of a few with the welfare of all. Indeed, an accompanying passage seems to me to contain a reminder of the Mellon "trickle theory," one Roosevelt used to delight in formulating over and over with ironic illustrations. Says Moley: "It cannot be emphasized too strongly that the policies which vanquished the bank crisis were thoroughly conservative policies . . . Those who conceived and executed them were intent upon rallying the confidence, first, of the conservative and banking leaders of the country and, then, through them, of the public generally." Baruch and Johnson had, I say, reeducated Moley, if not so successfully the President.

Our failure—Adolf's and mine—was exposed during the final months before inauguration by another developing situation. I shall not attempt to recount the various incidents associated with the agenda meetings for the London Economic Conference to be held late in spring, after Roosevelt had become President. I may, however, recall that much of the campaign strategy had been based on a certain view of tariffs and the international debts remaining from the war. This view inferred that the handling of these questions at the conference might somehow mitigate the world crisis. Roosevelt at one time had been somewhat put to it to meet the propaganda of the internationalists on the transfer problem involved in collecting the debts. It was their contention that not enough exchange could be made available to meet the payments of foreign governments to the United States as they would fall due. This Roosevelt answered by a rather free interpretation of the Democratic tariff plank, saying that reciprocal arrangements for trade would have to allow for this. The British and the French, particularly, were determined not to pay. We believed, all of us, that they not only should but could.

Those bankers whose Americanism is always faintly tinged with Anglophile or Francophile bias—especially those who represent the nationals of those countries here—set themselves to change Roosevelt's attitude. They did not succeed until their best representative came home from conferring abroad. This was Norman Davis, whose long efforts as Hoover's delegate to the disarmament conference were no doubt valiant, however futile they may have seemed. He was one of those Democrats who were practically indistinguishable from Republicans. And it must be granted that he, too, proved a better educator than we professionals, even with the long start we had in his subject matter. Roosevelt, of course, knew what he was doing. He never reversed himself on the debt question. His acceptance of Davis, however, was the beginning of foreign adventures I believed to be unwise; and this doubt rose to a conviction when, later on, Hoover's Secretary of State, Stimson, was made a Roosevelt confidant, and the acceptance of probable future wars began to appear. Roosevelt's navy years had familiarized him with international affairs. He had a wide acquaintance—even friendships—among the diplomats who during his stay in Washington had been secretaries and attachés at the embassies but who had now risen to senior rank. Davis and Stimson moved easily in these circles. Davis' adventures in Cuba could be matched by Stimson's in the Philippines; and, although Adolf had served with the peace delegation in Paris and had a polish all his own, Moley, Taussig, and I were certainly country bumpkins in such society; and Rosenman and O'Connor were simply lost.

More could be made of this struggle over foreign relations than is warranted by the issues. Roosevelt humiliated us a good deal in the course of it; and even after election he nerve-wrackingly delayed coming to policies sufficiently decisive. He did cut the United States loose from the international exchange speculators, resisted stabilization on French or British terms, refused to let the Economic Conference concern itself with anything but long-run issues, and initiated reciprocal trade treaties. But the internationalists had their victories too—notably in preserving the "most favored nation" policy and in the actual, if only nominal, forgiving of the intergovernmental debts.

It had been Hoover's thesis—or alibi—that the depression had "come upon us from abroad," as a result of dislocations following the war. We had met this argument by saying that the sins of Europe were at least shared by the United States, and that the Republican policy of disposing of surpluses by creating purchasing power abroad through loans was distinguishably among the causes of the trouble. This thesis always irked the international bankers, though in the worldwide crisis they fared so badly that they sang low for a time. In 1933 the issues were still alive; and, on the whole, still unsettled.

Roosevelt had no particular dislike for bankers. He was inclined in their case, as in that of other businessmen, to discriminate between the good and the bad. Anyone who does this must have a code to go by, whether implicit or explicit; and Roosevelt had his. The behavior of many people who were in charge of affairs during the ten years before 1933 was offensive by any test, even their own. They had got their positions by a kind of ruthless disregard for others. This was justified in such cynical and often-heard aphorisms as "business is business"; and the saying that none of them remained in it "for his health." This attitude extended to more than the David Harum-like attempt to get the best of one another; it included violations of trust, and the taking advantage of confidences and of "inside information." This contempt for the old accepted rules of an earlier regime became so commonplace as to be unremarkable to most people.

A businessman's word in the simpler world of day before yesterday had been "as good as his bond." Not even his bond was necessarily good any more. Such degeneration of customs in economic life might have been explained by a cynic as a natural evolution. The breaking down of restraints was to be expected, it might have been said, in a world whose premiums went to the dishonest. The development of new processes and techniques had separated out a class of enterprisers who no longer operated industries but only manipulated them or their securities for speculative profits. There were those who, looking around at the behavior of the powerful financiers, industrialists, and merchants during prosperity and now in depression, might have said that an honest—a "moral"—businessman was an anomaly. The rules of the game were such that a really scrupulous individual could not succeed; he would be eliminated in the selective process. But this was not Roosevelt's way of looking at things. Finance, to him, was normally something more than the glorified racket it seemed to me. Resort to double-dealing, fraud, blackmail, and force was not to him a necessary accompaniment of financial activity, even though he saw that such behavior had become very common. Its features were not less ugly when overlaid with the thick respectability of new-made wealth, and he was outraged as most Americans had refused to be so long as they shared a little—or even hoped to share—in the profits of the 1920s. They had neglected their professed code of behavior. And like Roosevelt, they felt that the troubles come upon them were caused by departures from accepted rules. That disaster was inherent in the industrial-business process was not and could not be believed. If it were so, the guilt was not only widespread but also irretrievable, short of fundamental change. That undertaking almost no one was prepared to encourage.

Roosevelt, when he said that he believed in the capitalist system, was saying something he could not conceive that anyone should doubt. The demands made on him for reiteration of his faith may have come from a genuine disbelief, on the part of financiers and industrialists, that the system could be saved except through some kind of dictatorship; and though he never went so far in suspicion as to identify these traitors, he often spoke of them. Many leaders among them undoubtedly felt that nothing short of a coup of some sort could fend off the wrath of a disillusioned people and prevent a redistribution of privileges. There was a good deal of vague talk, perhaps even some plotting, going on. Roosevelt, I am quite sure, although he knew what was up, never wavered about this. He intended some purging and punishing—these were necessary penances. As for the participation in the whole perverted business of so many decent folk, they had had their punishment in loss and grief. Aside from this, his code required a change of heart, or new personnel with better hearts, throughout the economy. He regarded this as possible, an optimism resulting from his Christianity. For he was a deeply religious person in the true experiencing sense. He was also guided by the Protestant ethic, and this led him to the conclusion that ill behavior in the economic world required regeneration. It did not occur to him that the Protestant ethic had been largely responsible for what had happened. He felt that men in great numbers had failed to live according to its requirements. They must begin again to practice the faith they professed.

His subsequent relations with businessmen are to be understood in the light of this attitude. For from his point of view, it must be seen, they refused to reform. They were doing one thing after another in pursuit of profit or other advantages; and it began to appear very soon that they saw no reason for change. They rejoiced in not having to, in "having got away with it." And Roosevelt was considered a crazy reformer for continuing to insist, when the better times of partial recovery came, that what they had weepingly promised in the fake repentance of a stormy day should now be carried out. No really worldly and realistic person should have expected the President's Reemployment Agreement and the subsequent codes, as they were formulated and managed, to produce a more ethical industrial system. There was no meeting force with force, no compulsion even when behavior was most outrageous. The most cynical aims and the most destructive methods were introduced without shame into the "partnership" of government with business; the government, indeed, was expected to join in legitimizing gains from the practices it had always condemned. Roosevelt did not quickly grasp the outrage which once more swept the country; and he never concluded from this experience anything he had not concluded from the depression. But he was hurt, just as millions of others were. And his attitudes sharpened under the repeated propaganda attacks of the now-recovered industrialists. He at last recognized unmistakable implacability in the enmity he faced, an enmity far worse because he was recognized secretly as the true, the curative, friend. For businessmen could now be unrepentant, raging against controls, cynical in subversion. Most of all they hated and feared the reformer who wanted to improve their morals.

Roosevelt's education went on in this practical rather than pedagogical manner. He was driven from point to point until his opposition appeared to be universal. It was not really that, however, because there was still no fundamental disturbance of code, no diminution of faith in individual regeneration as a cure for economic ills. Moley finally parted company with him on a curious issue, essentially nonrecognition of the plainest facts. He would have required of the President an appeasement he should have known was impossible, for it involved assent to what Roosevelt regarded as wickedness. Moley came to the point of regarding demands for plain ethical behavior as somehow threatening and unusual. On this Roosevelt's attitude continued to be bolstered by religion, by training, by everything moral in an unstable world. I came to the point, in my observation of attacks on him and evasions of responsibility on the part of businessmen, of wondering whether his code would stand the shattering impact; but it always did.

The unremitting drive from business on the forts of Roosevelt's courage usually presented itself to the world in the guise of a quest for "confidence." Those who had investments to make, who sought to control funds, who could start enterprises and create employment, would claim to be stopped from doing so because the President refused to speak kindly, because he would not confer his blessing, remove obstacles, forget and forgive. This kind of pressure proved ineffective because it opposed itself to something in him beyond his or anyone else's control.

His code of right and wrong was fully developed. This was often concealed by superficial amiability or by political flexibility. Every little while there would creep into print, or into that underground so characteristic of Washington, the whisper that things had changed; the President was now "going to be good"; he would fire his "radicals" who were always presented as people who "hadn't met payrolls" and were therefore not "practical." What was always hoped was that the President would come around to fronting for the speculators, the exploiters. At the end of it all Roosevelt remained serenely impervious to whispered stories, and to direct attacks, a man of unreality perhaps, and in this sense not educated, because this is not an educable trait.

On the contrary, Roosevelt set himself from the first to be the educator, rather than the educated; and if he could not convert the men of business, generate in them a sense of sin, he would go to the nation. This, I feel, is why he came to be so hated. This is what his undermining of confidence consisted in. For those very "economic royalists" whose measure he took were verbal supporters of the same code. They could not object to his standard; but their indignation knew no bounds when they were exposed—again and again—as its violators, flagrant and willful. Thus a man who believed in business, what he called "honest" business, became a reformist scourge.

To say this is to point to a certain numbness and cynicism in me; but in Roosevelt, with far greater provocation, it gained no hold. My capacity for indignation died down, much, I imagine, as does systemic reaction to a drug. I was educated by experience. But Roosevelt never was. His belief in a free press was shown by anger at each new unfairness; similarly his underlying faith in business can be measured by the capacity he retained for outrage at each new instance of wicked behavior. When such a man no longer becomes angry, I have often thought, then is the time to look for something spectacular. Until that happens he still looks for conversion and will do nothing basically dangerous.

Eventually I found myself in such a confusion about what I had always believed and about the possibilities I believed to be inherent in American life that simple withdrawal became irresistible. I could hope to find some certainty again if I escaped from the center of struggle. But Roosevelt remained in this respect untouchable, his certainty unimpaired, his ethics unchanged.

6

PROTAGONISTS:

ROOSEVELT AND HOOVER

Looking back, after several decades, some of the forces at work in 1932 can be much more clearly seen than they could at the time. Also the personalities operating in the peculiar circumstances of depression can be understood much better than while the campaign was going on. Hoover, of course, was on the defensive; Roosevelt was seeking to displace him; but even after Roosevelt had won, Hoover was determined not to abandon his principles.

It was impossible, as the campaign of 1932 progressed, not to spare a pang of sympathy for Hoover. We may have been furious with him at the beginning, representing as he did the smug immovability of reaction. But before the campaign was over he was more an object of pity than a respected antagonist. As the attack developed and replies were made, it dawned on many of us, to whom it had simply not occurred before, that Hoover was not an engineer at all in any factual sense, but a man of fixed principle. It had been a mistake to think that a scientific training implied social realism. He was genuinely convinced that consent to the mild measures of reform proposed by his opponent was immoral. It was immoral because there was almost no distinction, in his mind, between federal relief for the unemployed, for instance, and Communism. At the very least the one was a commitment to the other. He was to be pitied because he suffered.

Raymond Moley, returning from the preinaugural meeting in Washington between the President and the President-elect, spoke of the further immolation to be read in the President's face. "He

NOTE. This essay appeared in *The Antioch Review*, Winter 1953-54.

seems to me close to death," he said. "He has the look of being done, but still of going on and on, driven by some damned duty." The duty was to minimize as far as he could the disaster to the nation involved in the Roosevelt accession. It had frightened him during the campaign; it had ravaged his spirit in the months which had followed; and he did indeed look, at the end, completely spent.

There was such consistency in all we knew about him, and it led so inevitably to tragedy, that even in the busyness of those days, and even though we had resented his stubborn reluctance to meet the issues they had raised, we were moved by his ordeal. It had not seemed likely at any time after 1930, when the Democrats had carried the interim election, that Hoover would survive politically in 1932. It had been apparent from the time of Roosevelt's nomination in July that he would win and that Hoover would lose. He had won; and Hoover had had to struggle with the inadequate weapons he allowed himself, and against the harassments of a partisan and hostile Congress, to stem descent into disaster, even while he prepared to hand over power to a successor he profoundly distrusted.

When he heard that a Roosevelt envoy had been burrowing among the equivocal paragraphs of the 1917 Trading with the Enemy Act he said to Ogden Mills, so we heard: "Good God! They're going off gold!" There was scandal and heartbreak in the ejaculation. The permissive clauses had been brought to him—we found them underlined in red in the Treasury copy—and he had rejected the betraying alternative. As late as February he was proudly affirming: "Ever since the storm began in Europe the United States has held staunchly to the gold standard." "We have," he said, "maintained one Gibraltar of stability in the world."[1] To us that may have seemed a curious view of the situation in February of that year. There was no Gibraltar of stability for all those unemployed and their families, all those home and farm owners who were being dispossessed, all those holders of insurance policies whose companies were insolvent; there was none even for industrialists whose factories were closed. Presumably it was a Gibraltar for those who owned gold. But even the banks did not

1. Address of February 13 at the Lincoln Day dinner of the National Republican Club. *State Papers of Herbert Hoover*, edited by William Starr Myers (New York, 1934).

own enough. Within a month they would all be refusing payment to depositors.

It was, as a matter of fact, only five days after this breast-beating effusion that a long-hand letter to the President-elect was written. The letter began: "A most critical situation has arisen in the country of which I feel it is my duty to advise you confidentially." It went on to repeat his theory of the depression and recited repeated "shocks." We were, he said, "confronted with precisely the same phenomena we experienced late in 1931 and again in the spring of 1932."

The trouble was, according to Hoover, a lack of confidence. This was what he had been fighting all along. First the Democratic Congress had frightened business, then Roosevelt had frightened it even worse. Now there was nothing more that he could do. But the alarm could still be quelled and recovery begun "if there could be prompt assurance that there will be no tampering or inflation of the currency; that the budget will be unquestionably balanced even if further taxation is necessary; that the government credit will be maintained by refusal to exhaust it in issue of securities.[2]

This, we felt, was about as far as anyone could go in sticking to his guns while the ship went down. There was the clear implication that the Republican policy was to be absolved of all blame for the depression. That holocaust had begun as the aftermath of war, it had continued because of "shocks from abroad," and heroic efforts to overcome it had been frustrated by irresponsible Democrats. It is to be supposed, from the earnestness of the February communications, and their confidential tone, that Hoover did not believe dissent to be possible. He thought that Roosevelt and his helpers, as reasoning people, must accept his analysis and join in the obvious measures for the restoration of confidence.

Such obtuseness could only be owed to immersion in an ideology completely immune to events. The statement of the thesis was made repeatedly during the campaign; it was held to in the interval

2. This letter, now in the Roosevelt library at Hyde Park, is something of a historical curiosity, not only because it was handwritten and confidentially delivered in a great crisis, but because it was not answered, so that ten days later Hoover felt compelled to forgo pride and, in spite of the apparent discourtesy he had suffered, address another letter to the incoming President, indicating that the situation had deteriorated further. This last brough a reply and the explanation that the apparent discourtesy had been a secretary's oversight. The incident of this letter and the surrounding circumstances are discussed at some length in Moley's *After Seven Years* (New York, 1937).

before inauguration; it was even elaborated afterward not only in W. H. Newton and W. S. Meyers' account of the Hoover steward-ship,[3] but in the ex-President's own *Memoirs* published twenty years later.[4] Few men in our history have played a premier role in comparable circumstances and have kept their convictions so inviolate.

To read Hoover and the Hoover apologists it could not be inferred that there was another explanation of the depression. But there was. It was stated, rather cautiously but nevertheless unmis-takably, in the early Roosevelt campaign speeches. It was, in fact, stated in the first of them, the acceptance:

> In the years before 1929 we know that this country com-pleted a vast cycle of building and inflation; for ten years we expanded on the theory of repairing the wastes of the War, but actually expanding far beyond that, and also beyond our nat-ural and normal growth. Now it is worth remembering, and the cold figures of finance prove it, that during that time there was little or no drop in the prices that the consumer had to pay, although these same figures proved that the cost of production fell very greatly; corporate profit resulting from this period was enormous; at the same time little of that profit was devoted to the reduction of prices. The consumer was forgotten. Very little of it went into increased wages; the worker was forgotten. And by no means an adequate proportion was paid out in dividends—the stockholder was forgotten.
>
> What was the result? Enormous corporate surpluses piled up—the most stupendous in history. Where, under the spell of delirious speculation, did those surpluses go? Let us talk eco-nomics that the figures prove and that we can understand. Why they went chiefly in two directions: first into new and unnecessary plants which now stand stark and idle; and second, into the call money market of Wall Street, either directly by the corporations or indirectly through the banks. Those are the facts. Why blink at them?
>
> Then came the crash. You know the story. Surpluses

3. *The Hoover Administration* (New York, 1936).
4. *The Memoirs of Herbert Hoover: The Great Depression* (New York: Macmillan, 1952).

invested in unnecessary plants became idle. Men lost their jobs; purchasing power dried up; banks became frightened and started calling loans. Those who had money were afraid to part with it. Credit contracted. Industry stopped. Commerce declined, and unemployment mounted. And there we are today.

This, it will be seen, was a mechanistic, not a psychological, explanation of what had happened. It implied, consequently, that the remedies to be applied would need to be of the same sort. If there was a disparity between costs of production and the prices of goods, it would be necessary to force prices down. Only this would cure the stifling effect of this disparity. Price control by the federal government and some direction of investment were implied. If by this means corporate surpluses were reduced, they would neither be invested in unneeded plant nor flow into Wall Street to finance speculation. If all groups could buy the products of other groups and keep on buying them, continuous activity would have been established.

But there was another range of fact to be considered. And Roosevelt went on to consider it in the acceptance. It loomed larger and larger as the campaign progressed; and it was more important in shaping the New Deal program than the analysis just cited. This was the dislocation of established relationships involved in the deflation of the depression years. This involved not only the debts owed by individuals and groups to each other, but also exchangeability. It was reasoned by Roosevelt that panic had supervened when the value of securities had moved toward worthlessness, when debts contracted in dollars of low purchasing power could not be paid off in dollars of high purchasing power because debtors could not get enough of them.

It followed from this that if the dollars could be returned to the levels of their purchasing power when the debts had been contracted, debtors could get enough of them to satisfy their creditors. The incurring and discharging of debt—one of the central mechanisms of capitalism—could then go on freely. Reducing the value of the dollar was inflation. And the inference was that the new administration would resort to it in some fashion.

It was Hoover's contention that businessmen were frightened by both these inferences—that prices might be controlled, and that inflation might be resorted to. He maintained that this declining confidence made it impossible for the measures he sought to take in late 1932 and early 1933 to have any effect. The Roosevelt conception of cure made it impossible for the Hoover cure to work.

In 1952 Hoover summarized the items of his recovery scheme:

(a) to avoid the bank depositors' and credit panics which had so generally accompanied previous violent slumps; (b) to cushion slowly, by various devices, the inevitable liquidation of false values so as to prevent widespread bankruptcy and the losses of homes and productive power; (c) to give aid to agriculture; (d) to mitigate unemployment and to relieve those in actual distress; (e) to prevent industrial conflict and social disorder; (f) to preserve the financial strength of the United States government, our credit and our currency, as the economic Gibraltar of our earth—in other words, to assure that America should meet every foreign debt, and keep the dollar ringing true on every counter in the world; (g) to advance much-needed economic and social reforms as fast as could be, without such drastic action as would intensify the illness of an already sick nation; (h) to sustain the morale and courage of the people in order that their initiative should remain unimpaired, and to secure from the people themselves every effort for their own salvation; (i) to adhere rigidly to the Constitution and the fundamental liberties of the people.[5]

It should be noted that this summary was made in 1952 and so may possibly have exaggerated to some degree the promptness and energy with which the crisis was met. Certainly Hoover did "go into action within ten days" and it is true that he was "steadily organizing each week and month thereafter to meet the changing tides." It was this which wore him out by 1933. But that everything cited was done when it should have been done may be questioned; and wehther other measures were not called for, even on his own premises, is even more questionable.

But perhaps not, for it will be noticed that from *e* on, this list consists of qualifications. Many things suggested to him, or later

5. *Memoirs,* I, 32.

said by Roosevelt to have been necessary, were ruled out by considering carefully whether they might not result in the dollar ringing less true on some counters, whether they were reforms which were likely to intensify the national illness, whether morale and initiative might not suffer, or whether there might be some doubt about constitutionality. These were, indeed, not the sort of thing to worry Roosevelt too much, or at least to prevent him from acting when it seemed imperative; but they were for Hoover serious considerations.

Hoover returned to the debate of 1932 in his *Memoirs*;[6] he still thought he had had the best of it but that an impatient democracy had preferred to follow after a siren voice. This was the harder to accept because he felt so virtuous about the whole thing. He had said during the campaign, and italicized in the *Memoirs*, the following, which is typical of many other such affirmations: "We have not feared boldly to adopt unprecedented measures to meet the unprecedented violence of the storm. But because we have kept ever before us these eternal principles of our nation, the American Government in its ideals is the same as it was when the people gave the Presidency into my trust . . . We have resolutely rejected the temptation, under pressure of immediate events, to resort to those panaceas and short cuts which, even if temporarily successful, would ultimately undermine and weaken what has slowly been built and molded by experience and effort throughout these hundred and fifty years."[7]

This rather lofty moral position had been a vulnerable political one in 1932. Winning the election would need something more. That Hoover recognized this, and yet refused to compromise, is a measure of his inflexibility—or his devotion to principle. He undoubtedly did recognize what was happening. And he did become indignant. On October 25 Roosevelt said, with all the exaggeration allowable, certainly, in a campaign: "The crash came in October 1929. The President had at his disposal all the instrumentalities of government . . . He did absolutely nothing." That was too much. Three days later Hoover burst out: "It seems almost incredible that a man, a candidate for the Presidency, would broadcast such a violation of the truth."

6. *Memoirs,* II, chapter 20 and those following.
7. Address in Washington, August 11, 1932; *Memoirs,* II, 256-257.

Although his audiences were large, and there were known to be far more Republicans than Democrats, and although he felt he had resorted to every device allowable to him, and used them with energy and resourcefulness, he knew that he was losing. Only one event could save himself and the party from defeat. "Indeed, our only hope of winning the campaign was a rapid economic upturn. Only that would carry complete public conviction as to the rightness of our policies."[8]

Hoover was certain that such a change was occurring. He was relieved. The depression was defeated and recovery was coming. It was discernible in July. The only question was whether there would be time enough between July and November for public conviction to spread. He recalled sadly: "the upturn was halted by the Maine elections at the end of September which, in effect, went against us. The fears of the business world at Roosevelt's announced policies started a downward movement for the next six weeks which greatly nullified our hopes of mitigating the political influence of the depression."[9]

The look of death, fixed by exhaustion, on Hoover's face was gradually relieved when the pressures of responsibility were removed by the inauguration of his successor in March 1933; but he did not give up the argument. He saw, and others gradually came to realize, that a debate had been begun which, if it should be abandoned to Roosevelt, would end in the complete discrediting of Republican policy. To an extent not realized in 1932, Hoover and Republicanism were inseparable. This had been unconsciously admitted when the movement to supplant him with another candidate had failed at the 1932 convention. It was more and more openly acknowledged as the years passed. Another candidate was turned to in 1936—it was, after all, not necessary to carry too far such an acknowledgment. But Alfred Landon was a candidate after Hoover's own heart; and, anyway, he was bound to lose. The Roosevelt charm had not been dissipated by the cold logic of Hoover's position.

The Republican thesis that the depression was a Democratic creation was an article of faith no more to be abandoned than

8. *Memoirs*, II, 267.
9. *Memoirs*, II, 269.

other articles in the list. If it had been, the other party commitments would have been undermined and might have had to be abandoned. For if Roosevelt had been right in 1932, business had brought on its own debacle and complete freedom of enterprise was no longer a tenable policy for the nation. There was hardly a Republican in the land who would not rather have seen the party buried than yield Hoover's principles.

The candidates might temporize as one campaign followed another—1940, 1944, and 1948—and they continued to lose. But that Republicanism was the faith of business—that the two were identical—was evident. It kept the party alive and vigorous even in defeat. And when candidates wavered, and seemed to accept the New Deal, when even the platforms became equivocal on some doctrinal issues, the aging ex-President in the Waldorf Tower, growing more saturnine and even more fixed as he grew older, was always standing somewhere in the shadows to remind newcomers where their faith had to center. He appeared at successive conventions; he made speeches in each campaign; and in the interludes he made other pronouncements. He was still carrying on the debate against Roosevelt. He was always convinced that he had not lost that argument even in the minds of those who had turned against him. Their defection could be accounted for in other ways. They had suffered too much. They preferred to try the easy and immoral way out rather than the honest but trying struggle urged again and again by himself.

In 1952 he was still arguing. By then, in his *Memoirs*, he had "final proof." In a campaign won on precisely the grounds he had said it had to be won on, Roosevelt's defeat, and the defeat of all that Roosevelt had stood for, was accomplished. Eisenhower was of the true faith. Liberty could now supplant regimentation; business could be freed; the budget could be balanced, taxes lowered and the dollar redeemed. Moreover, the same policies as had been adhered to in the 1920s could be returned to. They could, because it was not true what Roosevelt had said, that they had caused the depression. What had caused it—at least its later and more serious phases—was Democratic behavior resulting in loss of confidence. This had to be believed, a psychiatrist might have said, because a return to the Republicanism of the twenties would otherwise cause a new depression. Democratic responsibility not only had to be accepted, it was true. There was faithful Hoover who had never wavered, still proclaiming the principles that Roosevelt had lightly tossed aside.

This was the proof in 1952: (1) that the Great Depression extended from 1929 to 1941 and was only ended by preparation for war; (2) that recovery from the Great Depression came quickly to other nations of free economy; but, as a consequence of the New Deal devices, it never came to the United States during peacetime; (3) that the primary cause of this failure was the New Deal attempt to collectivize the American economy.[10] The proof was supported by figures, collated patiently over the years with the neatness of an engineer's mind; they showed conclusively that what Hoover had always said was fact. It had been a Democratic depression, and the Republicans had been on the way to its conquest; but the Democrats had interfered and prevented recovery until war had intervened and saved them. It was quite safe to go back to the Republicanism of the 1920s.

There had been times when Hoover had seemed to stand almost alone, shouting occasionally, from high up in the Waldorf, what men must believe. By 1952 he not only had the vindication of political victory, but also the establishment, among perhaps the dominant intellectual majority, of the thesis he had been steadily proclaiming. This would be conclusive. It had been taught by so many pundits, elaborated in so many courses of schools of business, that it was by now quite casually repeated by radio commentators and financial writers. And an acute observer might have noted, about the time the *Memoirs* were published, something new. There was a certain peevishness. Some perverse intellectuals—a minority, of course—were still clinging to the Rooseveltain explanation. This might be expected of politicians; but to have the intellectuals still not right on this issue was downright dangerous. Heresy might spread, and anyone could see that if world events caused a new depression, a sudden resurgence of the Roosevelt contention might again find wide acceptance. If it did, and another Hoover should be defeated by another Roosevelt, it could

10. *Memoirs*, II, 471.

be seen that a renewed New Deal might really carry out the program Roosevelt had only proclaimed but had never been able to impose on the country.

For the alternative to Hoover's "proof" was the horrid suggestion that perhaps recovery had not occurred because actually there never had been any New Deal as Hoover defined it. That is to say, prices and investment had not been controlled and the resort to spending had never been sufficient. This would, it could be seen, account for the ending of the depression in 1941 and not before—1941 brought ample spending as well as a certain regimentation.

It is even possible to argue that Roosevelt could not attain recovery because he operated within somewhat the same limitations as did Hoover. He believed in the same private and public virtues; he had concern for the national character; he thought individualism precious; and he was unwilling to give up private enterprise.

There was evidently involved a matter of degree rather than of kind. Hoover could see unemployment grow past ten millions, see Hoovervilles proliferate, and know that human suffering beyond estimate was getting worse—and still not be shaken in what he knew to be right. It was not that he was an indifferent or an insensitive man. Human suffering had for him an intense meaning. He had spent much of his life, as a matter of record, in works of relief—even in Russia whose government he abhorred. It was simply that certain resorts were not available. Public authority must do everything to help people to help themselves. It must do nothing to help them directly. Better suffer or even die—and certainly better suffer political defeat—than compromise about this. So he haggled for most of his term with the Democratic Congress about relief and about public works. The government might make loans to the states but not grants, and not gifts to people. Public works must be self-liquidating. The Reconstruction Finance Corporation might support financial institutions but it might not supplant them.

Thus Hoover. As Roosevelt loomed on the political horizon, he appeared to be dangerously flexible in such matters. It was hard to say just why; and Hoover had some trouble during the campaign explaining his conviction that it was so, a trouble he would not have after 1934, when the dollar had been devalued, direct relief had been undertaken, and boondoggling had got under way. But during the campaign he had only the implication of regimentation and inflation to go on. And actually Roosevelt's Pittsburgh speech made a great difficulty. That came in October, and to Hoover it must have seemed a blow below the belt. For in it Hoover was attacked for having presided over two years of federal deficits, thus weakening the dollar and destroying confidence, and for having countenanced the foreign loans now being repudiated. Roosevelt had gone on to say: "I shall approach the problem of carrying out the plain precept of our Party, which is to reduce the cost of current Federal Government operations by 25 per cent."

That speech would return to torment Roosevelt; what is too often overlooked is the genuineness of the torment.[11] Those who worked with him were always aware of his feeling of guilt about spending, his belief in a balanced budget, and a sound dollar. He claimed to have made the reduction in expense promised in Pittsburgh "in current Federal Government operations." Even when expenditures for relief and works were being readied and made, salaries were being reduced, staffs were being cut, and operations generally stepped down. Lewis Douglas was chosen as Director of the Budget because he had a fervor for economy matched only by two other contemporary statesmen—Senator Byrd and Representative Taber. And for more than a year Douglas and the President appeared to agree about fiscal matters.

With what reluctance Roosevelt was forced into deficit spending, and how he resisted it at every step, Harry Hopkins, Harold Ickes, and numerous other New Deal administrators could testify. Their estimates of need were always pared down; and this project or that was taken off their lists. For a long time every project was regularly cut from 10 to 25 percent; and an earnest attempt was made to excise every research item from the budget with the explanation that this was the kind of thing universities ought to do.

During the Hundred Days $3,300,000,000 was appropriated for relief and public works. That may have seemed an astronomical

11. There is an amusing passage in Judge Rosenman's *Working with Roosevelt* (pp. 86-89) which refers to the commitment in the Pittsburgh speech. The frequent accusations that the President had broken his word rankled. When in 1936 another Pittsburgh speech had to be made he wanted it to be a vindication. After considering the matter Judge Rosenman gave up and told the President, "The only thing you can say about that 1932 speech is to deny categorically that you ever made it."

sum to conservative citizens; but Senators La Follette and Wagner—who were the real experts in this matter after two years of duelling with Hoover—knew that a much more realistic sum would have been about $12,000,000,000. They were quite right, if what was wanted was what was professed to be wanted—the relief of unemployment. That, if nothing else, was proved when expenditures of that order began in preparation for war a few years later.

Roosevelt's spending was never enough to provide everyone with purchasing power, and consequently to ensure recovery. It therefore in the long run had to be far more than it would have had to be if the initial attack had been logically and courageously carried out. The reason it could not be, and the reason there was always wavering and insufficiency, was that Roosevelt felt just as much convinced that imbalanced budgets were sinful as Hoover had been.

Then too, much of what was appropriated was not used in ways calculated to get the maximum effect. This again was for a moral reason Hoover would have approved. There were repeated and serious struggles within the administration, not always known about by outsiders, over this issue. There were those who contended that direct relief was cheaper, easier to administer, and quicker than public works, even those boondoggling projects of the Civil Works Administration and its successor organizations. But Roosevelt was adamant. People must *earn* their livings; the government must get out of the relief business. He was afraid of undermining character.[12]

There was a similar struggle when it came to the shaping of the Social Security Act. There were many hot arguments as to whether the government ought to make any contribution or whether a payroll tax should carry the whole load. Roosevelt, who was wholly persuaded of the regressive nature of sales taxes, was nevertheless determined that social insurance should actually be insurance—that is, paid for directly by those who were to receive the benefits. They should be deductions from, not additions to, wages.

12. It was because of a difference about this issue that Frank Walker left the administration during the first term. He believed economy more important than doubtful concern for the preservation of character. He also probably felt that the President was seriously inconsistent in not sticking to his professed principal concern for economy. Memorandum, Walker to F.D.R., September 10, 1935. Hyde Park Papers.

These illustrations are cited to show that if Hoover carried his principles too far, they were not different from the Roosevelt principles. The difference was that on occasion Roosevelt consented to modification. He was more of a pragmatist—or, perhaps, a better politician. The long debate, Hoover versus Roosevelt, is misconceived if it is thought to proceed from morals or orthodoxy on the one side against different morals or unorthodoxy on the other. If Roosevelt unbalanced the budget, devalued the dollar, and involved the federal government in the direction of enterprise, it was because these expedients were forced on him by depression and war. In resorting to them he was, in his own mind, doing wrong; and he was sensitive to criticism.

It is probable that Roosevelt changed in many of these matters. There is reason to believe that he came to accept the theory of the compensated budget, as he did not in 1933, although he understood the theory. He finally came to see that a federal agency presiding over the mechanisms of conjuncture was necessary, something he had not admitted in 1933.[13]

In those early years Roosevelt was far nearer to Hoover than either realized, or than historians have realized since; but differences, if less than is usually thought, were still significant. There was, for instance, that tendency in Roosevelt to recognize necessity.

It is well known that Roosevelt was the product of Hyde Park, Groton, Harvard, and Albany. What is not always understood is what it meant to be the product of those successive environments. It is true that he came from moderately wealthy people and occupied a favored position in society. It is not true that this tended to make him careless of others' well-being and insensitive to their sufferings. He was taught a noblesse oblige at home as natural to his father as the possession of the wealth which made it possible. Headmaster Peabody's influence at Groton reinforced his acceptance of social responsibility. This has sometimes been lost sight of in the obvious but more superficial evidence that he was

13. That was the neglected function of NRA which now goes under the name of "countervailing powers." The theorists who contemplate the development of such a system—advocated by David Lillienthal and at least explained by John Kenneth Galbraith—will discover that the presiding authority of government is necessary. NRA may well be reconstituted, but, of course, under a different name.

interested in sports and social goings on. Certainly he was. But note the following in Freidel's account: "At this period [when he was sixteen] Franklin was developing considerable interest in religious and charitable work. He had attended the Rector's confirmation lectures, been one of a class confirmed by Bishop Lawrence. Later he was elected to the Missionary Society which conducted church services in small rural localities nearby, managed a summer camp for underprivileged boys, and contributed to the maintenance of a club for them in Boston."[14]

There is the fact, sometimes also overlooked, that he had no outstanding successes at Groton. He was a good deal humbler youth—and more sincere—than he was afterward given credit for having been. Peabody remarked that much had been written about Franklin when he was a boy at Groton and that "it was more than I should have thought justified by the impression he left at the school."[15]

Like most schoolboy letters, Franklin's communications with those at home had to do with the exaggerated trivia of Groton events. It is impossible to read them, however, without gathering an impression of unusual warmth and concern that all his affairs should be shared by those at home. This continued to be true at Harvard and was intensified by the loneliness of his mother after his father's death when he was a freshman.

Then—or perhaps even before at Groton—out of the warmth he felt toward his family and friends, there began to develop a wider regard for the welfare of others. This would one day blossom first as an interest in conservation and then as a concern for his less fortunate fellow citizens. This evolution went on below a particularly deceptive surface and in spite of (or perhaps, in reaction, because of) many surrounding influences. The temptation was to use the family fortune and the assured social position as many of his contemporaries did. There were those who had known him as a young man who could never understand how he could be different from what they had supposed him to be. The appearance was that of a gilded youth without a thought in his head beyond dress, sports, social affairs, and easy friendship.

14. Frank Freidel, *Franklin D. Roosevelt: The Apprenticeship* (New York, 1952), p. 49. See also *F.D.R.: His Personal Letters, Early Years*, edited by Elliott Roosevelt (New York, 1947), p. 71.
15. Freidel, *The Apprenticeship*, p. 50, and *Letters*.

By a strong instinct too he soon was led to show no more of his inner nature to his mother than to others. This was undoubtedly because he knew very well how opposed she would have been to the conclusions maturing in his mind. At any rate, neither she, to whom he seemed so close, nor others with whom he had intimate contacts, had any notion of what was going on. And the student of his life has, in fact, to infer far more than he would like about the spread of the roots which must have gone on over many years without betraying the kind of tree his character and policies were to be. His characteristics begin to be plain by 1910 and through his Albany years; but they can be seen in full maturity only later—after his trial in the ordeal of physical disaster.

There is some inclination to seize on the struggle for recovery from infantile paralysis as a transforming episode, and to credit those around him with a miraculous change as he fought back to mastery of himself. This is very likely, again, somewhat exaggerated. Eleanor Roosevelt and Louis Howe were devoted persons; and Eleanor, perhaps, ought rightly to be sainted. It was compensation indeed to have them by him through the years of struggle. But inner convictions making Roosevelt the instrument of his nation's return to health were very deep, and they were his own, so determined and full fed, so ardently and with such artfulness fought for, that they can only have been the extension of his own nature, at last come to full maturity through suffering, contemplation, and conviction—not created by those experiences but ripened by them.

Walter Lippmann never in his life made a greater mistake than when he judged, in the spring of 1932, that the Governor of New York had no discernible qualification for the presidency other than an obvious ambition. His political cleverness, like his personal charm, misled many commentators. They missed a conviction of appointment and a dedication to service hidden beneath an expedient surface, but apparent in his history. There was, also, a deep religious faith assumed by most contemporary commentators to be no more than the nominal affiliation any politician would maintain. His Episcopal church did not ask of its members an ostentatious piety but his commitment to its precepts was absolute. The Roosevelt religion was consistent with gaiety and intellectual freedom; but it was nevertheless deeply held. And if it required nothing else as a norm of conduct it insisted on good works. It was thus a reinforcement, or perhaps partly the source, of the noblesse so characteristic of his life. How this could transform itself into a concern for human welfare strong enough to override any principle of government or any conception of business is not difficult to see. Nothing else was so important. Institutions were instrumental, and among them were both government and business, together with all their agencies.

Clues to the essential Hoover are to be found in revealing profusion through the first volume of his *Memoirs*. In no other part of his accounting is there the telling lift the dullest memoir must show in those passages when the pleasantest recollections are spoken of. But real verve is to be found here. Yet even about this volume one reviewer—a British one—remarked that the justice of some of its strictures would be admitted by most readers, but that they would "be apt to resent the holier-than-thou tone of some of his unfluent, memorandum-like chapters."[16] Most of his writing is memorandum-like. His state papers are heavy and awkward; that might be expected; but so, surprisingly, are his *Memoirs,* with the exception of the volume subtitled *Years of Adventure.* In these chapters the recollection of early hardships, risks, winnings and losses—the "adventure" of his title—overcomes the stodginess and constriction of his writing. It would be strange if it did not. He had two decades, almost exactly, of such a life as few men lead but most men dream of. There was not only the sharp joy of struggle in far places against nature and lesser men, but also the satisfaction of bringing about creative changes on a grand scale. Order was imposed on chaos everywhere he went because of his integrity, his single-mindedness, and his administrative genius. He rose from small things to great, from circumscribed responsibility to worldwide interests affecting men by the hundred thousand. And he savored every instant of those achieving decades.

Hoover not only led this kind of life, journeying now to China, now to Russia, and again to Africa or Malaya. From a point in London, he gradually created an organization extending his administrative control indefinitely. For the last decade of these years,

16. *The Listener,* February 5, 1953, p. 233. This criticism applies most aptly to the later chapters which take him into public life.

young as he still was, he was the head and arbiter of a group whose sole occupation was to go where business emergencies had arisen and settle them. Lesser men were always biting off more than they could chew and ending up, perhaps after the most convulsive struggles with creditors and stockholders, in a net of troubles, and it was the function of Hoover and his men to loosen and remove these, and set things right. The business was set going again or it was decently reorganized. What was done was the most that could be done in the circumstances.

Because of the reputation for being able to accomplish such prodigious feats spread, because the world is full of promoters and dupes, and because bankers cannot themselves untangle the webs their clients weave, the Hoover group was always in demand. The last time he ever asked for a job or sought a client, he said proudly, was when, at twenty-one, the mine where he was working after he had graduated from Stanford closed down, and he asked a California mining engineer to hire him.[17]

That was in 1895. By 1914 Hoover had long since passed through a partnership with the famous London firm of Bewick, Moreing and Company, and had for eight years been a free-lance engineer on his own with offices in New York, San Francisco, London, Petrograd, and Paris. He had accumulated a fortune and could select the most interesting of many opportunities.

In the seventy-five pages of *Years of Adventure* devoted to this business career, there is material for a dozen novels. Even though the most complicated and dangerous of the incidents there recalled, say the story of the Cabinet mines in Siberia, the Boxer Rebellion in China, or the occurrences at Hsipaw in upper Burma, are told in a few paragraphs or a page or two, the obvious related circumstances left to the imagination have fascinating implications. The old gentleman in the Waldorf Tower had rich enough memories for a dozen declining ages. This part of his life, the years of adventure, made and fixed his mind and character. He was strong, successful—and always right.

This period ended in 1914 when the First World War began. He became involved in organizing the return of Americans from battle-swept Europe, then in Belgian relief—and from his beginning as Food Administrator in 1917, he did not leave public office until

17. *Memoirs,* I, 27.

1933 when he left the White House to a successor he distrusted as profoundly as it was possible for one man to distrust another. For out of his experience he had generated an impatience and xenophobia he could not compromise. He had not only been an organizer of order, an emergency administrator, a rescuer of weaklings and a punisher of crooks, he had generated a profound dislike for politicians, a scorn for bureaucrats, and a dislike of "foreigners." He tended to trust engineers, especially the American variety, and almost no one else. He was impatient when lawyers and diplomats created tangles, and he came very close to believing that the world would be better off without them. It is impossible not to conclude, also, that he considered other peoples to be so lacking in integrity as not to be trusted in any dealings. Certainly the United States, in his mind, was the repository of the elements necessary to the human future.

All this happened in his mind in spite of his years of operating from London, his travels into all the strange places where minerals revealed themselves, his constant contacts with other peoples, and his almost unvaried good fortune. He rejected the thought of educating his sons abroad and underwent severe inconveniences to establish them in the American environment. He never thought, either, of making them anything but engineers. And in this he succeeded as in all else. There was, indeed, never a backward step, a check, a humiliation, or a disappointment in his whole life until he came to the presidency and fate played him the lowest trick she could reserve for a successful man. She had in store for him the revelation that the system he had helped to manage with such unvarying success, that had raised him to its most powerful position, was fatally defective. It failed at the crucial moment of his career. He could not believe that it was true; and he would not believe it to the day of his death. Much of the rest of his life would be spent in tortuous processes of ratiocination intended to show—and to convince others—that the obvious was not fact; and he would not be alone; the spokesmen for the undirected business system would be involved as well. It required decades for new ideas to replace those Hoover had so well represented.

The *Memoirs,* after the first volume, are one long dispute with Roosevelt, centering in the causes of and the cures for the Great

Depression. No violence is done, in a historical sense, if the two leaders are accepted as the protagonists of two drastically contrasting viewpoints. If Hoover was right, the Republican policies were right. If Roosevelt was right, the Republicans would continue to fail. They would not see, as Roosevelt came so reluctantly to see (even if the conviction was implemented so poorly), that an intelligent and democratic collectivism was the sine qua non of individualism and liberty, that it became so because of circumstances, that there was no return to the good old days without abolishing technology, and that failure to develop the instruments of collectivity would result in dreadful penalties—as it did in 1929.

The argument had gone on since 1932 with no cessation except for war. There had been no great differences about foreign policy, and there had been substantial agreement about domestic policy. The differences centered not in whether free enterprise should be encouraged but whether it should operate within a framework; not whether money should be "sound," but whether soundness meant anchorage to gold; not whether the budget should be balanced but when it should be balanced. In 1932 Roosevelt promised to be sounder, more economical, and more reformist than Hoover. Later Republicans have promised the same things if chosen over Democrats. The electorate, having two candidates to choose from neither of whom offended their sense of principle, have chosen that one who promised to find ways to make principle comport with solutions of the outstanding contemporary issue—in 1932 the depression; later, coexistence with equal power complexes.

It could not be said, after several decades, that the electorate had chosen for domestic policy either theory of sustained prosperity—that holding to 96 percent free enterprise, or that holding 86 percent to be a close enough approximation. The Republicans wanted only 4 percent leeway: they would bring the government to the rescue of business institutions when disaster threatened. The Democrats would not only have a Reconstruction Finance Corporation but a Relief Administration. Then they would have social security and welfare.

Neither suggested what President Roosevelt had abandoned under Supreme Court displeasure in 1935 and never again espoused: an acceptance by the government of the responsibility for economic conjuncture. Hoover went on claiming that the Roosevelt position was subversive; the Democrats pictured the Republicans as completely unsympathetic to labor, to consumers and common folk generally. The truth is that both gave way by enough not to remain ridiculous, and then the debate gradually became unrealistic, beside the point.

It ought to be noticed, however, that neither Roosevelt nor Hoover really gave up—they were superseded. It was the fondest of Roosevelt's hopes, nursed through one disappointment after another, that he could either transform the Democratic party into a progressive one or find the political resources to shape an alliance with disaffected liberal Republicans.[18] The original Roosevelt program in 1932 was drastically modified under pressure of orthodox progressivism; the same pressure perverted the administration of NRA and forced resort to inflation, both by devaluation and spending. These did not bring recovery; but that failure was masked by the expansion as war approached. The President knew that after the war new devices would be needed. He began to think again of the program of 1932; but then he died. His successor did not have to meet the problem because preparations for war began again almost at once and inflation again supervened.

Hoover was never reconciled. The Republicans gradually and reluctantly absorbed social security and other social minima but gave no ground on the enterprise front. In 1952 they won an election they chose to interpret as a businessman's victory. The car dealers, in Adlai Stevenson's phrase, took over from the New Dealers. The issue still remained to be settled by events; twenty years had not produced definitive answers. In 1953, on the financial page of the Chicago *Daily News,* there appeared an article under the headline: "New Dealers Still Blame Hoover."[19] A few sentences from it follow: "the induced deflation Roosevelt caused by his unwillingness to cooperate with Hoover and his bank policy was many times more severe than anything that happened under Hoover ... Billions were unnecessarily sacrificed in the bank assets in order that FDR could have his fun. But the man in the

18. In 1932 he commented to me that in eight years we might not any longer have a Democratic party but we would have a Progressive one. In 1944 Judge Rosenman was entrusted with a mission to begin negotiations with Willkie for a new party; this is related in *Working with Roosevelt.*

19. "Everybody's Business," a column in the Chicago *Daily News* by Phil Hanna, February 9, 1953.

street never got that picture. The present generation of New Deal writers probably never heard of it." This is straight Hoover. It might have been culled from the *Memoirs*.

The debate refused to end. A generation later, the feelings the protagonists had for each other earlier have a certain interest. It will be remembered that both Hoover and Roosevelt were members of Wilson's official family during the First World War. Hoover, of course, was the senior. He was not only eight years older than the Assistant Secretary of the Navy, he was Food Administrator and had a tremendous reputation as the organizer of relief for Europe. No one thought of him as a businessman. He was a singularly devoted and able public servant, an engineer with a flair for managing difficult enterprises, particularly if they had to do with the relief of human distress. Roosevelt admired him.

Because Hoover was part of a Democratic administration there was a widespread movement to get for him the party's nomination. It came particularly from the progressives. One of these was Roosevelt. He wrote to his friend Hugh Gibson (then ambassador to Poland) on January 2, 1920: "I had some nice talks with Herbert Hoover before he went West for Christmas. He is certainly a wonder, and I wish we could make him President of the United States. There could not be a better one."[20] What would a historian not give for a transcript of those talks in early 1920, even a memorandum, or someone's recollections at second hand. Said Mrs. Roosevelt in answer to a general question: "Franklin knew Mr. Hoover fairly well through Franklin Lane and Adolph Miller. I met him a few times and also saw Mrs. Hoover a little but I never knew her well."[21] There was some reciprocation, even if fairly formal. When, later in the year, Hoover had declared himself not to be a Democrat, and Roosevelt had been nominated for the vice-presidency, Hoover sent friendly felicitations.

There is also something worth historians' attention in the matter of the Construction Council headed by Roosevelt in the 1920s. This was one of those industrial organizations so plainly the forerunners of NRA, and there is a certain significance in the Roosevelt connection with it. That council, for instance, produced a

20. From a letter in the manuscript collection at Hyde Park.
21. Eleanor Roosevelt to Tugwell, November 19, 1952.

"code." But here it is of interest to note that when Roosevelt was elected as its head on June 20, 1922, he had already armed himself with a pronouncement from Secretary of Commerce Hoover. The telegram seems not to have survived, but the letter itself reveals that, in the opinion of the Secretary of Commerce, the interested industries might well organize on their own—that any interest shown by the federal government in such an organization would hurt it.[22]

Whether or not Roosevelt was disappointed, he took it very well. In the meeting on June 20 he wound up quite a long speech by saying: "I do not believe, quite frankly, that the Department of Commerce will accept the beau geste which we make in this resolution asking them to go ahead and do this work. I do not think they have the money, and I do not think our very good friend, Mr. Hoover, wants to go in too much for that kind of official reporting. He believes, as most of us do, that it is primarily the function of private organizations. We have put in that suggestion, however, because, after all, it is our government, we want their cooperation, and we make the gesture, if you would like to call it that, of saying, 'Mr. Secretary of Commerce, here is what we believe should be done: will you and your Department undertake it for the good of the United States?' And when he says, 'Thank you very much, I would like to undertake it, but circumstances prevent,' then we have the field open to do it ourselves, and we are assured of the very hearty cooperation of the government itself."[23]

The rather casual but, on occasion, cooperative and even cordial relationship of the twenties and before did not survive into the thirties. From the moment in 1928 when Roosevelt won the governorship in New York (although Smith himself did not carry the state) he was a logical and likely opponent of Hoover in 1932. During the Roosevelt governorship there were some acrimonious exchanges between Albany and Washington concerning power developments; but it appears that the only time the Governor and the President met face to face was on the occasion when the Governors' Conference was tendered a reception by the President. Mrs. Roosevelt, at least, carried away from that meeting no very kind recollections. Her husband had been herded into line in the

22. The letter is in the manuscript collection at the Hyde Park library.
23. Transcript from the collection of manuscripts at Hyde Park.

East Room by naval aides and made to stand for upwards of an hour before the President descended and made his way along the line shaking hands. Standing that length of time on steel braces was an ordeal a loyal wife would resent on behalf of her husband. Later on, when there was music and the musicians—artists of great reputation—were dismissed from the company, Mrs. Roosevelt built up what for her was a very hot indignation.

The Roosevelts, to put it mildly, did not admire the Hoovers in the White House. This did not make it any more difficult for Roosevelt as the Democratic candidate to accept his appointment as Hoover's opponent. Knowledge of the Roosevelt feelings, not well concealed, may have made Hoover's role as New Deal critic during the post-election years easier to play. As we have seen, Hoover regarded his opponent as inexcusably irresponsible, on occasion a prevaricator, and not to be trusted with serious affairs. There is animus in the *Memoirs,* more than is traceable to mere political ill-fortune, more than is accounted for by resentment at unkind and unfair fate, and more even than ought to arise from profound distrust. Its violence, I think, is accounted for by personal resentment. This emotion is so evident that it is likely to confuse the student of these relations. He is apt to take sides.

It is of no considerable importance, whatever its interest, whether these two individuals were or were not fond of one another or even whether they had a mutual respect. What is of importance is that they were—and are—the protagonists in an epic struggle of ideas. This struggle is to be defined in narrower terms than are sometimes used. Neither the protagonists nor the majority of those they represented were so separate as capitalism or socialism, for instance, as is sometimes said or implied. They both regarded themselves as liberal capitalists, even if the Roosevelt definition would have included planning and direction. They differed on a question of instrumentalism—what was end and what was means and what could therefore properly be manipulated and what had to be regarded as untouchable. If this seems narrow ground for so consequential a struggle it is nevertheless the ground on which it is taking place. It was—and is—that kind of struggle; and it was never settled. Both died, Hoover bitter and unreconciled, Roosevelt softened by justification, as he believed, but still puzzled by Hoover's ineptitudes.

7

THE COMMONWEALTH
CLUB ADDRESS
IN THE FIRST CAMPAIGN

One speech made during Roosevelt's important western trip in the summer of 1932 was taken then and afterwards as the most thoughtful and well-considered pronouncement he had ever made and was more favorably noticed because it had none of the usual marks of an appeal for votes.

In a buoyant letter to John Dalton (dated September 2), Robert K. Straus, one of our confidential helpers, noted that Baruch had seen one draft and approved it. Why it had been shown him I do not know, unless it was that Adolf Berle, who had put it in final shape, was now, in a sense, a member of the Baruch coterie. He had recently written to ask Roosevelt whether there would be any objection to his having Baruch as a client. Roosevelt had answered that there was none; but he doubtless noted this as another evidence of the web being woven by that persistent claimant for appointment. Straus was evidently allowing him to examine the speeches; and even Ray Moley, I began to suspect, was softening. He had been extremely hostile, earlier, because of Baruch's support of Smith before the nomination.

A marginal note on that same letter of Bobby's (we all called him that) said: "Raymond Leslie Buell at lunch today called it 'the greatest speech since Wilson.'" Perhaps it was; but I have never thought so.

One reason for giving it serious reexamination is that it was certainly not carefully considered by Roosevelt before it was made, as the commentators assumed. For one thing it was not in his style or habit. If it was well organized, it was that way because ne had had little chance to concern himself with it. Also several paragraphs were completely uncharacteristic; they expressed a conviction that the economy was now matured and that instead of policies calculated to develop it further, it was necessary only to consolidate the gains already made and turn them to public uses.

Bobby's note about Buell's approval could not have been written, I think, if Roosevelt had really worked on the final draft. The whole thing would have been very different; Buell, I am sure, would not have approved a genuine Rooseveltian treatment of the same subject; Roosevelt was far from believing that progress had stopped, even temporarily, and that it was a time for assessment, caution, and holding back.

In *After Seven Years* Moley has said some things of the speech that must be mistaken. These concern its preparation and the circumstances of its delivery. His divergence from what now seem to be the facts is not extensive, but still sufficient to explain why a thoughtful but uncharacteristic statement should have been made at a midpoint in the campaign. Roosevelt's general intention, repeated many times, was not to call a halt but to summon Americans back to their traditional optimistic and energetic work for progress. Nor was he meaning to suggest lines of thought reaching into the future; he had explicitly forbidden forecasting to us and forsworn it for himself.

The Commonwealth Club speech said that the confining bonds of devotion to an old moral order belonged to a preindustrial age. They were useful now only to those who opposed advance by the common people. Ours was an industrialized society without any chance of reversal and this required a new posture by government. It must become a servant of those who had been exploited rather than their exploiters. When certain of its citizens were in trouble, it must come to their rescue; it must discipline public enemies; it must help those whose disadvantages could be removed only by general intervention.

This attitude was posed as the alternative to the philosophy of noninterference, preached as a moral imperative by the Republicans and held by them to be the secret of American progress. Allow the individual full freedom, Hoover was saying, and when he rises by ability and initiative, he will become part of an economy that produces prodigiously and furnishes employment to those less competent and energetic.

Even the successful ones must obey certain easy rules, of course, especially if they serve other businesses; the government might regulate but must not displace them or direct their operations. Even when the system falters and stumbles to a stop, private initiative must be trusted to start it again and carry it on to new achievements. The principle of individual responsibility must apply to the workers as well as to the industrialists. They must find jobs; they must expect to look out for their families; they must carry the risks of their employment. Their employers might lose profits; they must be prepared to lose their wages.

Against this, Roosevelt was offering an alternative, developed in his experience as Governor, and reinforced by the argument that the business system had been wasteful, that it tended to unbalance, that this led to periodic paralyses, at which time the burden of risk was sloughed off by owners and managers and shifted to the workers who were least able to carry it.

Free enterprise also required, for its periodic deflations and slow recoveries, that those who had made investments should sacrifice them, or part of them. This included savings, equities in homes, businesses, and farms, and all the other equipment for carrying on economic activity. When bank accounts disappeared, when the assets of savings institutions and insurance companies were frozen, and the unemployed, wholly without income, were turned into the roads and streets, their reserves used up, their families destitute, and their hopes destroyed, government must not be expected to accept responsibility. It might assist out of pity but was not required to as a duty.

Roosevelt was saying, in direct contradiction, that government ought to prevent depression, and if it occurred in spite of preventive measures, recovery was a public responsibility. Prevention was not possible unless business was required to operate within a certain order. Competition must be limited when it threatened to become destructive. Exploiters must be held in check. As things had been, they had run to cover when the calamities they had caused occurred.

They demanded rescue; and conservative administrations labored mightily to give them what they demanded. Their principles did not forbid the rescue operations of the Reconstruction Finance

Corporation, only those that would have rescued the unemployed and the investors. For the victims of the system, they had no pity. Even the meager assistance that would keep families alive was given as charity when it was given at all. The grudging recognition of misery had to be forced from them by fear of rioting or some lesser manifestation of revolt.

First, the tendency to unbalance in a free economy must be controlled. Government must see to it that capital went to producers who needed and could use it, not to those who meant only to gain speculative profits. The risks remaining, even in a balanced economy, must be borne by government acting for the community as a whole. Men who lost their jobs must be helped to find others; meanwhile their families must not be expected to carry the whole burden of unemployment; and finally it must be recognized that unless a permanent flow of income to consumers was insured, there would be no continuous industrial activity because there would be no buyers.

This conception was already half-formed in Roosevelt's mind when our discussions with him had begun; it had been elaborated and systematized in our repeated reformulations. He knew what the requirement was. He had warned us, of course, that he had a problem about saying publicly what this must be. He had to contend with those who were devoted to free competition, and with estimates made by politicians of what the voters would find it agreeable to hear; also he had said that the first guide for campaigning was the getting of the votes that would turn a long-continued Democratic minority into a Roosevelt majority—if not a party one.

This was the background for the Commonwealth Club address. In the midst of a campaign devoid, so far, of practical suggestions for recovery, although the ends to be gained had been repeatedly referred to, it was a real shocker for those who simply assumed that free competition was no more to be questioned than home and mother. That is, it was a shocker for those who really took it in. Actually, it was extremely well received without much apparent understanding of its implications. Because of the praise it earned, it influenced the further conduct of the campaign. It made Roosevelt bolder, much bolder than he had been before. There was a marked difference between the early speeches and the later ones; and the speech at the Commonwealth Club was the dividing line.

Moley has correctly described its origin. Bobby Straus, listening to our discussions in Albany, had been disturbed because there seemed to be so little recognition of the contrast between Hoover's rugged individualism and Roosevelt's intention to use government as a social and economic regulator. He thought there ought to be one speech developing this idea, since it could be only inferred from occasional and separate references to such problems as power, railroads, the credit structure, and unemployment. The possibility was talked about several times; but Roosevelt was standoffish.

He still thought it wiser, even necessary, to shy away from outright statements of this sort. The rebukes of the professionals after the Oglethorpe speech had made an impression. His appeal to potentially dissident Republicans after that had been on quite different grounds. He had said for their ears that he was actually a more devoted and much more realistic individualist than Hoover who talked so much about it. We thought this an evasion and there was a general feeling among us that an honest contrast ought to be made, even if not in the specific terms I had spoken for. To do it would be to take advantage of the ridicule Hoover's trumpeted slogan had caused. Rugged individualism was by that time being repeatedly used in cartoons and in editorials to characterize his refusal to involve the government in rescue operations. It had really become so well-recognized a phrase that its reverse could profitably be formulated and capitalized on.

This seemed to us so sound an idea that Bobby was encouraged to develop a first draft, so that Roosevelt could see what we had in mind. This, with Dalton's help, he proceeded to do. His manuscript was passed on to Adolf, who then wrote a version of his own on the theme—including the passages I found objectionable concerning the maturity of the economy. This draft was being written just when preparations for the long campaign trip to the West Coast were in their last rather hectic stages, and the issue was not brought to any conclusion. Ray had not read Berle's draft, and Roosevelt had not agreed to make any such speech; in fact, we had the impression that he would not. Still, Adolf finished it so that it would be on hand if he should change his mind.

The prospects for a holistic turn seemed to us to be growing so much more favorable that Roosevelt's strategy might well be reconsidered. He ought to be preparing the public mind for the shift away from avoidance of responsibility for economic stability as well as unemployment. He had more than once spoken of interwoven interests. But he had not said what this involved—the changes in industrial organization that were required. We thought he ought to make a beginning. We knew the politicians would oppose it if they were consulted. They considered that things were going well. He would be elected if he just offended no one. Shocks must be avoided. Rising resentment would turn Hoover out.

He had intended to do no more at the Commonwealth Club than make a safe and friendly little speech about San Francisco and the West. It was, as he told us, a dangerous spot. There were no rules about politics in California. The extremes of right and left, easily differentiated elsewhere, were intermixed there. Politicians were touchy, responsive to no discipline, and skittish about party labels. There was Hearst, with newspapers and a fortune; there was Senator Hiram Johnson, who was a maverick; and there was a Democratic candidate for governor from Los Angeles—Culbert Olson—who was regarded by Hearst and McAdoo as wild and irresponsible. It was indeed a situation calling for caution.

It had been in California, Roosevelt recalled, that Charles Evans Hughes, the Republican candidate, had offended Johnson in 1916, an incident that had made the difference in that election. A similar mistake might do so in another. Roosevelt was confident of his skill in delicate situations; but this was comparable to a wire-walking act—one small slip might be fatal.

He had been warned, however, that the club expected a speech worthy of its reputation as a serious forum. So, in a last-minute appraisal, he inquired, or Ray did for him, what had become of that speech on individualism we had talked about several times.

An emergency call came to the Brains Trust headquarters in the Roosevelt Hotel; Adolf made a hurried final version of the draft he had prepared, and it was sent—I believe by wire—just barely in time for its use on September 23. What was finally used appears in the *Papers* not under the heading of "Individualism, Romantic, and Realistic," the original title, but under that of "Progressive Government." Ray must be right in saying that some hasty altering was done, because there is the folksy material at the beginning that Roosevelt characteristically used to get himself started and that no one could really imitate because no one could believe it was not slightly ridiculous. It always proved to be acceptable; but even Ray could not bring himself to imitate the corny phrases of a Roosevelt opening.

Otherwise, however, there was not much change. Many years later, considering subsequent events, I got to wondering what had happened. The development of the historical theme—most of the speech—still seemed, in retrospect, almost beyond contention; the recognition had by then become very general that industrialism was smothering the old rural culture, and that rural attitudes were inadequate for its containment or control. It was certainly not realistic to have said that industrialism had reached its furthest development and that the problem now was not to expand further but to be content with civilizing the factory system. It is true that industry was operating at only a small percentage of its capacity. Five times the goods and services being produced in 1932 would have required no expansion of facilities at all. To have projected a static future for such an economy as ours, however, was to assume that we had come to the end of our resourcefulness and, indeed, of our resources. Roosevelt did not believe that. Perhaps Adolf did, but I had not thought so.

I made some inquiries of those who had been concerned. There was what Ray had said in *After Seven Years,* making some point of the contention that the speech had had the same sort of consideration and revision that all the others had had. He stood on that. I could not accept this; so I wrote to Straus and Dalton, who between them had originated the idea and written a first draft. As a result, I have before me as I write not only the version printed in the *Papers,* the one actually used, but three others. One is the Straus-Dalton original, one is the first Berle version; the other evidently the one wired to Moley as revised after consultation. Dalton, for some reason, had carefully put them away. He sent them to me; and shortly afterward, he died.

All the drafts are more correctly called by the first title. The intention was to show that the individualism much praised by Hoover was so anachronistic as to be dangerous in a society in which most economic activities were corporate and so concentrated that they were controlled by a small managerial elite. How useful was individual initiative to a worker who was one of thousands working for a concern that was shut down? What was the position of the small businessmen Hoover talked about when they had no customers and no credit? What were the farmers to do whose markets had vanished? All this was in the speech. It said that equality of opportunity no longer existed and that it had to be reestablished. There were hints of social security, but not such strong ones as there had been in the Straus-Dalton version; and there were more references to the concentration of power that was Adolf's specialty.

There were, too, several paragraphs of real wisdom and strength that deserve to be quoted again and again as the Roosevelt philosophy. They foreshadowed much that was to happen later, much also that he expected us to flesh out, and much that I had supposed he would not even hint at during the campaign. It may be said that the statement only reaffirmed what had been said earlier, but there had been none of these occasions since the nomination. More than any other of his speeches it represents, I think, the conclusions he had come to about the economy and its management; it was what he had been making up his mind must be done; not in detail, of course, but in principle: "Happily, the times indicate that to create [an economic constitutional order] is not only the proper policy of Government, but it is the only line of safety for our economic structures as well. We know, now, that these economic units cannot exist unless prosperity is uniform, that is, unless purchasing power is well distributed throughout every group in the Nation. This is why even the most selfish of corporations for its own interest would be glad to see wages restored and unemployment ended and to bring the Western farmer back to his accustomed level of prosperity . . . This is why some enlightened industries themselves endeavor to limit the freedom of action of each man and business group within the industry in the common interest of all; why businessmen everywhere are asking for a form of organization which will bring the scheme of things into balance, even though it may in some measure qualify the freedom of action of individual units."

This, I said to myself, is the Concert of Interests, a phrase I had persuaded Roosevelt to include in two former speeches, notably his first in Minnesota. The fact is that neither he nor Moley wrote that paragraph. It is to be found in the Berle draft almost exactly as it appears in the printed version. It shows, I think, that we had arrived at an agreed conception of the solution. Roosevelt felt no need to rephrase Berle's formulation. But it also shows Roosevelt with more independence from the politicians than he had been willing to show even as late as August.

This was gratifying to me, and something of a surprise after my instruction in what was suitable for political purposes and what was not. I thought now the lesson might have been considerably overstated, or that I had taken it too much to heart. What made economic sense was not such disastrous political doctrine after all—although it might be, I reflected, when its implications were realized.

It made more interesting, if not more urgent, the commission I had been given just before the departure west. That commission, like so many of Roosevelt's, was an offhand one; and at the time, I did not really know whether its intention was any more serious than that of so many others I had been given and seen or heard given to others, the results of passing thoughts, to be forgotten, perhaps, by the time any beginning had been made. My instructions were to cultivate the progressives and to see whether closer cooperation might not be possible. They had not been notably enthusiastic in his interest up to now, and this augured badly for what must be done later on.

There was nothing to do about this effort, which I regarded as so all-important, but to assume he was really in earnest. I did assume that. It was why I continued in his service.

8

ROOSEVELT AND THE

BONUS MARCHERS OF 1932

The summer of 1932 was not especially uncomfortable, but for those of us who were working with Roosevelt it seemed very long. Matters without any obvious relation to campaign activities nevertheless affected everything planned and done. They nagged our minds and demanded his attention. The immolation of Mayor Jimmy Walker was one of these; but there were others.

The most difficult of them had to do with the depression, naturally, since it hung, a sort of miasma, over everything. For example, there were strange financial happenings taking place in Europe; the mysteries of international banking that were plotted in directors' rooms of financial institutions were difficult for outsiders to understand and especially amateurs like ourselves. Then business failures and massive unemployment in Britain and on the Continent were even more serious than our own; they were causing challenges to authority by shouting bands of blackshirts and brownshirts orchestrated by demagogues; and governments were actually being overturned. More of these violently erupting volcanoes were reported almost daily.

We had no time to study these carefully but it was evident that they portended something sinister. Besides, they had a frightening similarity to occurrences here at home; and ours had begun to have the same immediacy. The weakened economy had begun to collapse on those whose outcries were more readily listened to than the cries of the smaller fellows who until this point had suffered most. We ourselves watched the daily and weekly reports from the centers of trade and the issuers of statistics with intense interest; and every new indication was analyzed for its possible meaning. We made of it what we could and Roosevelt, widening his circle, took in masses of advice and information. For many of these developments he had no responsibility and so could not be blamed; but he was expected to have attitudes about them and, on occasion, to make appropriate pronouncements.

The worst were, of course, the simple ordeals of those who had to endure as best they could whatever anxieties and hardships the worsening times brought them. By this time, the millions who had no jobs were in an advanced stage of desperation. Summer was not so hard as winter; patched clothing and worn shoes did not have to keep out frost and slush; but food and shelter for a family were harder to provide. Private charities had practically exhausted their resources, and public agencies were rationing their meager appropriations.

By that summer the relentlessly progressing deterioration was squeezing many of those who had hitherto been immune or nearly so. Not only wages, but salaries too were being reduced when there were any jobs at all, and executives at the secondary levels were being put on part-time with the likely prospect of separation. In city after city, public employees were being asked to take salary cuts of 10 percent or even more. In New York they were asked for a month's work without pay. People who owed debts faced settlements with no way to meet them; they had to resign themselves to foreclosures of pledged collateral; and that might represent the savings of years, perhaps their business properties or homes. Graduates coming from the campuses in May and June had discovered that there were no jobs to be had, and that there was not much they could do but join their fathers who were sitting around a house that was only doubtfully theirs or an apartment whose landlord was demanding overdue rent.

It was this pushing upward of the crisis into income groups hitherto untouched that rang the alarm bells in offices and board rooms and caused the foreboding that hung over superficially cheerful editorial pages in the newspapers. In spite of forced official optimism and patent playing down of bad news, there was a darkness closing over the nation that Americans had no conditioning to endure. Were these the signs of collapse? Were the few riotings and protest marches the forerunners of a revolution such as had tormented European nations? Not even a lively political campaign was likely to enthuse people who were hopelessly walking the streets; nor were promises for the future likely to bring much cheer to those who were homeless.

Quite suddenly, however, in July, Hoover became convinced that deflation had run its course and that an upward trend was starting. For a time his optimism seemed about to burst into jubilation. We ourselves were convinced, after an intensive study by Adolf, that what was being relied on was no more than a flurry in the stock market, a false indication of resumed activity. Frances Perkins hinted darkly that it might even have been induced. She spoke of those who could still afford to spend something substantial if it would stop the loose talk of reform and reprisal being reported to them. Just then, she was having a heated controversy with federal officials about the number of unemployed, having detected a kind of reporting that resulted in underestimation by some millions. Much to Roosevelt's amusement, her challenge had had fairly wide publicity. Her engagement was really with Hoover himself who stood sponsor for the figures; and nothing could be better than to have the high priest of figures and reports discredited by an obscure New York State commissioner, and a woman at that. Roosevelt encouraged her; she was having much the best of the argument.

Continuing controversy over depression phenomena was background for everything else; but other events and controversies dragged along and refused to resolve themselves, further disturbing people's minds and adding to the prevalent confusion. Some were gradually concluded; but so many of those remaining were a discredit to Hoover and his supporters that we began to feel a furtive sympathy for the President who lately had stood on so high an eminence and was now so generally reviled.

There was a corresponding change in attitude toward Roosevelt. The general judgment that he was no great success as Governor, and that he offered no special promise of leadership, was rapidly being revised. He was now being looked at more carefully; what he said and did was being watched for indications of his policies; and even his record was being reassessed. True, the New York *Times* was not yet satisfied with his pledges. To the editorialists they seemed neither frank nor comprehensive, and he continued to be criticized for being evasive. It was now generally understood, however, that he meant to do something about the prevalent misery, that he was well practiced in government, and that he had a more sophisticated understanding of economic problems and a more studied approach than had been imagined. This turn had taken place even before he had had much of anything to say except in the mutilated acceptance speech. Regard for him seemed to spread in some mysterious fashion; but that it was spreading, those who were watching as closely as we were could not doubt.

We guessed that the change was not really traceable to any efforts Roosevelt himself made to impress the public with his prescience. He had hardly begun that effort and was, in fact, in no position to make curative suggestions. He was still uncertain. The improvement was owed more to a reassessment of his energy and intelligence. Now that he was being watched, he was seen to be a vigorous, mature, and competent public man, one who made no hypocritical pretense of not wanting office but frankly asked for it, offering himself as an alternative to Hoover. Above all, he was apparently not frightened by the country's plight, but regarded it as a challenge to American ingenuity. He and the people together would find ways to overcome the crisis.

Hoover's failures, it must be admitted, had been more of an asset than Roosevelt's promises. The judgment that his administration was a disaster deepened with every day that passed. The transfer of his presidential command, a reliance so much needed by all Americans, was clearly being prepared.

The false trumpeting of an imminent recovery, when it was exposed, further undermined public confidence, and even most convinced conservatives were skeptical; but the final failure, the symbolic end, I still believe, was furnished by a most unlikely, almost trivial incident. This was the mismanagement of the events associated with the Bonus March of that summer. People suddenly saw their President as a frightened and hapless executive resorting to violent reaction rather than the benevolent tolerance so obviously called for. Things had obviously become more than he could handle. He could no longer be relied on to keep his head; and this was no time for bad judgment.

For him, it must have been a terrible disappointment that the signs of renewed activity were so soon shown to be false. They did soon begin to fade—by September had all but vanished—and although they were persistently gilded by a slanted press, hardly anyone found his protestations credible. Conditions were, in fact, worsening; decay was reaching further and further into the foundations of industrialism, doubts and disillusions about the system itself were circulating from person to person, and more and more openly. The whole nation seemed to be sinking into a bog of despair.

To make matters worse, other unnerving things were happening; and all had the same effect. Each added its share to the weight bearing down on the Chief Executive. In the farm states, violence broke out repeatedly, and on a larger and larger scale, as prices fell to all-time lows. Then, in spite of Hoover's favorite rescue operation, the Reconstruction Finance Corporation, financial institutions with frozen assets continued to fail with spectacular repercussions. The RFC would be more effective when it really got going, but during these months results were not apparent. Besides, his concern with the Corporation had led him to minimize the need for relief funds. He was confirmed in people's minds as one who relied on the "trickle theory." During the last weeks before election this became a sour joke even among the least informed voters. He was sunk in a disastrous morass, pitiful to see.

The investigation of Mayor Walker in New York dragged on; no one knew then that it would presently turn into something of a triumph for Roosevelt, made complete by Walker's flight to Europe. The Republicans hoped for disaster; but they soon saw signs that it might be averted. The noisy controversy between Hoover and the Congress was ended with adjournment in July. Members went home unhappy, and even the Republicans found it discreet not to defend the President, when they started their own campaigns.

It was against this background that the Bonus March—otherwise not so sensational—developed into a nationwide spectacle. It became a test for the courage and competence of those in authority—and especially, of course, Hoover's. He failed, miserably.

This outcome was the stranger because Hoover's calling out of the military and the unnecessarily savage repression of the marchers would almost certainly, in other circumstances, have brought him extravagant acclaim. It had done so for other presidents in other times. When Cleveland, in 1895, sent soldiers to suppress Pullman strikers and there resulted a small civil war on Chicago's south side streets, he was warmly and widely praised as the protector of law and order. It was one of the few occasions during that President's second term when any considerable public approval came his way.

In 1932, however, there seemed to be some evil magic at work. Even actions that citizens might have been expected to hail as saving the nation from revolution brought Hoover only dispraise. There were early exaggerations of the threat to public order. These stuttered off into reluctant apologetics. It had been like using a sledgehammer to kill a fly, perfect material for such flamboyant orators as Fiorello La Guardia, Robert La Follette, and others who, as sentiment changed, commanded wide attention. Americans were uneasy, but they were not ready to concede imminent overthrow of the government by a few thousand indigents who, not long ago, had been its defenders. People might be having it hard; but they were not persuaded that their veterans were about to storm the White House or the Capitol.

There were, however, mutterings from both right and left that tougher treatment was called for. The rightists had taken to praising Mussolini for making the notoriously slack Italian railways meet their schedules; and the leftists were pointing out that there was no unemployment in the Soviet Union. Fascist and Communist alike offered order and security to those who were being made to bear the risks of a free economy. Mention of the accompanying regimentation was omitted, usually; and anyway what was so novel was that anxieties were now spreading to a surprised and resentful managerial elite. The real sufferers were strangely enduring even when their calamities were unbearable. True, the farmers were volubly objecting, but their demands were for a more equitable sharing—not for revolutionary changes.

Even the well-to-do were beginning to reject the daily doses of optimism administered by the press and were growing more and more apprehensive; and the unrelieved anxieties of the unemployed were obviously justified. Their hopes did not notably fasten to any foreign ideology; and they were hopelessly unorganized, so the fears of their betters were actually hollow. Even the labor leaders only sporadically voiced any indignation.

It was impossible to say how far disillusion with the administration had spread; but one in Roosevelt's position was bound to hear as much as anyone about the evidences. Tycoons and labor leaders, social workers and philanthropists, clergymen and press proprietors, farm organizers and office holders, crowded the Albany house and his anterooms in the Capitol. The advice they had to offer was sufficiently high-keyed and alarmist; but it continued to be unfocused and diffused. There was no agreement about remedies and, actually, no deeper disaffection than that calling for Hoover's defeat. More than anything, as Roosevelt said wonderingly, it was a desire for leadership. People—even those who held themselves out to be popular tribunes—wanted reassurance, an authority they could rely on.

The Bonus March, when it began to find its way into newspapers of cities along the route of its progress toward Washington from the Northwest, inevitably recalled the similar march organized by Jacob S. Coxey of Ohio in 1894. That descent on the seat of federal power petered out on the lawns of Capitol Hill, and Coxey himself was jailed as a vagrant. Early fears were dissipated in the end; even the hoots and jeers that betrayed the relief good householders felt soon disappeared from the front pages. In 1932 there was an obvious hope that the Bonus March would have a similar end.

The circumstances, however, were different. True, there were hard times as before; but W. W. Waters, who was the Coxey of 1932, had veterans of more recent vintage to count on. Besides, they were not demanding the consent of the Congress to a general easy money policy as Coxey had been; these veterans were only asking for the fulfillment of what they regarded as an obligation. They had been in the army no more than fourteen years ago. This brought them into their thirties; they were men who ought to have been in their busiest and most productive years. Their families were no more than half-grown, perhaps not even complete. Their inability to find any sort of work was a grievance made more acute by new conceptions of government responsibility and by recent years of rising prosperity. Above all, what they were asking for could be made to seem a just demand. Back in 1925, the Congress had "adjusted" the compensation for their military service and had authorized certificates to be payable in 1945. They were petitioning for immediate payment of an acknowledged but postponed debt; it was hard to picture this as an outrageous demand.

Like many others who watched the papers, we had first begun to be aware of the marchers when they got into trouble in East St. Louis on May 21. There were not many of them—a few hundred. They had been making their way east by boarding freight trains after the fashion of the depression's indigent thousands. They called it "riding the rods." They camped along rights of way and climbed into the empty box cars of slow moving trains. In good weather, passing freights had riders on roofs and others sitting in the doorways with their legs hanging out. This was against railroad rules, and even against protective laws; but train crews quite generally affected to be blind; they too might have to take to the road. No one had much security.

At East St. Louis, however, railroad officials had a sudden seizure of indignation and a guard was set up to prevent illegal boarding of east-going trains. Since this was a suggestion rumored to come from Washington, it seemed to the marchers a provocative cancellation of their unspoken arrangement with authorities; and the pacifist professions of the less stable marchers broke down. Gangs got together and soaped rails, uncoupled cars, and generally made nuisances of themselves. This brought in the police and trouble resulted sufficient to become national news.

It must be understood that all over the country there existed a kind of hushed expectation that something dreadful might come of all the cutting of ties with places of work and with settled homes. Even the most secure of citizens could understand the humiliations of indigence and of hopelessness that had no promise of an end; and they were frightened by the implications. The signs at East St. Louis were small ones; but they were ones among many; and they were peculiarly sinister because these were men cut loose from traditional ties and were more or less organized; the veterans' initiative might spread.

The Baltimore and Ohio Railway guards were successful enough in repelling boarders so that the municipal authorities had to do something about their unwanted tourists. They resorted to traditional methods. Marchers were crowded into trucks and sent out of town—eastward. After a few miles they were unloaded; and jungle camps outside other towns were suddenly a problem. The publicity about the St. Louis incidents insured a close watch as the marchers made their way toward Washington. Officials prepared to meet the invasion much as St. Louis had done; but now the problem was more formidable. Other unemployed veterans suddenly felt that the country they had fought for owed them something better than they had been getting. From many other towns on many other railways, volunteers gathered and started in the same direction. It became a movement.

The Waters contingent from Portland, with its accretions, amounted to about a thousand when it finally reached Washington; but from almost every arriving freight, coming from all directions, a dozen or more joiners dropped off in the railway yards looking for their comrades. Very soon there were two thousand, then five; and by July there were something like eleven thousand. By then a large slumlike community was well established on the flats beside the Anacostia River and some sort of order had been achieved. When there was no more room, other sites were found and simply squatted on. These had no water supply and only primitive sanitation, and the Potomac Valley's summer sun beat down on the tents and shacks, producing, almost under the noses of congressmen, Hoovervilles they could not ignore.

What amenities there were in these camps resulted from the sympathetic efforts of the decent and kindhearted man who chanced to be superintendent of police in the District: Pelham Glassford, who had been the youngest and one of the ablest brigadier generals in the Expeditionary Force of 1918. He chose to regard the campers not as tramps, but as old soldiers fallen on hard times. He rode among them on his big blue motorcycle, gave them advice, and got for them what supplies he could from all the sources he could think of. He was easy and humorous.

He was regarded as a friend and protector. One was needed, because their growing numbers were regarded more and more by householders in their vicinity as a menace. Anacostia and other small "cantonments" became more crowded, the summer heated up, and the effluvia from garbage heaps and latrines became almost unbearable. Arrivals increased daily and moved into any empty lot or abandoned building they could find. Commander Waters said there were nineteen such sites. He also said the numbers had grown to 23,000; Glassford thought 11,000 nearer the fact. Even that many, having presently lost any reason for pleasing the Congress by being orderly and submissive, grew harder and harder to control. The District commissioners were disinclined to support Glassford's tolerance and finally they simply ordered him to disperse the visitors by a date in the near future. The whole country was watching. It was an intolerable situation; also, however, it seemed insoluble.

Only two among the authorities knew what to do about it. They needed permission, of course, and finally after an incident or two—ones, it afterward appeared, that were provoked—they got it. The two were Secretary of War Patrick Hurley and Chief of Staff Douglas MacArthur.

While fears had been rising and excited publicity conditioned the public to demand drastic action, the Congress had been considering the bill authorizing immediate payment of the bonus certificates. In June, it had passed the House; but in July, it was rejected by the Senate. Members of the Congress then went home and left the problem to others. The Marchers no longer had the same excuse for staying in Washington; but most of them had no reason for leaving either, and now they had a grievance. Besides, their number went on increasing. The momentum would be hard to check.

Glassford thought something more humane was called for than seemed to be contemplated by the federal authorities and the District commissioners, and he conceived the idea of reconditioning an abandoned army camp not far from the city where some sort of life for those who were quite homeless could be organized. Before he could make much progress, however, the inevitable infiltration of real radicals began, and when John Pace of Detroit, a notorious agitator, persuaded some two hundred like-minded fellows to gather outside the White House, Washingtonians became as hysterical as Chicagoans had been in 1895 when Cleveland and Olney had chosen to regard railway strikers as rebels.

Armed guards were set to watch the White House and hasty high-level conferences were held. The imaginary threat to government became front-page news. Within a few days the whole country was watching the President. What could he do?

Hoover, harassed by advice from disoriented assistants and impatient generals, could think of nothing better than suppression. And on the morning of July 28, MacArthur, with Major Dwight Eisenhower and Captain George Patton in attendance, personally directed the deployment of cavalry, infantry, and tanks on Pennsylvania Avenue. They systematically routed squatters from the buildings they had been occupying along the avenue, then marched in column up Capitol Hill and went on toward Anacostia. Arrived there, they unslung rifles, flung tear gas bombs, then seized and carted away all those who resisted. That done, the veterans and their families—such as had come along—had to watch the soldiers raze and burn the poor shacks and tents they had used for shelter.

For days the roads leading into Maryland were crowded with refugees, herded and harried by Maryland police. Thousands dispersed into Washington streets in spite of blocks, and made their way west out of the city. The mayor of Johnstown, Pennsylvania, a veteran himself, had watched the proceedings with growing indignation; he now offered a refuge in one of his city parks, an offer vetoed at once by a fearful city council. Since this was the only suggested haven for the refugees, they had nothing to do but trudge along the highways, begging for rides, many quite literally starving. No one took pity on them; and soon they were forgotten in the press of other problems and were somehow absorbed into the miserable refuges so prevalent in the countryside.

The week of these happenings, the last in July, had been one of the pressures and problems in Albany too. What we knew of the Battle of Washington was what we read in the *Times.* Such warmhearted spectators as La Guardia, La Follette, Wagner, and many others, outraged but impotent, told us in detail what had happened. I discovered that, in spite of other matters that would not wait, Roosevelt had been told too, or had read the *Times,* and had drawn his own conclusions. On July 29, the expulsion occupied many columns, and there was a whole page of photographs.

On that same morning, there was a report of Mayor Walker's reply to the Seabury charges, something that must have immediate study. It would be on Roosevelt's desk when he got there. Yet about 7:30, when Roosevelt called from his bedroom and I went in, the page of pictures was open on his bed. They looked, he said, like scenes from a nightmare. He pointed to soldiers stamping through smoking debris, hauling resisters, still weeping from tear gas, through the wreckage to police wagons; women and children, incredibly disheveled and weary, waiting for some sort of rescue. In the lower right hand corner, the victorious general, one of the few in our whole history who had led armed troops against civilians, stood nonchalantly by a fence, immaculate and smiling among the vagrants, drinking from a paper cup.

Roosevelt, spreading a hand over the picture page, reminded me that we had been going to talk more about Hoover, but so far as he was concerned, there was no need now. He ought to apologize for having suggested him as candidate in 1920; but he had seemed then just what was needed. No one in sight had had such a reputation as he. He had managed a massive rescue operation. He had shamed generals and lazy officials; he had done what no one thought could be done. He was the world's most admired humanitarian. What hadn't been realized was that the man was actually a sort of timid boy scout leader. Since he had done so much for people and on so immense a scale, he was supposed to be a kind of superman.

Roosevelt went on to recall that the whole country had still admired Hoover in 1928; what he had accomplished in the Commerce Department had been notable; by then he had become the Great Engineer instead of the Great Philanthropist; and that was just what the country needed. He was the strong and honest man in the Harding and Coolidge cabinets. The contrast with the others in those administrations—except for Charles Evans Hughes in State—was obvious to everyone.

Even when the depression had come along, it had seemed something Hoover could handle better than anyone else. This was his specialty—economic management. No one saw it as the disaster it turned out to be. But, said Roosevelt, from the crash in 1929 to yesterday, when he had set Doug MacArthur on those harmless vets, he had depended altogether on his business friends; he still talked about principles; and he organized charities; but actually he had not done anything that was nearly big enough. Now look where he was. He had surrounded himself with guards to keep away the revolutionaries. There was nothing left inside the man but jelly; maybe there never had been anything else.

Roosevelt went on to say that he himself had a political problem smaller than he would have believed before this incident had happened. MacArthur and the army had done a good job of displaying Hoover to the country as a timid leader; he could not be reelected now. If the Battle of Anacostia had happened a little earlier it might even have prevented his renomination.

I made some objection. There were all those registered Republicans; they were pretty traditional. Wouldn't they vote the party ticket anyway?

He said no; this went deep. They would not like to vote for a Democrat; but they would like even less to vote for Hoover now. And his name was Roosevelt—still almost as much a Republican name as a Democratic one. If he did say so, it stood for energy, for action. He pointed at the pictures in the *Times,* reminding me, as he had done before—pridefully—that during his four years as Governor in a state troubled by depression, he had never called out the National Guard. The fat cats had wanted him to, several times, when they were scared; but he never had. His answer had always been that suppression would not be effective when there were real grievances. It would only make matters worse. They went on suggesting that the country was in danger of revolution and that discipline was needed, but he had refused.

I asked what he actually had said to those who urged him to act. He grinned for the first time in that talk. He usually let them go on, he said; if he argued too much with them, they would go away and say he was a softie, a coddler of radicals. A good many suspected that anyway; but now that Hoover had been frightened by a few poor unorganized fellows, and the reaction had been against him, there was no need to say any more than had been said by the reporters.

I guessed he was right. There was a Hooverville bigger than the one in Anacostia down by the Hudson River just below Morningside Heights. The people there lived on scraps in shacks built of bits and pieces. Their clothes were rags. But they were too beaten to be dangerous except to health. The difference in Washington was that this fellow from Detroit, Pace, had got some of them to march around the White House. Wouldn't people sympathize with the President? Wouldn't they consider him justified in using force?

Not in these times, Roosevelt said. What Hoover should have done was to have talked with Waters when he asked for an interview. Then when those two hundred marched up to the gate, he should have sent out coffee and sandwiches and asked a delegation in. Instead he had let Pat Hurley and Doug MacArthur do their stuff.

He might even feel sorry for Hoover, he said, if he did not feel sorrier for those people—eleven thousand of them, the paper said. They must be camping right now alongside the roads out of Washington. They must be sleeping cold. And at least some of them had families. It was really a wonder that there had not been more resentment, more radicalism, when people were treated that way. He smoked. Then he said that anyway, they would make a theme for the campaign.

He wasn't interested any more, he went on, in analyzing Hoover. He had been turned inside out. Everyone could see what was there; and they wouldn't like it. Neither did he; he would not feel sorry for him even in November.

If Roosevelt had had any doubt before about the outcome, I am certain he had none after reading the *Times* that day. But his last word was something to the effect that either Hoover had been very different in the war years or he himself had not known him as well as he thought. He was just a bit wistful.

9

TRANSITION:

HOOVER TO ROOSEVELT

Our experience during the fall and winter of 1932-33—Raymond Moley's and mine—would never be repeated. Beginning shortly after the election, and continuing until Roosevelt's inauguration in March, Moley was, for all practical purposes, a cabinet in one person, and I was his second. There was no real third. O'Connor and Rosenman gradually dropped out; Charles Taussig did not have Moley's confidence; Adolf Berle was not always available; General Johnson went back to working with Baruch in Wall Street and we saw no more of him.[1]

The situation of any President-elect is delicate, but Roosevelt's was especially so because the worldwide depression deepened. This brought many momentous issues to the decision stage before responsibility could be matched with authority.

This was the last of the long intervals between presidential election and inauguration. The stretch of some four months, devised

NOTE. This essay appeared in *The Centennial Review,* volume 9, number 2 (Spring 1965).

1. Raymond Moley, professor of government at Barnard College, Columbia, had been the organizer of the Brains Trust in the spring of 1932; Basil O'Connor, partner in the law firm of Roosevelt and O'Connor, had been a helper during the campaign; Samuel I. Rosenman, who had been Roosevelt's counsel as Governor and a speech writer in his gubernatorial campaigns, was now a New York Supreme Court Justice. Charles Taussig was a New York businessman with attachments to Roosevelt and with ideas he frequently put forward without much success but with Roosevelt's tolerance; Adolf Berle, the third member of the Brains Trust, having been drawn in from his professorship in the Columbia University School of Law, was best known for his recent analysis of corporate power, *The Modern Corporation and Private Property,* written with Gardiner C. Means, who later joined me as a consultant at the Department of Agriculture; General Hugh Johnson, an assistant to Bernard Baruch, was loaned to Roosevelt during the campaign as speech writer and liaison with businessmen and later became administrator of NRA.

for a people who traveled mostly on horseback, or by boat, was a dangerous hiatus in the circumstances of 1932-33. Hoover was discredited. Other governments were reluctant to deal with him, with his Secretary of State, Stimson, or with his Secretary of the Treasury, Mills, lacking knowledge of Roosevelt's attitude. As far as the carrying on of legislative business was concerned, the Democratic majority lacked any direction except Roosevelt's cautious off-the-record suggestions.

The 72nd Congress began its final session in December, a hopelessly futile lame-duck body. Leadership could hardly be expected from the southern Democratic leaders who, through seniority, had risen to committee chairmanships. Their purpose in life for two years had been the impeaching of Hoover's administration. They had no mental resources adequate to the developing crisis. The Congress seldom does; but the weight of the depression in 1933 had paralyzed it completely.

Parliamentary countries provide for such situations; hostility between executive and legislature branches cannot become serious when governments not reelected disappear almost immediately. President Wilson had made an arrangement for deferring to his successor in 1916 if he failed of reelection; and Lincoln had thought of an immediate resignation in 1864. We heard that Hoover was considering something of the sort after the election; but if he was, nothing came of it. He went on as he had been; and Roosevelt became conscious almost at once of a serious effort to persuade him that he ought to endorse policies he would have to reverse as President. Yet a crisis was approaching with frightening rapidity; and it was difficult to evade making some statement of his intentions.

Among other things, it was by now clear that public expenditures for relief were hopelessly inadequate; that the freezing of debts had made inevitable widespread bank failures; that insurance companies were insolvent; that the situation of farmers, homeowners, and businessmen who could neither borrow nor pay was becoming more desperate every day; and that something drastic would need to be done about the international debts left over from the war. On hardly any action concerning this tangled complex could Roosevelt agree with Hoover. Yet he was constantly pressed to cooperate in Hoover's proposed actions lest the country fall into complete chaos.

No one knew better than Ray Moley and myself that we were poorly equipped to understand several simultaneous crises on a nationwide, even on an international, scale. Yet we were almost as well prepared as Roosevelt himself. He, of course, had some advantage in his acquaintance with diplomats, officials, and politicians during the Wilson administration when he had been in the Navy Department. I had the least preparation; Ray, after all, had done a good deal of public work, and Adolf Berle, who next to me was depended on most, had a history of public service running back to a precocious participation in the work of the Peace Commission in 1919. But Ray's jobs had never been national in scope and Adolf had had no recent contacts in Washington. Roosevelt said to us that we at least did not begin with a determination to justify the policies of the past twelve years. We were free to consider the condition of the farmers, the workers, and the businessmen who were caught in the grinding machinery of a system unsuitable to an interlocked economy. We had the advantage, too, of knowing what Hoover would not admit, that the old ways had failed.

Our situation, Ray's, Adolf's, and mine, was complicated by Roosevelt's habit of asking comparative strangers to "look into" something or to consult with some person or group and then neglecting to tell us about it. We often heard of others who claimed, with or without reason, to be his "representatives." Some consequences of this lighthearted delegation were as annoying as might be expected, but sometimes we were forced to admit that this resulted in getting done work we could not have organized in any regular way. Its informality gave it a certain nerve-wracking quality, but all of us came to recognize that it was something we must accommodate ourselves to. The alternative was to quit. This we did sometimes consider; but I, at least, gradually found out that the sensation of being out on a limb was quite ordinary for those who served successful politicians; and I have since learned that Roosevelt's was far from the worst behavior in this respect.

Ray was most annoyed by this irregularity. After all, he was responsible for coordination and delegation; but he also tended to be irritable under strain—and strain had been unremitting for months. The discovery that an ex-congressman, a political boss, a banker, or even another professor was making contacts and perhaps commitments of one sort or another in the President-elect's name, and "helping to get ready," was not calculated to improve a temper he himself described as "Irish." He grew positively irascible as the weeks stretched out and the burdens were increased. It seems remarkable now to recall that he and I went through it all without any quarrelling serious enough to have stayed in my recollection.

I had gone back to my work at Columbia after the election, assuming that we were finished. A colleague has since reminded me that I said to him about this time, when he asked me whether I expected some advancement, that "there could not be any, because, as Professor Robert L. Schuyler had once said to me, it was impossible to promote a Columbia professor." I think all three of us felt that way.

Roosevelt had discussed the agricultural situation with me repeatedly when we were formulating campaign policies. He now asked me, without giving me any precise directions, if I would "try to see what could be done about getting some relief legislation passed at the current session." The lame-duck Congress, he said, could be expected to do little else. I pointed out that Garner, the Speaker, who was Vice President-elect, was actively promoting sales taxes as a way of paying for relief, but was showing no interest in a farm bill. Still, as Roosevelt said, the agricultural bloc was nonpartisan—had been for years—and it might be possible to get this one thing done now. As things looked, there would have to be a special session immediately after inauguration but it would have a banking crisis to deal with, and if farm relief could be out of the way before then, so much would be gained.

I had this to do, then, while he was away on a postelection cruise in the Caribbean, and, as best I could, I accommodated it to my university work.[2] The prospects were not favorable. There were acrimonious differences among the farm organizations that all our pacifying efforts during the campaign had not meliorated.

2. This postelection cruise on The *Nourmahal*, Vincent Astor's yacht, lasted from February 5 to 16. On his return to Miami there occurred the shooting incident that resulted in Mayor Cermak's fatal wounding but in Roosevelt's escape from injury.

Also, to complicate things, Henry Morgenthau, who was Roosevelt's State Commissioner of Conservation, was negotiating with the farm leaders all on his own. It should be said that he had done this before my time and was therefore not out of his legitimate sphere. Furthermore, he had been chairman, during the Roosevelt governorship, of an Advisory Committee on Agriculture. It was difficult to work with him, both because his academic relations were so exclusively with the Agricultural College at Cornell and because his fierce ambition, linked to Roosevelt's career, made him elbow everyone else out of the way when he could. I had trouble finding out what it was that he and the Agricultural College people wanted. Later on it came out clearly enough that they were money reformers and were opposed to the adjustment scheme Roosevelt was committed to. What was most needed, they believed, was a device for raising prices, and they considered that this could be done by manipulating the gold content of the dollar. Our domestic allotment device would require the federal government to intervene on a wide scale. It would depend on a nationwide administration directed from Washington, and this they contemplated with horror. It violated their laissez faire principles.

If agricultural relief had depended on Morgenthau, or on the Cornellians, there would never have been any; but what mattered at the moment was that he was anxious to place himself at the center of negotiations for reasons clear enough to everyone: he wanted to be Secretary of Agriculture. Roosevelt spoke to me about this, saying that it was obviously impossible and not to pay any attention to it. This gave me the opportunity to suggest Henry Wallace, as several of us, including M. L. Wilson[3] and Ray Moley, had agreed that I should do at the first opportunity. At this time it was a mere hint, but I could see that it was taken seriously. I still feel that if I had not made the suggestion at that time the secretaryship might have gone to George Peek who felt entitled to it, and who had others pressing his claim—including Baruch and Johnson. He had for years spent money and time working as a lobbyist, and sheer seniority was all on his side. He had been far on the

3. M. L. Wilson was then a professor at Montana State College but had the freedom, apparently, to conduct a year-long campaign for domestic allotment, the device we adopted and persuaded the Congress to accept. Wilson later succeeded me as Undersecretary of Agriculture.

periphery of our campaign activities, but that was partly because he was a Republican and partly because then, as later, he was scandalized that professors should have been allowed to speak up at all. He could hardly bring himself to associate with us. The animus in his notes at the time, published later in *Why Quit Our Own* (1936), amounts almost to hysteria. He was as bitterly opposed to domestic allotment as Morgenthau—but he wanted relief left to the processors of farm products. They would raise prices paid to farmers, he said, if they could in turn raise prices to consumers without fear of the antitrust laws.

When I talked with Roosevelt as he was leaving, I suggested it would be better if I withdrew entirely and left the legislative chore to Morgenthau—except that I must point out his opposition to the kind of relief bill we were proposing and that Roosevelt himself had agreed to. He answered that he knew about the difficulty Henry was making but that he was obligated to Henry and his father because of their long service; and he hoped it would be possible for us to work together. In any case, he wanted me to take the lead in conferring with people like Marvin Jones, chairman of the House Agricultural Committee, with the senators of the farm bloc, and also with Fiorello La Guardia, leader of the House progressives, who, he was sure, would be helpful. If we got the farm leaders to agree, we could all work together to produce a bill and we might perhaps get it passed.

I then said that I thought it would be best not only to have a meeting of all these people in Washington but to have Wallace and Wilson present. He liked the suggestion and asked me to take the responsibility for all of it while he was away. Morgenthau isn't going to like it, I told him; but he only laughed and said that Henry's jealousy was getting as bad as Louis Howe's. We just had to ignore it.

I spoke to him then about something that had been bothering me for some time. Most of those I was dealing with—not only Morgenthau, but also Wallace, Wilson, the several senators and representatives, and the farm leaders—were old-timers in the struggle to get some sort of justice for the farmers. They regarded it in just that way, whereas I thought of it strictly as a recovery measure. In their fraternity I felt myself something of an interloper;

their concentration on getting a government advantage for farmers made all other considerations irrelevant. Then too I was a New Yorker—a city man. Morgenthau was at least the proprietor of a farm paper and a state commissioner; Wallace was the editor of an old respected agricultural journal; Wilson was a professor in an Agriculture College; and of course the farm organization men had got to where they were by the most intense concentration and by in-fighting of the fiercest sort. I was an outsider.

Roosevelt's answer was that I was useful for the very reason I had cited as disqualifying me. The others were all too involved. Each had some sort of interest or ambition. You go ahead, he said, and see what an amateur can do—and remember, I am an amateur too. Just between us, the justice to farmers these fellows talk so much about appeals to me too mostly because it means justice for a lot of other people as well. You and I really believe in that concert of interests I have been preaching about.

As it happened, practically all the leaders to be assembled were in Washington arguing endlessly about the form of a bill to be introduced as an emergency measure—not that they could expect Hoover to approve it any more than he had former ones, but the gesture would have been made, and gestures were important to organization politicians who had their constituencies to think of. They were as argumentative as usual; none had been persuaded by the others; and now that Roosevelt was promising action, their tempers were more uncertain than ever.

I asked Wallace to come and enlisted the help of Mordecai Ezekiel, then attached as an economist to the Farm Board. Ezekiel was familiar with the reasons for the failures of Hoover's Farm Board and he could at least furnish warnings. He was, besides, an old friend of both Wallace and Wilson. During the next two months we formed a team. We knew that unless the farm organizations agreed to the domestic allotment plan Roosevelt would not press it on the Congress and our present effort would end. In all our meetings, and especially in all conferences with farm organization men, where the attitude of the new administration had to be outlined, we presented our case. We tried not to offend Morgenthau; but his opposition to the plan was obvious. He often sat looking dour (and he could look as dour as anyone I ever knew) while we schemed to get the legislation we believed was needed. His Cornell advisers were represented by young William I. Meyers, who was kept by his side throughout the proceedings.[4]

As soon as Wallace and Wilson arrived in Washington, we began conferring with the farm leaders, putting to them the dictum of Roosevelt that they must agree. "But," they always demanded, "what does he want?" In my conversations I cited the acceptance speech and the Topeka declaration on agricultural relief, and indicated, as Morthenthau squirmed, that these were commitments to the domestic allotment plan. Then I could say that the two people who knew more about the scheme than anyone in the country were in the same room—M. L. Wilson and Mordecai Ezekiel.

We did not really get to work until there had been two whole days when each of the officials, in his turn, made a long and usually passionate speech expounding his own proposal for relief. These were already lying dead in the committees of the Congress as referred bills, but we could not escape the deluge of talk. At the end, however, they finally agreed to consider whatever bill should be drafted on the principles we had laid down; and F. P. Lee, Washington lawyer for the Farm Bureau Federation, was engaged to help us do the drafting.

No special difficulties appeared in this, but one of another sort did become visible. Marvin Jones, as Chairman of the House Agricultural Committee, would have charge of the bill. Morgenthau and I had had some indeterminate conversations with him and got along well enough; but it seemed to me that his interest in farm relief, though earnest, was not of a sort to welcome any novelty. He wanted simply to compensate farmers' disadvantages with federal subsidies. What was really sinister was that he was known to be in constant touch with Peek's crowd, who were doing all they could to channel the coming effort into a combination of marketing agreements with processors and arrangements for dumping in foreign markets, meanwhile agreeing to temporary subsidies. Peek had the millers, meatpackers, and cotton manufacturers ac-

4. He would afterward succeed Morgenthau as governor of the Farm Credit Administration. Later on he would leave the administration, of course, and become one of its most hostile critics.

tively with him. It was a well financed and efficiently operating opposition.

It would have been difficult to make acceptable so complicated a scheme as ours even if it had not involved restriction on production, the feature most opposed by all the farm lobbyists. Jones finally said, however, that if that was what Roosevelt wanted, he would do his best. He pointed out that he had already prepared a bill for an immediate subsidy. He could hardly back out of the commitments involved in this, so he suggested that this should be Title I of the bill and the domestic allotment plan Title II, not to go into effect until the second year. This suggestion was enthusiastically agreed to by our conferees, although Ezekiel and I pointed out that there was a whole year's supply of cotton and wheat in existence and that the bonus provided for in the bill would bring on an attempt to sell all of it immediately. The cost to the Treasury would be far more than the income from the tax provided for in the bill. Roosevelt's campaign promises of a balanced budget were still embarrassingly close behind. We doubted that he would approve.

As the bill emerged from committee, it had one significant and some minor changes. They were for the worse. Provisions for individual contracts with producers were dropped; so were those for state and county allotments; and the voluntary local committees for enforcement were not mentioned. I felt, however, that, for the moment, we had done the best we could. Perhaps amendment, either in the House or the Senate, would be possible. I hoped that our lobbyists would stay on the job, would object to any further modifications, and would press for the restoration of allotments.

I urged Wallace not to involve himself too much in further controversy. He knew, for whatever it was worth, that his nomination as Secretary was being pushed by Ray and myself. He also knew as well as we did the difficulties in the way. Several of the farm leaders were candidates themselves; so was Morgenthau; and Baruch meant to see that Peek got the job. Having his man in the secretaryship was worth a great deal to him, and there were times when it seemed more likely to be Peek than anyone else. I had developed a strong respect for Baruch's influence. I had not much more to go on in my hopes for Wallace than the feeling that

Roosevelt might appreciate the irony of having as his Secretary of Agriculture the son of a former Secretary who had been humiliated by Hoover. Nevertheless, since we had hopes, Wallace ought not to incur any unnecessary enmities.

Roosevelt, I am sure, did not really expect much from our effort in Washington. He said as much when I told him of an interview with Cotton Ed Smith, the Senator from South Carolina who was chairman of the Senate Committee. Cotton Ed had been there so long, Roosevelt said, that he thought he owned the Capitol. In this particular matter, Cotton Ed's links with speculators rather than any concern for farmers was what determined his attitude; but he was successful with his constituents, and it was well known that Baruch was one of his backers.

It was Roosevelt's belief that quarrels about farm relief would settle themselves. They had gone on for years now and the issues were fairly well clarified. The processors and speculators had prevented action about as long as they could. When farmers took to dumping milk and refusing to market hogs as they were doing now, the end was in sight. The Middle West was showing signs of revolt. That at least would frighten the opposition.

There was something else that would settle itself. There would be no trouble at all about an enormous relief program: the "fat cats," as Roosevelt called them, were really scared by the winter's miseries and the resulting unrest. Still it was one thing to give temporary relief but quite another to get acceptance for the reforms he had in mind. He was trying ideas and testing possibilities in talks with those same "fat cats." A succession of them were coming to Albany and Hyde Park. He was cordial but noncommittal.

I had the uneasy feeling that agriculture by now was not a central concern. It was the business system that had to have attention. It had at least allowed the depression to happen and perhaps had caused it. The country's financial institutions were all insolvent; and the intergovernment debts were an added problem. The bankers were telling him they would have to be canceled because they could not be paid.

In the matter of these intergovernment debts, I was acting as second to Ray. The settlements made by the Debt Funding

Commission after the war were background, and we studied these in detail, consulting many of the people who had been principals, and trying to assess the various petitions for reduction—all this aside from the claim that it was impossible to make transfers of the necessary funds.

The excitement before inauguration was caused by the presentation—beginning on November 10 and continuing through several succeeding days—of notes from other governments asking for reexamination of the debts. When these were received, Hoover was still in California where he had gone for the election. He telegraphed from his returning train requesting Roosevelt's cooperation and suggesting that the Debt Funding Commission be reconstituted.

It happened that on the day this message came I was in Albany with Professors H. Parker Willis and James Harvey Rogers, whom I had brought to Roosevelt for a general discussion of possible banking legislation. Willis was known to represent Senator Carter Glass's point of view and had, in fact, worked with him in preparing not only the Federal Reserve Act of twenty years before but the new act Glass was now urging. Rogers represented quite a different viewpoint from Willis' conservative one; but each respected the other; and it pleased Roosevelt to hear them argue.

He was just recovering from one of his frequent attacks of influenza. We had all of us been invited to lunch; but he excused himself, and Mrs. Roosevelt did the honors. After lunch he called me into his study and showed me the Hoover message. He had been studying it. He asked me to think over during the afternoon what might be done and suggested that I stay over so that Moley could be sent for and we could all discuss it in the evening.

There followed general conversation concerning alternate proposals for banking reform, Willis and Rogers differing sharply. We finished with Roosevelt asking Willis to convey his best regards to Senator Glass, but making no commitments as to support for his bill. The reason for this was obvious. It would raise reserve requirements, limit classes of discountable paper, and contain various other provisions of a restrictive sort. The effect would be deflationary, and one thing not needed at the moment was further downward pressure on prices.

Rogers was much less interested in banking than in money; but the discounting device in the Federal Reserve System tied banking and money very closely together. This was especially true in a country like ours where upwards of 90 percent of the exchange transactions involved the use of bank checks rather than currency. He did feel that banking reform was desirable but he thought that restrictions ought to be loosened rather than tightened as the Glass bill would do. Roosevelt found his argument more congenial than Willis'; but he recognized the prestige of Glass with the financiers.

The conversation went on for a couple of hours. As we were going out, Roosevelt called me back and said something that showed he had all the time been thinking of another matter while the talk about finance had been going on.

He spoke for a moment about the contrast between Willis and Rogers. Then he went on to say, thoughtfully, that it seemed to him Hoover's invitation to meet ought to be accepted. He could stop over in Washington next week on his way to Warm Springs. What would I think, he asked, if he took Ray Moley with him to the conference. I questioned him a little to see whether he had considered all that was involved, but then told him that I was pleased that he thought of taking Ray. He could not possibly take along any banker, and in fact a technician was not called for since that would make it appear as though responsibility was being accepted. Ray was sufficiently innocent of knowledge about financial affairs to indicate that the meeting was only for information.

When, that afternoon, he announced his intention to the press, the newspapermen realized the implication at once. The efforts of the international bankers to take what they believed their rightful place as advisers to the forthcoming administration had been ignored, even if in typical Roosevelt fashion—by indirection.

Before his press conference that afternoon, he had only one other caller, Cardinal Mundelein of Chicago, with whom he talked for a long time. After the Cardinal left, at about five, we had tea in his study—the Roosevelts always had tea—and then sat for more than two hours before a fire. It was raining outside. He was sniffling from his cold, but feeling, he said, somewhat better. He spoke about the Cardinal's liberalism—such ecclesiastical support would be important and the Cardinal had better be kept informed. Presently he came back again to the depression and how recovery could be started. This gave me an opportunity to say that the raising of farm prices would certainly make a good beginning; but the real trouble, as I had said before, was not so much low farm prices as the contrast between them and other prices. It was high prices for industrial goods that was restricting markets. Many factories were shut down entirely because they could not sell what they made. Until some sort of selective process has been established, pulling some prices up and pushing down others, activity would not be resumed. At the same time ways had to be found to provide incomes for the remaining unemployed. Until that was done demand would not be sufficient to keep factories going. I admitted that I had been impressed with Adolf's insistence that the assets of savings banks and insurance companies must not be further deflated. That had less to do with recovery than it did with savers' security; but it was important. Some middle way was indicated. I would like to see pressure both ways.

He said the financial men were telling him that investment had practically stopped. He himself knew of many people who were looking for some profitable way to use their funds. This led him to speculate on what first steps could be taken with general acceptance. There would have to be some way of halting runs on banks. Their assets would have to be thawed out—but that expression really meant, he said, that the values of their holdings would have to be guaranteed; but only recovery could really do that. Actually the whole complex situation could only be resolved by getting activity started again. I said the answer to that—for a first step—was in getting income to the unemployed and to the farmers. This was something we had agreed on from the first. I said I wished now that he could take back the promises of economy he had made in the Pittsburgh speech; relief expenditures would have to be substantial. He said he was depending on the savings to be made in federal expenditures—cutting down employment and reducing pay. I objected that this would diminish incomes and so the demand for goods. It would have precisely the wrong effect.

He ended by saying that there might turn out not to be any real choice. He laughed, but I could see that he meant it. The crisis might make its own conditions. All this was in a way repetitive. We had gone over and over it during the spring, but tension was rising. What we had been discussing more or less theoretically for months now had become an immediately reality.

Missy LeHand and Grace Tully were at the table, and the conversation was general, but afterward we spent the whole evening again on the problems of recovery. It was mostly speculation concerning devices that might be tried. We discussed at considerable length, I recall, a fact that seemed significant to me. This was that the funds he had spoken of as seeking some place to go—at least a great part of them—had been for the past few years going into the money market to finance the frantic speculative boom of the late twenties. All this had come about, I said—and here I went back to an old thesis again—as a result of rapid technological advance. There was no norm of relationships between prices and costs, reduced by new methods and new machines. Profits had been so high that abnormal corporate surpluses had been the rule rather than the exception.

I pictured a board of directors deciding how to dispose of their company's earnings. Profits, I said, might be distributed as dividends, of course; but it was fairly usual to divert a large proportion, before distribution, into reserves to be used for new plants, or the improvement of old ones. This was not a way to make earnings larger when markets were contracting. The new or improved plant would be idle. Realization of this resulted in the diversion of those free funds to the open money market. I pointed out that some big corporations had been found, at the time of the crash, to have been loaning hundreds of millions, sometimes at interest rates as high as 20 percent.

The significance of this was that earnings were used not to buy finished goods—that is, ultimate products—but to finance further expansion, or to lift the price of securities; and neither of these helped to increase activity. We went on from this to the connection of these corporate habits with our customary moralities. There was a curious carry-over of individual desire for security. When corporations saved for a rainy day, however, it resulted in surpluses that had to be disposed of somehow. When industrial activity was put at the disposal of directors who regarded their organizations as individuals, their behavior set the whole system to rocking, first one way, then another, until it approached a smash.

As we speculated about devices, he clearly foreshadowed for me the setting up of self-planning agencies for each industry, in order, as he said, that planning might be taken out of private hands and that the fair exchange I was always talking of might be brought about by mutual trades and pressures. I again spoke of my scheme for self-government in industry, but pointed out the danger of overestimating the foresight of businessmen as contrasted with financial people, to which he answered that they were beginning to be frightened enough to act more rationally by now; and that confident public leadership would, he thought, be accepted. In any case, the government must always be the senior partner in all such organizations. This went back, of course, to the Oglethorpe speech before his nomination, whose proposals he had afterward abandoned for the campaign. It showed that he had paid more attention than I thought to the memorandum I had given him just after nomination. It had not been acceptable campaign material; but here it was in his mind again as the need for action approached.

Ultimately, our talk turned to questions raised by the Hoover message. I ventured the suggestion that all the problems would probably have to be discussed together—intergovernment debts, the stabilization of currencies, tariffs, and perhaps regulation of staple commodity production throughout the world. Also, there was disarmament; I thought that we had enough to offer in the other matters to get concessions on this traditional American policy.

He countered immediately that his view was just the opposite. He went on to work out a distinction I at first had difficulty in following. Some questions, he felt, could be settled as rational economic matters, but others had become so sensitized that any economic solution would have to be politically prepared and probably postponed for some time. These would compromise the others and ought to be kept separate. He talked perhaps for half an hour before I began to be impressed; and then I was not persuaded that this was the way to proceed. Since he had evidently reached a conviction, I ventured the opinion that the intergovernment debts were the most urgent, and if it was his intention to separate this question from the others, that could certainly be done; but we had better begin at once. Yes, he said, this had to have first attention.

When we had finished with this we fell silent; it was late and the fire was nearly burned out. It was not only I who felt a significance in the moment, perhaps, for after some time he said, without turning his head: "You know we ought to have eight years in Washington. At the end of that time we may or may not have a Democratic party, but we will have a Progressive one; and some day we will have the planning you want." After a silence I spoke of the conservative party elders, but not with any conviction, for I saw, before he pointed it out to me, that now they had no other place to go, no way to share in power except through him. He did not yet see that they might prefer Republican times; and he obviously did not foresee how party bonds would stretch when he threatened privileges they felt themselves bound to protect. "They will have to go along. You'll see," he said, "we will get our job done in the time we have." I had no experience to combat this judgment. I was listening to a sophisticated politician.

Moley arrived when we were about to go to bed. He came in out of the cold and, standing close to what fire was left, began talking in the slightly nasal but pleasant way he had, about something not very important. After a little Roosevelt winked at me, cocked his head to one side, and interrupted. He flourished his cigarette and said with a mock serious air: "Ray—have you got any striped pants?" While Ray was off balance and looking to me for an explanation, Roosevelt went on: "As a matter of fact, Rex, he will need a top hat too. I'll bet he doesn't have one of those." Ray mumbled something about *his* not being a cake-eater—which was ignored entirely, because by now Roosevelt was off on a characteristic elaboration of the fantastic. He called McDuffie, his valet, and sent him to see whether he had extra striped pants, and measured Ray with his eye for fit. Then he said with false casualness, "You know, Rex, they say Hoover is very formal. We could not afford to have our expert dressed wrong." Ray looked at me and I nodded.

This was his notification that he was going to the White House meeting with Roosevelt. His elation was hard to conceal and we were a long time settling down for the night. Next morning, early, Roosevelt began again about proper dress for the occasion. "You know, Ray," he said, "Tom Lynch gives me a plug hat every time I am inaugurated. You'll have to wear one of my old ones. But what worries me is the spats. The State Department boys will be wearing theirs. I won't have to wear them because Hoover won't. But you will . . ." He spilled cigarette ash on his old gray sweater as he leaned back in bed laughing.

This sort of thing went on for a couple of days—we stayed until Saturday—getting more and more complicated and making Ray more uncomfortable. He was quicker than most people to know what was to be taken seriously, but he was not certain that he might not really have to dress, as he said, "like a monkey." Roosevelt knew protocol, but both of us were innocent of Washington manners.

We were gathering material and discussing procedure during most of the waking hours, and talked a good deal with Roosevelt when he could escape his routine. When he left to go to Hyde Park, Saturday afternoon, Moley and I went on to New York and worked most of the following three days until he left to go to the White House meetings on Tuesday.

I should report that he went in no fancier dress than he ordinarily wore when he went to his classes.

In the succeeding weeks and months, as we worked on this series of related problems, both Moley and I came around to Roosevelt's view about their separation. He had realized from the very beginning that people generally, and particularly the Congress, were determinedly set against cancellation, or even modification, of the war debts. There was also the corollary fact that the English and French were determined not to pay. These were facts and must be dealt with.

The general American attitude was very simple; it was still much the same as Coolidge had described it when he remarked that since they had hired the money they ought to pay it back. And the attitude abroad seemed simple too: the United States had made little enough contribution to the war, and the least its government could do with any grace was to forget the collection of money sent in place of men.

This seemed to me an impasse. Our opinion—Ray's and mine—after a good deal of research was that most countries were able to and probably would meet their payments on December 15. We thought the transfer difficulties had been exaggerated and we had no reason later to revise this opinion. After the White House conference Moley went on to Warm Springs with Roosevelt. When they came back we found ourselves deeper than ever in the complexities of international economic relations.

By this time, Roosevelt had convinced us that public opinion would not allow cancellation. Actually it was hard for its advocates to explain how interest and amortization payments on some 15 billions of *private* debts could be transferred anually—an amount it was difficult to estimate at less than five hundred million dollars—when it was wholly impossible, they said, to transfer approximately half that amount for the *public* debts.

We were doubtless irritated by the propaganda of the foreign representatives. We never knew the sources of the many approaches made to us—at least I never did—but it was not too difficult to imagine that the investment bankers and the diplomats were working together. It was an easy inference that forgiving the public debts would make the private ones more collectible.[5]

Our judgment may have been affected by our annoyance; but anyway, in our discussions with Roosevelt, we agreed that he ought not to join Hoover in any of his suggested moves. The position of the British warranted more leniency than that of the others, they having made arrangements at a time when the nation was more prosperous than France and having consequently contracted for a rate of interest at least twice as high. Generally, we felt that Roosevelt ought not to take a dogmatic stand about any of the payments succeeding those of December, but we were strongly of the opinion that the negotiation ought to be done after inauguration, and not, even then, by any special commission. So emotional a problem ought not to prejudice the more permanent arrangements to be made at the forthcoming World Economic Conference to be held in London.

I was delegated to explain this to E. E. Day, one of Hoover's delegates to the preliminary meetings at Geneva. Across a table at the Harvard Club, I argued as lucidly as I could for separation, pointing out that if we wanted the World Conference to have any result it would be necessary to damp down the emotions surrounding the war debts. Otherwise, the Europeans would be

5. I here call attention to W. G. McAdoo's discussion of the debt matter in *Crowded Years* (Boston, 1931), ch XXVII.

thinking of nothing but cancellation. He objected to so flat a statement. He still thought the debts ought to be included in a general negotiation along with other related issues. I replied that I had felt that way until I had become convinced that this was more a political than an economic problem.

I went on to say that disarmament had seemed an even more worthy cause; but here, again, I had become convinced that Roosevelt was right to keep its discussion apart. It was true that it was one of the most admirable of Hoover's efforts. I had begun by assuming that, since international negotiation was something of a poker game, we ought to further arms reduction by trading debt concessions for it; but I had changed my mind. One reason for this was that any forgiveness of debts would be permanent and that disarmament was not. Even if we gained something, it could not be guaranteed that we could keep it. We might make concessions on the debts and get something in return; but there would be nothing to prevent new crises in Europe from starting another arms competition and then all the gains might easily be lost.

I thought I had made an impression even though none of our suggestions had been explicitly accepted. Both Day and Williams (the other delegate), I felt, ought to talk with Roosevelt himself as soon as possible.

It began to look, about the tenth of December, as though Hoover had not given up. There were intimations that he was getting ready another communication insisting on the reconstitution of the Debt Commission and on tying all the issues together in the agenda for the Economic Conference. I warned Moley of what I had heard from Day, and a meeting with Roosevelt was arranged. It was to be on Sunday, December 18, at Hyde Park.

On that day Moley was ill and had to stay at home. On the train from New York to Poughkeepsie, Day, Williams, and I encountered Adolf Berle and Will Woodin (who was to be Secretary of the Treasury, although none of us knew it then). Will was one of the "Friends of Roosevelt" who had contributed $10,000 apiece to the preconvention campaign. He was president of the American Car and Foundry Corporation, a delicate, small man, an amateur musician, and as little like a corporate executive in appearance as could be imagined. He and Adolf were to discuss some railway matters with Roosevelt. All of us gathered in the big library. There were fires at either end, and it seemed a more leisurely day than most we had had lately. Our talks were friendly and understanding but nevertheless definite.

As to the agenda, Roosevelt stated the position much as I had done. And both Day and Williams indicated that they felt obligated to accept his instructions. We also went on to lay out a tentative schedule for discussions leading up to the conference. While Roosevelt was thinking out loud, I made notes: "We were to have informal conversations with the British in order to come to the tentative arrangement with them that seemed essential to the success of the Conference, French intransigency being what it was. However, these conversations were not to begin until late in February so that they could be made to last until March when the change in administration would take place. The final agenda meeting ought to be held in London about March 15, and the Conference itself delayed until July. Before that time we would have bilateral meetings with the representatives of as many nations as possible so that the Conference might not fall into dissension."

Before the conversation with Day and Williams, Roosevelt asked me to wheel him into his small office-study where he showed me a long telegram from Hoover, the communication I had been warned about. It also contained the suggestion—interpreted by Roosevelt as a threat—that refusal would cause the issue to be laid before the Congress. Hoover would certainly use such a meeting to further his own point of view. It seemed unwise to agree.

We went back to the group before the fire and Roosevelt asked Day and Williams whether they would not try to postpone the meeting he understood they were to have with Hoover and Mills on Tuesday. We do not want the conference to fail, he told them; in fact, we feel that a great deal depends on it; but time must be allowed to negotiate the debts and, if possible, reach tentative settlements; and we should like to carry through the disarmament conversations Norman Davis had been having in Europe since the Geneva Conference of last year; we ourselves must have time to consider all this. They agreed to try and left soon after.

Roosevelt had asked me to stay when the others went, and he then called in Adolph Miller, an old friend who had been a member of the Federal Reserve Board since its organization. Miller had lunched with him that day and was in another room with the ladies. It was necessary to prepare an immediate answer to Hoover's message, and Miller, who had been shown the telegram before I came, had prepared some notes while the rest of us were conferring. These he left with us since he had to leave almost at once. Roosevelt looked at the notes and then said they were not likely to be helpful and that I had better get something ready. I told him that I should like to communicate with Ray Moley. I felt it was necessary for continuity, since he had been present at the previous meeting with Hoover and Mills. He agreed; and, since Berle was returning to New York, I gave him a copy of the Hoover telegram to take to Ray. The plan was that I should work on the answer with the Governor that night, going with him to Albany, and then go down to New York in the morning and consult with Ray telephoning back any amendment he might suggest.

When I got to work, it seemed best to outline our general point of view, then to set up each specific question in turn and state our position on it. I worked out the draft in this way. Roosevelt asked for the reasoning on each point, but we were so well agreed that only minor changes were necessary. Ray, next day, offered some minor amendments, but somehow these did not find their way into the final text.

The matter did not end there. The influenza that had been bothering Ray then invaded my system and I had to go home. Someone—Ray was certain it was Frankfurter, since he was then in Albany—persuaded Roosevelt to issue a statement supplementary to the message. In it the sharp division set up between our policy and that of Hoover was badly muddled. At any rate, the exchange with Hoover was made public on December 23, together with two supplementary telegrams. Roosevelt was still puzzled, when I next saw him, to know why it was that Hoover insisted again and again on the setting up of a commission on the debts to carry over from his term to another when he knew that the policy was to be changed. Among my notes, I find that I said Hoover seemed not to grasp the notion that the political considerations had the importance that Roosevelt thought they had. He answered that it must be the engineering mind.

During this conversation I had a chance to speak of another matter. Lewis Douglas, Congressman from Arizona, had ridden with us from Hyde Park to Albany on the night our answers to

Hoover had been prepared. While I thought about our reply, Roosevelt and Douglas had talked across me. I was preoccupied, but I did understand that Douglas was probably being considered for a cabinet job—I thought it must be the Treasury—and that they were speaking of the economies to be made by a thorough reorganization of federal departments. Afterward, I had talked with Douglas briefly. I was struck with the almost vindictive way he spoke of bureaucrats and the way he lingered fondly over the possibilities of economies. He had the same bias, I concluded, as Baruch and others who thought that the federal government was overexpanded and that recovery could be started by reducing its expenditures. This seemed to me absurd in view of the problems to be faced. I said so to Roosevelt.

About Douglas, I remarked that he seemed not to be interested in administration but only in reducing its cost. "You know," Roosevelt said, "you are quite wrong about that; Hoover, who is strong on administration, has been able to accomplish very little in the way of reorganization during his four years in Washington. I think you will find that a good deal more may be done during our time; and Douglas will be helpful. I have been in the federal government before and I think we must have a shakeup. It may result in real economy."

He went on then to repeat something which had disturbed me in the conversation with Douglas. "The federal government has no business to be doing research, for instance. Enough of that is being done by the universities. I think we ought to cut it out altogether." I said I could not agree at all, though my impression was that some departments allowed projects to linger too long after their usefulness was past. But that was easily corrected, and anyway it could not be extensive. I made a really spirited speech about this but I could see that the impression I made was slight. We soon went on to other business.

My notes, written on that December 23, include this sentence: "The difficulty will be that he will not always be careful to have continuing assistance. He is apt to make use of me at one time, Ray at another time if we are not together, and if neither of us is handy, some Senator or Congressman who happens to turn up at an opportune moment." I should also have added: "Douglas," whose counsel was certainly the worst of all.

Early spring that year was the most miserable time of all for the unemployed, but the agonized cries of the well-to-do, the managers and submanagers of the economy, were louder than theirs. There was a terrific tension. But we were quite aware of a strenuous effort being made to put off the crisis until after inauguration. The Republicans unanimously wanted it to be a Roosevelt crisis.

Realistic merchants, however, did not wait to thin down inventories still further, and prices continued to fall. Insurance companies began to refuse policies. They had no place to invest new funds. Every one of them was bankrupt by any liquidation test. The RFC was deluged with demands for help. Bankers and businessmen knew their enterprises were insolvent but they hoped a government loan might give them a few more weeks or months of life. The RFC responded bravely to these appeals. But what it could do was not nearly enough.

Presently the hoarding of currency became a problem. During January it was disappearing at the rate of about 100 million dollars a week. This was a most impressive indication of fear among those who meant to have at least a little cash when the banks closed. This had gone so far that by February the entire banking system was in immediate jeopardy. On February 14 the banks of the whole southern peninsula of Michigan were closed by a governor's proclamation. This area included Detroit and involved institutions with assets of a billion and a half dollars. A suspension of such size naturally affected other areas. Panic spread rapidly.

The prices of stocks and bonds plunged lower in succeeding days and hoarding increased. On February 15, Roosevelt got back from his southern trip, and on the same night he called me to him in the 65th Street house. Hoover had asked him once more to make a statement "to restore confidence." The implication of this phrase was quite plain: the crisis would have been over and recovery under way if Roosevelt had not frightened the business community. We were aware of rumors that we were intending to go off gold, even that nationalization of banking was being planned; but he thought we should again reject the Hoover appeal. He would do nothing until he could do it as President. I agreed.

We talked of his southern trip and about his escape from the attempt to assassinate him in Miami. Then presently we considered what he should say to Hoover. He was equable and unhurried. He was, I thought, well rested and fit for the coming ordeal. Since he had concluded that nothing was to be done except to make everything ready for swift action on March 4, that was what we must now do.

When I went down to the Roosevelt house again on the morning of March 3, however, our readiness was far from complete. For the cave-in of the whole country's financial institutions had spread out from Michigan, and the state governors everywhere, at bankers' insistence, were declaring "holidays"—a euphemism for permission to refuse depositors' demands. It was hard for anyone to think of anything else.

Yet Henry Wallace and I in preceding days had managed another of our mutually exploratory occasions. He had been in New York seeing various people in whom he was interested and hiding from reporters. So was I, for that matter. We walked in the streets together, visited in my apartment or office when it seemed safe, and, once or twice, went to the theater. His painful shyness was wearing off and his stiffness softening a little. Those traits he could not have overcome altogether even if he had wanted to; they were part of him.

A few days before, in spite of intervening shyness, we had mutually approached what for him was a considerable difficulty— the matter of clothes. How did a member of the cabinet, a presidential intimate, a statesman—and we both laughed at the word—dress? I thought of Moley's striped trousers and told him the story. As a result, I said, I was now in a position to give accurate advice. Would he like me to go shopping with him? He certainly would, he said, with relief. And he was outfitted with satisfactory completeness, although he admitted to some discomfort.

During our conversations, I could see that he was feeling for a device that would cheapen money and I wondered if the Cornellians might not find him an ally. By this time Moley and I were beleaguered arguers for a "sound" position. But I was quite sure Roosevelt was going to do something about gold. What I did not foresee was that my economist colleagues would think me involved. After all, an Assistant Secretary of Agriculture had no voice in fiscal policy. What would determine that, anyway, would be Roosevelt's own attitude. I had had a chance to say to him whatever I thought and felt. But that phase was over now. There would be a cabinet. Ray's stewardship was really finished, and mine with his.

The 65th Street house was somewhat chaotic on that dull March morning. As the friends and political associates, new and old, of the Roosevelts prepared to make the ferry crossing and take the Baltimore and Ohio train from Jersey City, I am sure no outsider would have believed that every bank in the country was closed and that nothing yet had been done to reopen them. Our inevitable excitement was sharpened by our knowledge of a national crisis; but it was the first time that some of these people had met and the amenities had to be observed. The Wallaces in particular knew none of the others and had to be introduced all around.

Not half a dozen people on the special train knew what might be done before the week was out or whether anything was planned. Roosevelt himself had assumed an air of confidence, even of jollity, which I thought, for one unsettling hour, was so preposterous as to risk ridicule, although it is true that at least two of the numerous proclamations to be issued in days to come were already roughed out. One of them had to do with the convening of a special session of the Congress on the ninth and the other with a nationwide bank holiday. This last made use of the Trading with the Enemy Act, which forbade anyone to "pay out, export, earmark, or permit the withdrawal or transfer in any manner or by any device whatsoever, of any gold or silver coin or bullion or currency or take any other action which might facilitate the hoarding thereof."

I had had some part in preparing for this. Roosevelt had sent me to Washington in February to find out, if I could, whether a suggestion made by Rene Leon that the Act of 1917 had not been fully repealed was true. Did the repeal end with a semicolon before the gold controls were described, or did it go on to the end of the title? I consulted several senators and got in touch with Daniel Bell in the Treasury, through Herbert Feis in the State Department. Bell had in his desk a copy of the Act. Certain passages were underlined; the same ones Leon had spoken of. This led me to think Mills and Hoover had considered forbidding the export of gold on this authority but had dropped the notion. I went back to Roosevelt with the guess that this had been because the international bankers had objected. But, I confessed, no one could say authoritatively whether the clause was repealed or not. Nevertheless a proclamation had been based on it.

In the President's public papers, there is a note to the effect that he consulted with Senator Thomas J. Walsh about this. This is mistaken. We were never able to get in touch with Senator Walsh before his sudden death on March 2. He had been traveling and could not be reached. There had been, for two days, almost continuous conferences between the new Secretary of the Treasury, Woodin, and the outgoing officials of the Treasury, Mills, Ballantine, and Awalt. Moley and Berle had also participated, but I had heard about them only at second hand. Homer Cummings, who took Walsh's intended place as Attorney General, was not appointed until the last minute and he was probably not consulted until after inauguration.[6]

Feverish conferences went on as the inaugural train rolled southward. Roosevelt was still considering exactly what contingencies might arise, although it must have been a relief to have at least two proclamations drafted. It has often been suggested that when all the banks were closed Roosevelt ought to have kept them closed, and to have liquidated once and for all a monopoly so fatally abused—that of creating the nation's medium of exchange and making a profit on it. A dozen alternatives to the course he took must have been discussed, but it is my belief that what finally determined his decision to support the existing banking structure was the rising hysteria, together with his previous failure to put together a comprehensive alternative. Besides, he must have asked himself, who could help to execute it? And this last may even have been conclusive.

There were many people on the inaugural train, and many others who were to see the President within the next day or two, who would not have enough currency to pay their hotel bills or to meet the other expenses of their trip to Washington; and this was so ridiculous that it caused more joking remarks than foreboding ones. Nevertheless, well-to-do people were terribly frightened. The

6. Moley differs on this point, *The First New Deal,* p. 146. But he did not seem to know of my own explorations into the Trading with the Enemy Act. The confusion of these days made it impossible for everyone to know what others were doing.

poor had few dealings with banks. Their worst time had come earlier when they had faced far worse possibilities than that of not being able to pay a hotel bill. Why people had until now been so orderly under provocation was a matter Roosevelt speculated about. He was later inclined to think, as he looked back over that period, that disappointed hope, rather than despair, creates revolt and that what prevailed then was accurately to be described as despair. Now there was hope and he knew he must not preside over more disappointment.

The question had been raised whether the elaborate inaugural parade ought to be held. His answer to that had been short; of course it must. It was better to risk criticism than the added fear cancellation would produce. And so, as we reached Washington, the whole trainload of Rooseveltians was put into automobiles; and I, at least, had my first experience of a presidential cavalcade with motorcycle outriders.

It was cold in Washington—miserably cold and wet, as was usual in early March. During the night and all the next day conferences about the financial situation continued to go on at the Mayflower where most of us stayed. I was not among the conferees. So far as the financial disturbances of the next three weeks went, I was a spectator. Wallace and I were fully occupied with our own prospective jobs. He did have a chance to say something in the first cabinet meetings; I merely looked on with disappointed resignation.

On the fourth of March, in the morning, we took over our department. That is to say, he went to his office and I went to mine; and we saw our predecessors. I had a comical moment when R. W. Dunlap, the Assistant Secretary I had come to replace, informed me that he had no thought of resigning but expected to continue to occupy his office. Of course, I had not yet been appointed nor had any public announcement been made, I retired in bad order.

Within a few days, the *Congressional Record* carried the notice, however, and meanwhile I had been getting acquainted with my new colleagues. Dunlap had occupied an office in one corner of the department building. It was at the opposite corner from that of the Secretary and I thought it too far away. For his uses it had been admirable, I presume; anyway, when he seemed more reconciled to leaving, I asked him what an Assistant Secretary's duties were. He said that he signed the road contracts (agreements between the states and the Bureau of Public Roads) and presided at the hearings prescribed in the Packers and Stockyards Act. That, he admitted, was about all.

I am afraid I assumed that he meant to be funny. A troubled look seemed to travel upward and lose itself somewhere in the bald spaces above. "You will find," he said, "that an Assistant Secretary can't do very much. I spend some time out in Beltsville, too"—a remark I appreciated only after a little inquiry disclosed "Beltsville" as an experimental complex a few miles from Washington in a state of arrested development. He undoubtedly felt more at home in the fields and stables than in the office he was so reluctant to give up. When I prepared a few days later to move in, he objected that his resignation still had not been asked for, and he thought his salary ought to be paid until it had. He went away reluctantly, however, and I had a desk of my own.[7]

My seat at the inaugural parade was in a grandstand directly opposite the platform where the new President and the cabinet members sat. Roosevelt that morning had begun the process of restoring a nation's confidence in itself. There was, he had said, "no failure of substance." Nature still offered her bounty but generous use languished in the very sight of abundance. And then he tramped hard on those who were responsible. Primarily it was "because the rulers of the exchange of mankind's goods have failed through their own stubbornness and their own incompetence, and have admitted their failure, and have abdicated."

I have not been able to reconcile this speech of his with the policy of the first months. It was directed single-mindedly to the reestablishment of confidence in the very institutions he denounced. My only suggestion is that he had lost no faith in the institutions, only in the men who ran them; and that he believed the country to be of the same mind. Was that what was meant when he said that "the money changers" had "fled from their high

7. This was not the last I heard of Dunlap. He ran for Congress in 1934 and on what could only be described as an anti-Tugwell ticket, as I accidentally discovered afterward from the reports of a friend in his district. This is not simply that by that time I should have achieved either isolation or indifference—merely to point up the comic element in my ridiculous dignification as a symbol of all the Republicans hated.

seats in the temple of our civilization. We may now restore that temple to the ancient truths"? No man who did not feel to the utmost the solemnity of his responsibility would pour into the ears of a listening nation an invitation to such a comparison. But what "ancient truths" were to be restored? In two paragraphs he recalled Americans to the ethical standards they had neglected but had never ceased to profess. "These dark days will be worth all they cost us if they teach us that our true destiny is not to be ministered unto but to minister . . . There must be an end to a conduct in banking and in business which too often have given to a sacred trust the likeness of selfish wrong-doing."

Were banking and business sacred trusts? They had not been thought to be. They were profit-making occupations—and the more profits the better. And the wide separation of ownership from management in the modern corporation had not helped to "humanize" or to make business more ethical. Those who received dividends found it easier and easier to ignore their source in the overcharging of customers, the exploiting of labor, or the deceiving of investors. His hearers were left to recall the other sentence of the parable. That he had the whole of the tenth and eleventh chapters of Mark in mind could not be doubted.[8] For in the tenth it is said, "and whosoever would be first among you, shall be servant of all. For the Son of Man also came not to be ministered unto, but to minister, and to give his life as a ransom for many." And in the eleventh chapter it is related that as Jesus came to Jerusalem after his triumphant progress, "he entered into the temple, and began to cast out them that bought in the temple, and overthrew the tables of the money changers." And he taught, and said unto them, "Is it not written, My house shall be called a house of Prayer for all the Nations? But ye have made it a den of robbers." Had the new President pondered the next sentence of that story: "And the chief priests and the scribes heard it, and sought how they might destroy him; for they feared him"?

There came billowing up Pennsylvania Avenue, in the chill of the March afternoon, squads and squadrons, marching clubs, fraternal

---

8. The same story is told—with some variations—in Matthew, Luke, and John; the reason for thinking that he had Mark in mind is the previous reference to "ministering" found only there.

drill teams, silk-hatted Tammany chieftains, Gifford Pinchot in his spectacular governor's car, waving a hand to the Junior Progressive who was now President. There were bands, platoons of soldiers, sailors, and marines. There was all the gaudy color of American life. For four solid hours Roosevelt sat on a shooting stick or stood on his crutches, silk-hatted, broad-shouldered, erect, laughing and waving, watching the parade. The mood was certainly in contrast with the morning's solemnity. His "So help me God" as Mr. Justice Hughes had held out the Bible had come clearly from the amplifiers in his high tenor.

As he liked afterward to tell the story, he woke next morning to a sense of urgent need for getting to work. When he had been wheeled across to the executive office and was seated, for the first time, behind the President's desk, he found himself alone. It was Sunday. His desk was bare and no one answered the bells. For many moments he sat there, a little unnerved, with no one to take orders, unable even to make notes. The whole capitalistic system was smashing up. He had offered himself as its savior. And here he was, helpless!

But on Monday the Hundred Days began.

10

ON THE VERGE

OF THE PRESIDENCY

Early in the day on March 4, 1933, Roosevelt asked Divine blessing on his new official family. He might well ask for such assistance; no other seemed adequate to the national condition. The degeneration of the economic system had not been stayed by the prospect of a change in Washington; if anything, conditions had worsened; and this was certainly true of the whole financial system.

Until February, the sickness had been kept fairly far from the centers of finance by one means or another,[1] but it was now reaching those well-guarded citadels, the metropolitan banks. The trouble, like a flood, was rising higher and higher, inundating one another of the supposedly safe islands of the economy. Just during the few days preceding March 4, the governors of additional states had proclaimed what were euphemistically called "bank holidays"—meaning, in ordinary language, that the banks were closed to prevent the drawing out of funds by depositors who no longer considered them safe. Withdrawals had reached such proportions that further out-payments would be impossible.

Many of the anticipatory Democrats who had invaded Washington to enjoy the taking-over were unable to pay their way and

NOTE. This essay appeared in *The Antioch Review,* Spring 1956.
1. Mostly by allowing the banks in small communities to fail. Their assets were heavily weighted with foreign bonds and other doubtful obligations sold to them by the metropolitan banking houses.
Not all the banks were insolvent; that is to say many of them had assets enough to cover their obligations. But these assets could not be realized immediately and the demand for cash had exhausted the available reserves of currency.

there was some embarrassment. The spectacle of silk-hatted and formal-coated politicians scrounging around for the cash they needed to meet their bills had its comic side; but it can hardly have seemed comic to Roosevelt and those with him who were now picking up responsibility as Hoover and others of the outgoing officials laid it down. He may well have prayed more earnestly for assistance on that day than on any of the other occasions when he had assumed new public duties.

He had a choice to make; or, rather, he *had* had a choice to make, for about certain matters his mind was already made up and he was praying for help, not for guidance. He had concluded that it would be best to attempt the restoration of confidence, gradually reopen the solvent banks, and wait until later for serious reorganization or even for reform. He might have used the crisis in another way. He might have set up a substitute for the old system, so easily destroyed by pressure. He might have thought it time for a genuine national banking structure, since the semiprivate one had failed so disastrously. He chose not to attempt such a tour de force for reasons known only to himself. Perhaps the most credible suggestion is that the restoration of some order in the economy was, in his mind, so urgent a matter that he felt it necessary to adopt the quickest and easiest means to this end. A redesigned banking system might not work well at first, and might need repeated changes. This was not a time for risking doubt of the new administration's competence or of his own.

It may seem to a later generation absurd that there can have been such urgency. To suppose that in the United States known to them there can have been such a breakdown that familiar institutions—police and justice, supply and distribution, transportation and communication—might so largely cease to function as to create an emergency may seem to them to have been a fantastic forecast; but those who lived through that time and had some responsibility will always recall the narrowness of the escape from chaos.

What do people do who have no money? There were those who had been wondering about that for several years. Upwards of twelve million were by now unemployed, and many had been so for a long time. They had no income as of right. They might get something from the local authorities or from private philanthropy, and they might benefit from the sporadic and scattered efforts to start public works, but there was nothing to be counted on and assistance was for many not to be had at all. There were, indeed, those who had had to learn what to do without money.

There were interim makeshifts—selling household goods, borrowing from usurers, trading with one another—but when these failed there was only the last resort of soup and bread lines for food and Hoovervilles for shelter. The lines by now had lengthened until they stretched down streets and around corners, and often supplies ran out before the hungry had all been fed; and the Hoovervilles were sprawled on the garbage dumps and wastelands of every city's periphery.

The strain on people's bodies and minds from endless insecurity and hardship had tended to intensify and to spread. Unemployed men and women could not pay rent unless they were helped; nor could they buy food or clothes or provide shelter unless they were helped. The help, even when it came, was never enough; and when landlords and storekeepers were not paid, neither were the builders of houses nor the manufactueres of goods. When these could not collect, they could not repay loans at the bank or meet their other liabilities. This was why factories were closed or were on part-time schedules; it was why building had stopped; it was why, finally, the economic sickness had spread to the banks.

So it was no longer only the unemployed who had to learn what to do without cash. People much further up the scale of living were having to find out too. There was still a vast difference between them and the unemployed. They had claims on income, at least, and the poor had none; but they were frightened as they had never been before. Both, on inauguration day, were in fact equally moneyless—the one group because they had none coming, the other because what they had coming was frozen.

Some unusual devices were used when currency was no longer available because banks were shut: two of these were barter and the issuance of script. Barter was useful when there could be direct exchanges; but it was only by the merest chance that in a highly specialized economy sellers and buyers could meet. People who lived in cities hardly ever had any contact with the producers of food in the countryside; anyway, industrial goods came from factories and individuals seldom had them to dispose of. Barter was used to a certain extent, however, where conditions permitted. Script, issued by groups or associations, was found to be somewhat more useful. It could represent goods and could pass easily from hand to hand. When, however, too much was expected of it, exchange broke down. It had to be guaranteed. And when it got too far from the source of issue, recognition for it was only doubtfully granted. There was a time, at the worst of the currency shortage, when in rather wide areas these resorts proved indispensable.[2]

Conservatives were indeed worried almost as much by the various ingenious devices for meeting the emergency as by their actual troubles. It was an added reason for demanding that something be done at once. Their voices, as a matter of fact, were louder than those of the workers, who, on the whole, had undergone their ordeal with amazing patience. The President-elect knew about the unemployed. If, in his travels, he had not noted the smokeless factory chimneys, seen the idle on the street corners, and glimpsed the empty freight cars on remote sidings, he had those by him who could tell him about the state of the once proud economy.

So he knew. He knew also about the farmers. They had tired of poverty, of debts they could not pay, of losing their land and their homes by foreclosure. They were strongly inclined to approve the *status quo ante;* they wanted nothing changed except their own present inability to make a profit from farming. They were also diehard individualists, the thorniest of all citizens for bureaucrats to organize; and a majority of them were Republicans, as befitted citizens with such predilections, even if many of them had, in anger and resentment, voted against Hoover. Conservative as they

2. Part of the same improvised machinery were the self-help workshops set up in various places. Some were naturally more successful than others, depending on the management. That in Ohio finally began to look something like a system within a system. The unemployed worked to produce things which other unemployed could use; and these, in turn, produced to exchange—this was clearly an alternative to formal capitalism. It was viewed with the expected suspicion by conservatives and tended to wither as relief became more easily available and as works projects were developed. But it was one of the chief counts of the critics of Harry Hopkins' successive organizations to care for the unemployed that in various places these improvisations had been encouraged. Those who managed the local relief agencies, however, were usually undoctrinaire folk. Anything, they felt, which would assist those beaten down by the failure of industrialism was to be fostered. These were the heroes of the long depression. They were already hard at work before Roosevelt came to Washington or Harry Hopkins had been heard of outside New York.

might be, however, their resentments now had taken control, and it was they who were showing most conspicuously the symptoms of indiscipline, their usual preference for order making their violence much more terrifying than it otherwise would have been. Many a foreclosure sale, undertaken with all due process, was stopped by interference with authorities. Until a conspiracy among newspapers to maintain optimism got under way, there were many available accounts of such happenings during the winter. At farm sales in Pennsylvania, the auctioneers were bid five cents for a cow, five cents for family furniture, and five cents for the farm buildings. Hard-faced neighbors circulated among the crowd to see that no one bid more. Out in Iowa milk trucks were stopped on the highway and dumped. Not for starvation prices, the farmers said, would they furnish any more produce to the city markets.

Incidents of this sort had multiplied. They were now a daily occurrence in many neighborhoods.[3] It was true that Hoover had proposed, and the generally hostile Congress had agreed to pass, a bill to ease bankruptcies. It would have some effect; but it had not yet taken hold. The Reconstruction Finance Corporation was lending parsimoniously to states so that the furnishing of relief should not entirely stop. Furthermore, large loans were being

3. The following paragraphs are quoted from *Time,* February 6, 1933, p. 17.

"Near Bowling Green, Ohio, 800 ugly-tempered farmers last week assembled at Wallace Kramp's place to watch a finance company foreclose its $800 mortgage. Bidding began at 15 ¢ for a spring harrow. When the company's representative raised it to $1.55, somebody shouted: 'That's the guy what holds the mortgage.' Promptly the bidder was marched well out of the bidding range where he was rescued by a sheriff. Wallace Kramp's neighbors bought in all his things for $14, handed them back to him.

"At Nampa, Idaho, where a United Farmer's League was in process of organization, one William Ai Frost jumped up and shouted: 'Just give me a six-shooter and four red-blooded men who will have the nerve to follow me and a will to make the legislature put through any law we want.'

"At Overton, Neb., any outsider who dared to bid at the foreclosure sale on Mike Thinnes' farm was threatened with a ducking in the horse trough at the hands of 200 farmer friends. Mrs. Thinnes bought in cows for 10 ¢, horses for 25 ¢, tractors for 50 ¢—at a total cost of $15.

"At Perry, Iowa, approximately the same prices prevailed at the foreclosure on George Rosander's place when 150 of his friends collected to restrict the bidding. The holder of a $2,500 mortgage collected precisely $42.05.

"At Le Mars, Iowa, 25 farmers gathered to block foreclosure on a mortgage on the home of Dentist George Washington Cunningham. They explained that they all owed Dr. Cunningham for professional services.

"Events such as the above were what John Andrew Simpson, president of the National Farmer's Union had in mind last week when he told the Senate Committee on Agriculture: 'The biggest and finest crop of revolutions is sprouting all over the country right now.' "

made to businesses, to railroads, and to manufacturers, as well as banks, to keep them going. And all these measures might have had some effect except that the spreading paralysis all the time outran the measures taken to check it. Unemployment increased; loans were soon exhausted, and more and more were called for. There was no end in sight, not even any visible slowing of the decline. Enormous loan funds seemed to disappear without trace, leaving only an unpayable obligation.

In such circumstances those who knew how fast the degeneration was spreading could hardly be blamed for grasping at immediate remedies and forgetting for the moment their cherished reforms. That, at least, was Roosevelt's reaction. It was he, more than anyone else, on whom responsibility was descending with the momentum of a juggernaut. He may well have prayed, in the old church across Lafayette Square from the White House, for time as well as for wisdom; but there was no time. Such wisdom as could be managed must be used instantly. And wisdom to be of use must already have been available for several days.

One skeptical historian, Richard Hofstadter, later remarked that what seemed to the nation on that day the inspired and winged words of Roosevelt's inaugural address were actually trite and commonplace. Exhorting Americans to abjure excessive caution and once more to be bold and forthputting; telling them they had nothing to fear but fear itself—this was, as can be seen in the chilly light of later scholarly assessment, only another version of that "restoration of confidence" which had been Hoover's ruinous theme. It was the same idea businessmen were always harping on.[4] It was what Bernard Baruch had counseled as a campaign device. It had been the burden of the Pittsburgh speech during the campaign. Restore confidence, the line ran, and business will recover. When business recovers, unemployment will disappear and the banks will again be secure.[5]

4. It was what a whole parade of business leaders counseled before a lame-duck investigating committee of the Senate over which the retiring Reed Smoot of Utah presided, but which, after March 4, would be chaired by Pat Harrison of Mississippi. It was as pitiful an exhibition of futility as can ever have been displayed by the responsible men of a leading nation. See for extended reporting the New York *Times* of various February dates.
5. Hofstadter, *The American Political Tradition* (New York: Alfred Knopf, 1948), chap. XIII, p. 312: "When Hoover bumbled that it was necessary only to restore confi-

How was it that when Roosevelt asked for confidence, courage began to reinfuse the whole nation? There can be no doubt that it happened; the signs were unmistakable. The access of good feeling was, it must be admitted, largely just that—a feeling, traceable to the relief people felt in knowing there would now be a change. No one, for a long time, had believed that Hoover knew what to do, or that, if he did, he would be able to do it. He was discredited. Roosevelt would at least make new efforts without being stifled by preconceptions. Also—and this was important—he would have the power to act, because the Congress was Democratic too. Moreover, he had given an impression of vitality and initiative from the moment of his nomination when he had broken precedent, flown to Chicago to accept the party's designation, and spoken heartening words.

There was a most astonishing improvement in this way. The week before inauguration was one of despair. The sinking spell seemed to be more and more beyond any human control and fright was almost palpably present in the air. The week after inauguration, the reversal was like the incoming of an ocean tide in high latitudes. Did Roosevelt's words cause the change? Why, if this was to be so, did not the *prospect* of his accession have more effect? The historian dislikes having to answer such questions as these. He dislikes especially admitting that the trite words of a man, flung out into the air for a listening people, could so change the course of events. Yet the change in those March days has to be admitted; and there is no explanation other than an access of hope.

Such a reversal is certainly not easy to start; and it is even more difficult to sustain and to enlarge. The words of the inaugural may have been only another version of the threadbare confidence theme, but there was this difference between what Roosevelt had to say and what his predecessor had been saying: Hoover had addressed his exhortations to businessmen; Roosevelt addressed his words to others in the community. In fact businessmen could find little comfort in what he said; to them it sounded as though his promises to others would require of them some novel humiliations. Others, however, very obviously found comfort in

---

dence, the nation laughed bitterly. When Roosevelt said: 'The only thing we have to fear is fear itself,' essentially the same thread-bare half-true idea, the nation was thrilled."

the same words. Later skeptics lacked the impression of the strong, war voice speaking to the crowd before him and to all those who sat by their radios and waited. A miracle was so much desired that perhaps his listeners created it; but it certainly occurred.

Then, too, the accusations he made may have helped. The devils were whipped again as they had been during the campaign. Businessmen had abdicated their responsibilities. No one, henceforth, would be allowed to carry on as the wicked ones had in the years just past. "We are," he said, "stricken by no plague of locusts . . . plenty is at our doorstep, but a generous use of it languishes in the very sight of supply." This was because "the rulers of the exchange of mankind's goods have failed through their own stubbornness and their own incompetence."

He went even further. There was the much-quoted passage about the "money changers" who had "fled their high seats" in the temple. "We may now," he said, "restore that temple to the ancient truths." He then went on to speak of those who had betrayed their sacred trust. To such conduct there must be an end. There could be no confidence while it was tolerated, for confidence "thrives only on honesty, on honor, on the sacredness of obligations, on faithful protection, on unselfish performance."

There must be a change of attitude, he said; but actual results would require more drastic changes. Above all, "this nation asks for action, and action now." Then he got down to the hard policy. He summarized it in two paragraphs:

> Our greatest primary task is to put people to work. This is no unsolvable problem if we face it wisely and courageously. It can be accomplished in part by direct recruiting by the Government itself, treating the task as we would treat the emergency of a war, but at the same time, through this employment, accomplishing greatly needed projects to stimulate and reorganize the use of our natural resources.
>
> Hand in hand with this we must frankly recognize the overbalance of population in our industrial centers and, by engaging on a national scale in redistribution, endeavor to provide a better use of the land for those best fitted for the land. The task can be helped by definite efforts to raise the values of agricultural products and with this the power to

purchase the output of our cities. It can be helped by insistence that the Federal, State, and local governments act forthwith on the demand that their cost be drastically reduced. It can be helped by the unifying of relief activities which today are often scattered, uneconomical, and unequal. It can be helped by national planning for and supervision of all forms of transportation and communications and other utilities which have a definitely public character. There are many ways in which it can be helped, but it can never be helped merely by talking about it. We must act and act quickly.

It was said later that this was not much of a program to offer an almost fatally sick nation, and this, I think, must be admitted. Part of it was inoperable, part was trivial, and none of it went to the heart of the matter in a remedial way. It is, however, a fact attested to by everyone who lived through that time, that the sick nation enlarged the words and the intentions far beyond their face value and that the effect was just next to miraculous. The cure, whatever it was, then and there began to take effect. When all is said, there must have been some magic in mere words.

That morning Roosevelt called at the White House and he and Hoover rode together in the big open car to the Capitol. Roosevelt seemed to be chatting cheerily; Hoover, tired almost to death from his long immolation, appeared hardly to respond at all. Later, Hoover sat among those who listened while the new President took the oath on the old Dutch family Bible, repeating after Chief Justice Hughes the solemn words of consecration (instead, as was customary, of only saying "I do"). Hoover's face was a study in distrust as Roosevelt launched into his speech. He almost visibly winced as the "money changers" were referred to. There was only dull resignation as the "program" was elaborated. Afterward, he made his way, forgotten and alone, back to the White House and presently out of Washington, while Roosevelt rode triumphantly down Pennsylvania Avenue through cheering crowds to take possession of the presidency. There was a New Deal.

What the biographer has to acknowledge at this juncture—beginning on this day—is that he begins now to deal with entirely different phenomena than he has dealt with before. The man whose career he has been following has, up till now, been an entirely accountable person. He had got where he now was by scheming, by conforming and compromising, by hard work, by faithful performance of his political business—all of this attended by good luck. Every step can be understood, even the election to the presidency, which was much more a vote against Hoover than for Roosevelt. Now, however, the man whose inaugural speech was so poorly composed became overnight the embodiment of American aspirations. The person was lost in the President.

Naturally when, by election, the people were choosing a new leader, he moved in a heightened glare of publicity. There had been endless curiosity about him and about his family for months before inauguration. The smallest detail had been news. The Governor of New York had had little privacy; but he had had a good deal more than the President-elect. The sense of ownership felt by people about their president is a far more demanding sentiment than is centered in any governor. On the morning after election, the Secret Service of the United States had taken charge of his person. Thereafter the security controls would never be lifted until his death. The alert young men always near, trying to be inconspicuous, but watchful of his safety, were evidence that he was public property.[6]

What Americans saw was a man well schooled in being a public figure and well equipped to assume great office. Since his nomination there had been a show of energy, of fearlessness in the face of adversity, and even of gaiety, which contrasted with the defeat they had seen in Hoover. The contrast was about as complete as it was possible to conceive. Cold aloofness was being exchanged for an eloquently expressed intimacy; and they liked it. Even the hostile press was kind. The reporters were always mostly friendly; and the publishers knew how much their readers longed for a change. Their conservative principles were in abeyance—for the time being.

The reporters knew, being professionals, that the air of confidence and cheerfulness was mostly assumed, that actually Roosevelt could not possibly be so sure of his ability to cope with the crisis as he seemed; but they could not be certain how far into the causes of distress he actually saw, or the completeness of his

6. Two chiefs of the White House detail during Roosevelt's presidency have written accounts of their stewardship: Colonel Starling and Michael Reilly who succeeded him.

planning for the future. He might be better prepared than they had thought. The fact was that some preparations were further along than they guessed by inauguration day, but that others were far from being ready; only their outlines were beginning to be visible. The optimism was not assumed, but the confidence was.

Normally the Congress would not have met until the following January; and in the usual circumstances the new President would have had months to prepare a program of legislation. Until the last moment such an interval was anticipated. For effect, it had been supposed, he would call a special session, but it would be limited to a few agreed projects—relief, mostly, and public works. Even when the banking crisis widened the demands on the special session, there was not at first any intention of asking for the varied performance put on during the following weeks. That spectacle would be improvised as events developed. But the economic situation had by then become so acute that it was regarded as no more than response to emergency.

Once more the nation had found a champion in time of need. There was even a little complacency mixed with the prevalent praise. The blessing of good fortune did not have to be deserved; it was America's due; people were inclined to feel that some luck was justified after the hard years just past. They had endured their ordeal with a certain stolidity. Now the time had come for something to be done.

Accession to the presidency is a tremendous happening for the new president, but also for the electorate. There nearly always tends to be general euphoria, intensified when, after an exciting campaign in which strong contenders have been engaged, the choice has been right. Consequently inauguration is very often attended by the belief that democracy is being justified. Regardless—or very nearly regardless—of the start made by the new leader, good wishes flow to him and he is borne along into his first term on a strong tide of support.

Reciprocally he discovers, sometimes quite suddenly, that he is responsible not only to his party, or to those who voted for him, but to all the people, even those who opposed him. In this discovery there is a kind of exhilaration which, if he is well prepared and knowledgeable, will stir him to the formulation of an actionable program in a hurry. If he is not prepared, and not a quick learner, the period may pass without any real accomplishment, and disillusion will settle over his administration.

The first months of new administrations have long been called "honeymoons" to describe the bemused mutual regard of people and president. Political writers apply the term more narrowly to the temporary abatement of the perennial quarrel between the executive and the legislative branches. They are apt to ascribe it rather cynically to temporary conformance of the legislators in expectation of favors to come. Favors are certainly to be had, patronage being among the most important. But the real secret of congressional tameness is the uneasy sense among the members that they are excluded from the obvious union of president and people. They resent it, but for the moment they are helpless. He has, after all, been elected by all the citizens, they by only a few. In his single person there is concentrated the whole mystique of representation. Legislators, being politicians, are impressed, in spite of themselves, by the formidable potential of this oneness. They behave with almost comical circumspection. But hard and experienced eyes are nevertheless watching for the inevitable weakening of the bond, ready to assert themselves at the first opportunity. Legislators will go as far in attrition on the executive, then, as they dare. Infrequently, they trespass prematurely, rouse his ire, and cause him to "go to the people." They retreat sullenly from their positions if he succeeds—and if his case is well put, he usually does.

New presidents differ enormously in their understanding of the situation. Many have come to office without appreciating its requirements. The sudden transformation from pleading politician to national leader is beyond the capability of all but the professionals. The inexperienced will have wasted the honeymoon period, have lowered the prestige of the presidency, and have passed into history as "weak" incumbents. Those who, on the contrary, loom large in history have been those identifiable as "strong." What this means is that they understood their representative nature, understood, also, the inherently divisive nature of separated powers, and used the strength flowing to them from popular regard to coerce all the unwilling diverse interests into yielding consent to a national program.

There have been presidents who started off badly and then took hold; and the rapidity and extent of their recovery was the measure of their intelligence. Those who were initially weakest seem often to have been made that way be having been legislators. They are ambitious, as they take office, to reduce the tendentiousness of their former colleagues. Harding and Truman were two of these. But there have been presidents without this experience who have started out in the same way—Cleveland was one and Eisenhower was another. So the cause is doubtful; but the fact is not. The best reputed presidents have been the ones who have had an initial comprehension of the necessity for leadership; but there have been several who did make quick and complete recoveries such as was made in a few months by Kennedy—not that it did him much good; his time was too short.

These general remarks are made to place Roosevelt at the time of his inaugural. Obviously he falls into the category of those who understood the realities of the situation before entering on it. He was prepared to exercise leadership at once and without more mealy-mouthed equivocation than was necessary to comply with the amenities. A good legislator to him would be one who would go along; a bad one would be a reluctant cooperator. He did not expect policies, or the laws to effect them, to come from the legislature. They would originate with him, or in his neighborhood, and it would be his responsibility to see that they were passed. More realistically than any president of all the line, except his predecessor Theodore, and further back, Jefferson, he grasped the fact that presidents are inescapably chief legislators. An understanding of his initial intention to dominate the situation makes much more intelligible his dominance during the special session.

The preinaugural interval did not produce policies for all the problems to be solved; but much more was done than was generally realized. Some of it was not wise and had to be abandoned, but that it was done at all demonstrates that the new President clearly accepted his new responsibility. It is true that everything was, so to speak, compressed or syncopated, and decisions were hurried because of a fiscal crisis so demanding that much else was delayed or neglected; but there was never any doubt about the decision-making power or about the forthcoming of essential directives.

John Nance Garner, feeling his oats a bit as Vice President-elect, was persuaded by his business friends to start an agitation for a national sales tax, something they had hoped and worked for ever since the income tax had become burdensome; now that even Hoover's budgets were unbalanced, and there were obvious new obligations coming up to be paid for, they were trying again. Roosevelt, without such emphasis as would embarrass Garner too much, let it be known that he expected to balance the budget by reductions of expense, or, if necessary, by increasing the income tax. Half of this the knowledgeable were too realistic to believe, and the other half was distressing to the conservatives; but the progressives were loud in approval.

In this difference, there was an intimation of a schism. It was not created at this moment; it had been latent all along; but it would enlarge and become more and more difficult to compromise. It is impossible to estimate the proportion of his time over the next decade that Roosevelt had to spend holding together the uneasy, mutually hostile, elements of his support; but it was very high. It was exhausting too. Both sides were unreasonable and demanding. But he never quite reached a position where he could do what he must have wished to do innumerable times—make a choice and let the reactionaries go.[7]

He could see what was happening even so early; and it was only by finesse that he prevented an immediate split. It is arguable whether the resulting compromises were worth the effort; but they were inherent in his political method. He would always take what he could get and bide his time for the rest.

The conservatives may have been made suspicious by the small evidence of intransigency furnished by the sales tax rejection; but about some other issues they could not complain. One of these was the handling of the banking crisis. The measures determined on did not solve the problem. There began a long struggle about

7. Not, at least, until his third term was ending and Wendell Willkie had been rejected as a Republican candidate. He would then feel the time right and begin negotiations with Willkie. Willkie's death—and his own shortly afterward—intervened and nothing resulted. See Rosenman, *Working with Roosevelt* (New York, 1952).

inflation—or, rather, about the means to inflate. During this time the shades of Silver Dick Bland and Cross-of-Gold Bryan seemed to haunt Washington; and throughout the monetary crisis Roosevelt's temporizing rated as an extremely skillful straddle. The sound money advocates emerged more unhappy than the inflationists; they had to accept repayment in cheapened dollars of the debts owed to them; but private banking had, been saved and this was a rich favor.

Inflation as a policy was not settled on at once; but it was obvious to sensitive watchers that something of the sort was moiling about in Roosevelt's mind. It could not be pinned down; he was evasive; he sometimes seemed, even, to be on the other side—had he not made that speech at Pittsburgh during the campaign castigating Hoover for allowing the budget to become unbalanced and for not having reduced government expenses? This seemed to lead straight to acceptance of the "restoration of confidence" principle for which Baruch, Young, and the others stood. On the other hand, the progressives in the Senate and the House were waiting with obvious impatience to renew the push for enlarged federal relief and for enormous public works undertakings. These would require higher taxes, and, even with that, a horrendously unbalanced budget.

The original sponsor of the Federal Reserve Act, Senator Carter Glass, had a revision of the Act almost at the passage point in the lame-duck session. Roosevelt earnestly explored the bill and promised support for its passage. But somehow Glass did not trust him. He had heard disquieting rumors; and ever since the election he had taken a sour view of Roosevelt's publicity in his passages through Washington. During them, Democratic leaders had been "sent for." Cordell Hull might comply with such a request; but Glass regarded the President-elect as a probable radical and certainly an ignoramus about finance. He said so; and kept his distance. He was probably amazed when, in February, he was offered the secretaryship of the treasury. So, when they heard of it, was everyone close to Roosevelt. It was even more inexplicable than the offer to Hull of the secretaryship of state. Glass grumpily refused. Whether Roosevelt was relieved, no one knows. But Hull accepted, and whether Roosevelt was gratified, no one knows. One thing is certain. With both Glass and Hull in his cabinet, it is impossible to think of him doing what was subsequently done, and what, even then, he must have been considering.

Why then did he ask Glass to be a member of his cabinet? This and other selections can only be understood—and then not altogether—by exploring somewhat more at length his probable theory about his official family. It is only possible to infer what this was. In this, as in so many similar important issues, he confided in no one unless it was Howe who never talked. He might have to change his mind and it would be embarrassing to admit inconsistency. It was much better to act without saying why. He was sometimes annoyed by the resultant guessing among the newspapermen—he told one pursuer of logic to put on a dunce cap and stand in the corner—but his freedom was maintained even if with some difficulty and occasional embarrassment.

His first selections were obviously intended to consolidate his coalition and to make it likely that even the most reluctant members would accept his directions. It was weighted heavily with the southerners whose support he had to have—southerners would chair all congressional committees—and who would be most reluctant to swallow the medicine he expected to prescribe. It must be said, however, that he had less anticipation of difficulty with them than he ought to have had. His almost illimitable confidence in his own ability to get along with people led him to underestimate the conflicts sure to develop between North and West and South. Actually antagonisms would prove to be so irreconcilable that he could only occasionally find a *modus vivendi*. But trouble of this sort did not begin until after the honeymoon period. During the banking crisis and the good feeling of the first few months, only the unreconstructed reactionaries were frankly opposed to his proposals; and they were few. The trouble began somewhat later.

Most of the southerners were amenable to discipline at first. They were all good party members; and they were experienced in Washington. If they could not hope to produce a president, they did control the legislative branch through seniority. No northern Democrat in the White House could afford to ignore such strength. Roosevelt had to bargain. He had, in fact, begun his trading at Chicago where he had yielded the vice presidency to Garner of

Texas. An extension of this recognition yielded the southerners three cabinet posts, and would have yielded four if Glass had not refused. These were Cordell Hull of Tennessee, Claude Swanson of Virginia, and Daniel Calhoun Roper of South Carolina. Of these Hull and Swanson were out of the Senate (as Glass would have been; also Walsh, who died on the eve of becoming attorney general) and could be supposed to be influential with that body. This was especially true of Hull, who had long been a faithful party elder.[8]

It is probable that Roosevelt at this time did not think of this as compromising but rather as a gathering of resources to fortify his own position. His other selections emphasize that probability. Harold Ickes was the choice of the congressional progressives for secretary of the interior. He was suggested by Senators Johnson, Cutting, Wheeler, Norris, and Costigan, after at least two of these—Johnson and Cutting—had refused. This post was especially valued by westerners because of its implications for land and water development; and by the progressives because of their hostility to financiers and other traditional eastern enemies. George Dern, former governor of Utah, was not so well known as a progressive, nor was Henry Wallace of Iowa; but neither could be thought of as conservative. Wallace embodied, because of his father's martyrdom to Hoover in the Harding cabinet, the whole agricultural movement of the Midwest. Homer Cummings, who was substituted for Walsh at the last moment, was a stopgap; he had been slated for governor general of the Philippines. He was a Connecticut politician with solid party ties.

The most difficult of the cabinet posts to fill, because of the current fiscal troubles, was the secretaryship of the treasury. William H. Woodin, who was finally chosen, was a kind of compromise among many possible choices. He was a businessman and a financier but he was not a banker and he was untouched by the contemporary scandals. Moreover, he was one of the small group who had made large contributions to the Howe-Farley activities so important in maintaining the early momentum of Roosevelt's candidacy. He added no strength; but also he was not vulnerable and not so averse to unorthodox procedures that he

8. He had, for instance, been chairman of the National Democratic Committee back in the twenties.

could be expected to make trouble if some of the fermenting measures should actually be decided on.

This was the list, except for Farley and Frances Perkins. The postmaster generalship by tradition had gone almost invariably to the political manager who had acted for the president. He sat with the others less as the head of the postal service than as the vice-head of the party. Farley's reputation was, at the moment, high; and his widespread organization was ideologically neutral. He was as favorable to southerners, for instance, as to Democrats from New York, when it came to party matters. The one difficulty was in the West, where progressivism was at least half Republican even when it was wholly Rooseveltian. Farley found it impossible to understand that the La Follettes, the Wallaces, and others like Norris in Nebraska and Olson in Minnesota were more important to Roosevelt than Democratic leaders in their respective states. The coalition of West and South in his mind was all within the Democratic party. He could not comprehend mavericks. This, in the end, would prove to be one of the reasons why he and Roosevelt would have to part company. For the moment it was only a lesser problem among many requiring some attention; but Roosevelt had no real apprehension about this or any other political difficulty. He could depend, at any rate, on himself.

In the matter of the secretaryship of labor there were several considerations. The first of these was that Roosevelt was not really sympathetic to organized labor. He did not trust labor leaders and had none of the rapport with them he felt at once when farm leaders sat down across the desk from him. He said to the farm leaders at the very first: "Make up your minds what you can agree on and we will see that it is done." That was the line he followed throughout. But he felt no such trust in labor men. Moreover, there were several claimants to labor's prerogatives. In other recent administrations the secretaryship of labor had gone to a union official, as the secretaryship of commerce had gone to a businessman and that of agriculture to a representative of farmers. And no union man could be chosen without offense to rivals.

Roosevelt obviously did not accept the theory requiring the choice of a union leader; he would have said that interests—except a political one—should not be represented in the cabinet. This difference between his attitude and that of some of his predecessors was important. It accounted, also, for his not choosing those who seemed to commentators at the time the most likely selections. His selections were not accurately forecast by any of the guessers. Those who were prominently suggested included his rivals for the nomination, starting with Al Smith and including Wilson's secretary of war, Newton Baker; Governor Ritchie of Maryland; and Senator Byrd of Virginia. Also prominently mentioned were Owen D. Young and Norman Davis, both of whom had been well-publicized visitors since election. Most often mentioned of all was Bernard Baruch, who had been so prominent in Wilson's administration and who was still known to control a bloc in the Congress.

When the list was announced the two omissions most noticed were Smith and Baruch. It had been regarded as inevitable that a place would be made for both; and Roosevelt at once began to betray some uneasiness about Baruch's reaction. Concerning Smith he had no qualms. Smith's followers, he thought, could be reached in other ways. Baruch, however, had made of himself a kind of symbol. He was supposed to be a wise and disinterested statesman—a thought carefully cultivated by his publicity agents. Actually, it was well known that he influenced congressional votes for at best whimsical purposes, and at worst ones not unrelated to his business interests. Roosevelt would not have the disposer of such influence present in his intimate counsels. Heads of departments could be troublesome enough when they were thrust forward by the groups gathered naturally behind them; it would be intolerable to have as secretary of state, for instance, a person who could be suspected of manipulating the international exchanges and who had intimate Wall Street connections.

A certain tribute in favors was paid to Baruch's influence, but not such a price as would have had to be paid if he had been a member of the cabinet. Baruch's apartment at the Carlton Hotel was something of a headquarters, already, for his intimates among lobbyists, old politicans, and new administrators. The need for Baruch's support would be acknowledged when Hugh Johnson and George Peek were named as heads of the two most important recovery agencies. This was a substitute for giving Baruch himself a post; but it was a mistake. Inside a year both had gone or were going amid a vast hullabaloo; and Baruch was busily setting up opposition to the whole New Deal program. Progressive measures of all sorts suffered; many of them had to be abandoned; and favors went to those whose opposition in principle to all Roosevelt stood for was notorious. He pretended to be oblivious; occasionally he had Baruch to lunch or asked him to do some special job; but never until the final stages of the war did he consider inviting him into the official family, and then he changed his mind before actually making the offer.

Baruch, or Young, or even Baker as secretary of state or of commerce would have been regarded as fronts for an interest. If Roosevelt would not have a representative of labor or of agriculture, but rather chose "experts" in each field, how much less would he have a representative of business when business was so low in the public regard, and was, as a matter of fact, about to be brought under investigation and discipline. For the commerce post he chose Roper, who was an old-time Democrat from South Carolina, a smooth and effective politician of conservative bent. He was not suggested for the post by anyone except possibly himself; he had been one of the early and expectant visitors to the President-elect who had been marked by the reporters.

The principle of selection did not prevent an interesting deployment of the businessmen who had been Roosevelt supporters, even though none were asked to join the cabinet. Jesse Straus, who wanted terribly to be secretary of commerce, and who could see no reason why he should not follow other businessmen in that post, had to be satisfied with the embassy in Paris. Similarly David H. Morris went to Belgium, and Barry Bingham to London. On the whole, the official family in Washington did not personify any but political interests. The scheme would not prove wholly successful; but it served well enough during the earliest stage of Roosevelt's administration.

Roosevelt understood, even if he did not wholly accept, the prevalent additive attitude. To an extent he shared it, as who would not, having had his education and experience. There was very little in all he had been taught to suggest that wholes are more than sums of parts. Everyone around him all his life had been of the view that general well-being was arrived at by the separate achievements of many contributors, his teachers no less

than the politicians and businessmen with whom he had associated. His teachers expressed it by accepting and elaborating the
theory of free conpetition in economics and territorial representation in politics. The putative hidden hand spoken of by the
economists led individuals, in pursuit of their own ends, to the
common good. It was, really, a euphemism for nature; and the
processes of competition were supposedly controlled by natural
forces.

These laws, elaborated by generations of economists, had
justified the operations of business enterprise. They formalized
and sanctified free enterprise. Fairness for all was ensured when
sellers and buyers, producers and consumers, workers and employers, bargained freely with one another. Every bargainer would
get all he was entitled to; therefore the system was fair to all. This
was a moral and well as an economic concept. It was translated
into political principle as laissez faire. The state would only upset
the natural balance achieved by the market if it interfered. Matters
would come right only if bargainers were left alone.

Even though this had been the accepted doctrine of all those to
whom Roosevelt had owed regard, his practical sense made him
somewhat doubtful. As governor he had had trouble mostly with
the utilities, but also often with the banks. It was obvious that
much regulation was necessary if fairness was to be maintained.
Practical considerations—in the field he had studied most, electric
power—had led him to conclude, even, that public ownership
might sometimes be necessary. He had not become a socialist. No
one ever heard him advocate public ownership of *all* business or
even all the power business. He advocated a "yardstick" policy.
Even outside the utility field, regulation might be needed, perhaps
beyond the mere establishment of freedom. Stringent protection
for workers in New York State was one example. But the
depression had furnished the same lesson concerning banking and
finance. Just now there were turning over in his mind various
approaches to these problems not to be found in the teaching of
his Harvard professors.

One phenomenon would doubtless puzzle the historians of the
future: American adherence to individualism in theory even while
approaching collectivism in practice. Reiterated belief in free
competition did not interfere with the development of business

empires of enormous size. One of the necessary characteristics of this progress was the swallowing up or destruction of competitors, and those who were thus swallowed or destroyed could not have regarded themselves as possessing the freedom they heard so much about. The antitrust laws had been intended to stop this kind of thing; but they had notoriously not succeeded. Not even the most convinced believers in laissez faire had been able to say how big an enterprise must be before it should be disciplined or broken up. Growing, therefore, could not be stopped, and incidents along the way, such as the elimination of competitors, could not be prevented. Because they were small they could not survive. They were comparatively inefficient; and efficiency too was an American objective, quite inconsistent with free competition.

Nevertheless, theoretically and officially, Americans clung to free enterprise. Socialism was a word with opprobrious connotations. Collectivism was a dangerous idea. No politician could survive who did not proclaim his devotion to the small businessman, and denounce monopolists and socialists alike. Our leaders had emphatically not told us that Americans were, in fact, members of a collectivity, that each lived in a close and necessary association with others, and that the good of one had become the good of all. This was the more remarkable in 1933 because of the particular experiences of that generation, the most startling of all being the very depression they were in the midst of and completely mystified by. There can hardly ever have been lessons more thoroughly misunderstood. Because this was so the remedy most favored was more of what had caused the disaster.

The depression had affected more than a few persons and enterprises; it had touched all of them; its destructive power had indeed reached far beyond the confines of one nation. This had not happened because of anything a few individuals had done. It was a sickness of the whole. And nothing could be clearer than that general remedies, not those directed to individual rescues, would be needed. They were being considered; Roosevelt had to think not only of ways to relieve hardship—although he often spoke of that—but also of ways to reactivate the economy. If the economy "recovered," there would be employment, higher incomes, improved well-being, better business. Such was the conclusion of traditional theory; but the economy was an inclusive concept.

The industrial system was only just beginning to be regarded—largely as a result of the depression—as an organism subject to management. Those who so regarded it might be a small circle, but they were influential. The Taylor Society, for instance, made up of efficiency engineers, had lifted their eyes from shop management to economic policy; and academic economists were becoming knowledgeable about business cycles. There was current talk about stimulation, stabilization, and similar approaches to recovery. Each had its own devices. Stimulation, it was argued by some, could be administered by direct additions to purchasing power, and it might be better to find the funds for this by inflating, since this raised the price level and enabled debtors to get more dollars to pay off their creditors. Getting rid of the current load of debt was an important preliminary to the resumption of loaning; and until loaning began, business would be restricted. Stabilization was to be reached by getting prices into balance again so that each industrial group could make fair exchanges with other groups—so that each could work for the other and each would be the others' consumers. This position had been taken by the original members of the Brains Trust.

Roosevelt had been exposed to more such theory during the preceding year—proposals for recovery involving general principles—than in all his previous life; and although the end sought was practical, still the ideas were inclusive and had to do with the general good rather than that of any individual or group. The national economic health was in question. If it improved, the situation of everyone and every group would improve along with it. This was the holistic view.

Roosevelt was not really very much at home with ideas. He dealt much more easily with physical arrangements of people and things; and he had a predilection for hanging on to conclusions he had worked out in the past. This, however, was not so strong a leaning that he failed to see new facts or to grasp the obsolescence likely to overcome concepts. On the whole, it has to be said that by the time he became President he had an equipment of traditions, preferences, attitudes, and values—as well as an array of talents and a fund of experience—peculiarly suited to the tasks before him. Perhaps as important as any item of his equipment was his immediate reaction to challenge. This forbade inaction when there was something to be done. Then there was the noblesse his father had taught him and which was part of the Christianity he professed. It was wrong to tolerate injustices. With all this he had the politician's indifference to inconsistency. The public memory was short and he could change his mind without penalty if he had not made—as he seldom did—embarrassing public commitments.

So he considered the nation as a whole but also had a genuine concern for troubled men and women. He thought of agriculture; but he remembered that there were farmers. He saw that finance was a system; but it was operated by financiers—well or badly as the case might be. His holistic or collective thinking thus ran concurrently with his older assumptions and understandings. It was pleasant to think that relief for the unemployed put a stop to hunger and cold and at the same time stimulated productivity. He did, however, continue to suspect that character was undermined if people were not required to earn the incomes they received, and so he favored work relief rather than grants.[9]

This and other illustrations of a similar sort show how varied and mixed his ideas and preconceptions were. His make-up, although it had been given structure and substance by Groton, Harvard, Columbia, and his experiences as a wartime administrator, was so generally practical that new facts, thoughts, and experiences flowed into it and were tested quite readily and quickly for usefulness. Sometimes they were rejected, sometimes accepted; the bias was not—as in so many minds—toward rejection. Yet there was no understanding him if it is not always recalled that what was accepted *had* been evaluated and that the evaluation had been in terms of the ends to be sought.

Those ends were political and moral. There was the good of the nation to be considered. The government should be fair, even generous, in dealing with its citizens; but they too should be just to their government. People should have duties as well as

9. He clung to this notion even when it was less practical, certain that he was right when trusted friends differed with him. Frank Walker, one of the most loved of them, felt strongly enough about this very point to leave his official family later on—but still without changing the President's determination.

privileges; they owed something to each other and to their country. He saw his own immediate duty as a double one: to assist the unemployed and to bring about recovery. So he consented to a system of temporary relief, both for individuals and business; this meant not only grants to the poor, but also loans to distressed businesses, moratoria on old debts, and assistance to owners of farms and homes. All of these would be attended to in a first rush of legislation. He went further. Presently he urged a Civilian Conservations Corps to take youths off the city streets but also to improve the forests; he sponsored the Tennessee Valley Authority as a sample attack on the various ills of a distressed region; and he consented to vast public works that would improve all the facilities of common life. Following on, much more general ends were sought through the AAA and the NRA. It was necessary not only to recover but to lift the nation toward new levels of living, toward stability and security.

This seemed to be complicated enough, although its elements, if not its details, had become fairly clear by inauguration; but there were other intentions hardly anyone suspected. Americans, most of them, were struggling with disaster, and few of them could spare consideration for anything beyond immediate recovery—for themselves and for the country. But the President must consider the nation's security along with its well-being. Almost alone among his countrymen Roosevelt was beset in 1933 with uneasiness about events occurring abroad. Almost alone he understood that their implications for the nation's future were very serious indeed. He had for years watched the militarists gain power in Japan; and it should be remembered that Hitler came into power in Germany just thirty-three days before he himself was inaugurated in Washington.

As he looked about the world he would have to deal with as the shaper of foreign policy, there were, indeed, strange new phenomena to evaluate. There was Communism in Russia, Fascism in Italy, Nazism in Germany, and totalitarianism in Japan—all aggressive and all activated by fanaticism. There was, in fact, very little democracy left anywhere except in Britain, France, and other western European nations, and this was complicated by dissolving empires ingloriously disputing with colonial peoples.

Even the nearest neighbors were dictatorships, many of them naked and cruel ones. South of the Rio Grande there were few practicing democracies.

The new administration inherited many ongoing arrangements made in accordance with tradition or with Republican interpretations of it. These must be appraised; but Roosevelt was clearer in his own mind about foreign policy than he was about domestic problems. A representative instance of this was the Disarmament Commission so long at work at Geneva. This had been a matter of special concern for Hoover, who was a Quaker, and who had hoped for some achievement to mark his administration as having made a notable contribution to peace. But results had been disappointing. It happened that one delegate of the United States was an experienced diplomat and was also a Democrat. This was Norman Davis. Soon after election Roosevelt began to explore with Davis the probability of further progress. The prospects did not seem favorable, especially since the League of Nations was so evidently disintegrating. The aggressors—especially Japan, Italy, and Germany—were in no mood to submit to checks even if the other powers had had the courage to attempt them. Armaments seemed more likely to increase than to diminish. It was true that a treaty limiting navies had been negotiated in Harding's time; but land armaments, although the Treaty of Versailles had called for reduction, had been for twelve years the subject of temporizing committee meetings with no result.

Hoover's move to reactivate negotiations had been made early in 1932. These proposals called for "the reduction of armies in excess of the level required to preserve internal order by one-third, together with the abolition of certain 'aggressive' arms." Concerning this, years later, Hoover had to remark sadly that: "The conference adjourned to meet again late in the year, by which time I had been defeated in the election and was without power to carry on."[10]

Roosevelt hoped to pursue Hoover's beginnings to a conclusion. He kept Davis on the job; and after studying the possibilities, he made a new appeal on May 16, 1933, not through the somnolent League but directly to the heads of states.[11]

10. *The Memoirs of Herbert Hoover; The Cabinet and the Presidency,* pp. 34f, 356.
11. Hoover always considered that Roosevelt had done something unethical in not acknowledging that he—Hoover—had invented the formula for abolishing offensive land

But it was all too obvious that the totalitarian nations were intent on objectives inconsistent with disarmament. They meant to expand, by force if necessary. This intention would have to be opposed. It was not clear in the winter of 1933 that aggression at any cost was an irrevocable determination of the Germans or the Japanese, although in August 1932 Germany had withdrawn from the disarmament compact. But the signs were ominous, and they had to be watched with constant concern. About Japan Roosevelt had fewer doubts; and he did not hesitate to associate himself openly and without reservation with what was called the Stimson Doctrine.[12] This was the first glimpse Americans had of the approach to foreign policy of the incoming President. Some of them liked it, but more did not—those who paid any attention at all. It required no particular foresight to anticipate that ultimately much more serious differences would arise from the decisions just now in the making. These might even bring war. This too Roosevelt accepted without hesitation as possible, even probable. From the very first he felt that preparations must be made; only appeasement would avoid conflict, and that probably only temporarily. Appeasement was an inglorious policy for a great nation. He had no intention of accepting it.

These decisions were only shaping; and just possibly there might be a change in Germany or Japan; meanwhile, the nation must steadily oppose totalitarian aggression. These were the beginnings of fateful policies. Terrible as their implications were, Roosevelt adopted them without hesitation. They must have been ones he had considered in the past and thoroughly settled on without anyone having been consulted; they could not possibly have been improvised.

Another impending matter needing attention was the London

---

arms. In a rather sour note in the *Memoirs* (p. 357) Hoover said: "The nations apparently ignored the proposal, and I was informed that they considered the League should not be so sidetracked. In any event, all American pressure was discontinued, and all American interest was allowed to die."

12. An account of Secretary Stimson's concern that his Far Eastern policies should be perpetuated will be found in his memoir *On Active Service in Peace and War* (New York, 1948), pp. 282f. Roosevelt was quite ready to check Japanese aggression directly. Perhaps I may note that I was one of those who objected seriously. I thought the liberal forces in Japan ought to be built up; and the Stimson Doctrine played directly into the militarists' hands, making war much more likely than it might otherwise have been. I thought it was not our business to intervene between the Japanese and the Chinese. The Chinese in the long run would take care of these invaders as they had so many others.

Economic Conference. To this he had been alerted since his first meeting with Hoover soon after election. Gradually his differences with the old policy had become clearer; in negotiations at the conference the war debts owing the United States could not be thrown into a general bargain with monetary stabilization, trade relations, and disarmament. Hoover had agreed with the Europeans that they made one package. Roosevelt was determined not to jeoparadize the rest by bringing in the debts; and all of Hoover's efforts to commit him had been rejected. There were, in the fall of 1932, negotiators in Geneva working on the agenda for this London conference to be held in the spring. He must take them over, revise their instructions and, before the meeting actually took place, devise a comprehensive economic foreign policy. Here too, however, he was further along toward a conclusion than anyone realized—or would realize until he sent the "bombshell" message to the conference itself. Where the conclusions came from puzzled everyone; but there can be no doubt that he had them.

This was much more characteristic than is usually recognized. The propensity for arriving at settled attitudes without consultation was hidden by the extensive consulting he carried on all the time. What was missed about this was that when he opened subjects for discussion he was often already far along in making up his mind; but for public reasons, he had to be secretive. Added to these considerations, there were private ones. Exposure was repugnant if it led to the opinion that he was weak or uncertain; he must always appear to have confidence in his own judgment. It will be recalled that this was true when as governor he made the utilities the object of persistent pressure. When he talked with expert advisers about the behavior of the power companies it was only to stock his armory. He had already come to his conclusion. It was so about Japan. When he talked with Stimson on January 9 at Hyde Park, he was already a convinced adherent. This might surprise the Secretary; but it would not surprise him more than it would others who had thought themselves in Roosevelt's confidence.[13]

13. See *On Active Service*, p. 293: "The most important point to Stimson was Mr. Roosevelt's quick understanding and general approval of his Manchurian policy. Stimson warned him that the League was approaching a final statement; Mr. Roosevelt promptly agreed and promised that he would do nothing to weaken Stimson's stand. The following week the President-elect went even farther in a public statement in support of the

Many times as President he would "spring" decisions on the public and even on those close to him; but he had been doing this for a long time. It had not been noticeable when he had been a lesser figure and the decisions of lesser consequence; but in a governor, and even more in a president, it was a notable, even a disconcerting, characteristic. It tended to remove decisions from rationality, to enlarge the role in them of instinct, of gathered values, of preconception. Roosevelt was certainly an exaggerated example of nonrational decision-making.

It is of moment, therefore, to assess his values, attitudes, and stores of experience. This is something difficult to reduce to generalization. It is, however, easily illustrated. Consider, for instance, his instant but persistent reaction to Hitler, as that demagogue made his bid for world leadership. It is striking not only how concurrent their emergence into national leadership was; but also that their estimates of each other were made once for all as they were first ranged in opposition.[14] Throughout the ensueing years, as each gathered power in his own way, each was also to fix his nation in a position of such implacable opposition to the other's that trial by force could not in the end be avoided.

How much an antagonism of traditions, tastes, and personalities this was can be seen now by looking back along the era just opening in 1933. A merely casual examination of the incidents involving both nations during that time reveals a steadily deepening repugnance, a gathering of resolution, and a growing

---

administration's Far Eastern policy. 'It was a very good and timely statement and made me feel better than I had in a long time.' (Diary, January 17, 1933). In a second meeting in Washington on January 19 Mr. Roosevelt remarked that 'we are getting so that we do pretty good teamwork, don't we?' I laughed and said 'yes'."

14. Hitler was allowed to form a cabinet by the aged Von Hindenburg early in February, so as Roosevelt was choosing his cabinet, Hitler was also choosing his. It may be worth while to recall Hitler's list, considering how much its names were to mean: Vice Chancellor, Von Papen; Foreign Minister, Von Neurath; Interior, Frick; Defense, Von Blomberg; Finance, Von Krosigh; Economics, Hugenberg; Labor, Seldte; without Portfolio, Goering.

There was a general election on March 5, the day after Roosevelt's inauguration. This election had been preceded by a campaign of outrageous violence, including the Reichstag fire, and was won by the Nazis—that is they gained 92 Reichstag seats, so that with collaborators they had a clear majority. Hitler then assumed dictatorial powers, suspended by decree most of the Republican constitution, and entered fully on that desperate career of international aggression and internal hoodlumism which was to alienate most of the world and finally bring a belated retribution. Hitler had been rising since the 1920's on a tide of German resentment against the Treaty of Versailles. He now considered himself loosened from all restraints, with the approval of his people.

unwillingness to seek accommodation. But this progression, so obvious to the backward look, was not apparent then. Roosevelt was not well enough known, for one thing, to have his apparently casual comments or his oblique references widely understood. Nor, in fact, was there enough attention being paid to any of the developments abroad so that his concern would be much noticed. When it was noticed, there was no premonition that actual conflict might be involved. Americans took leave, as they always did, to make light of foreign peculiarities; and Hitler almost at once became a comic figure. He was never comic to Roosevelt, whose approach to him was, in fact, a curious mixture of detestation and dread. His dislike was such that he could not consider serious collaboration in recovery; yet he understood the mighty force such a man of malice might ultimately have at his disposal in the German war machine.

The active antagonism, it must be said, was mostly on Roosevelt's side at first. Hitler was in process of making the same double mistake his predecessors had made before 1917, of first ignoring and then misunderstanding the American temper, and of underestimating the current American leader.

Wilson had gone to war for reasons quite other than had developed in Roosevelt's mind, and with much more reluctance than the younger man had approved. When he first sized up Hitler, Roosevelt saw in him a personification of the same traits he had regarded as so revolting two decades earlier. And this time they appeared in exaggerated form: Hitler seemed almost a caricature of the insensitive, overbearing, gross, unsportsmanlike, and aggressive German. This was the picture so endlessly detailed in later years by cartoonists and correspondents; but it was seen at once—long before American reactions had become stereotyped—by the new American President.

There was, however, one difference between Roosevelt's and most others' estimates. He had enormous respect for the organizing genius of the Germans even under the control of so fantastic a character as Hitler; he had, after all, been a schoolboy in Germany for some time. He noticed, and spoke of, something not many others saw—that behind Hitler was the whole of German industrialism. The great capitalists gave Hitler financial backing. They regarded him as perhaps unsavory but still a useful front for their oligarchical designs. This connection meant much to one already sensitized to the sinister machinations of the international financial system and the worldwide cartels centered in Germany.

Another thing: Roosevelt understood from the first that there were in the United States those who would find totalitarianism congenial. Many of them for years had been admiring Mussolini for seeing to it that "the trains ran on time," a kind of symbol in their minds for a discipline they thought the United States could do with more of. These admirers were of various sorts: for one instance, those who had some actual association, perhaps well hidden, with the Germans; and for another, those who had ideological sympathies with Nazism. The first were powerful but few; the second were, however weak at the moment, potentially many. There are always the ignorant, the malicious, the unstable, and the envious to whom appeals of the Hitlerite sort can be made with effect—appeals to racial prejudice, to jealousy, or simply to hate and to vengeance for fancied wrongs.

Huey Long, Father Coughlin, Milo Reno, and John Simpson were plying the trade of agitation; and they had many lesser collaborators. America was far from immune to the virus working in Europe. It may well be that Roosevelt dreaded, more than anything else, as he entered the presidency, the inevitable encounters with this spreading disease. He knew how difficult it would be to counter it; but he knew he would have to try—not directly, at least at first, but indirectly. He studied the means at his disposal with the dispassionate eye of the expert.

One thing can be said—and it was a matter of immense importance to the country after the winter they had just lived through—he was not awed or paralyzed by the complexity or the vastness of his responsibility. He was like a strong swimmer in a rushing stream. He liked the opposition. It was something to overcome with zest because he was so much alive and so competent to meet the challenge.

11

THE COMPROMISING

ROOSEVELT

The problem of ends and means in political life focuses sharply in the American presidency. Ends tend to become especially enlarged for the president since, being elected by all the people, he is expected to see that whatever has to be done in the general interest is accomplished.

Because of this compulsion—felt more and more strongly by presidents as they struggle to shape a program and to overcome inevitable opposition in carrying it out—there is constant temptation to use the means readiest at hand for getting their way. There is the further desire, felt by every president, to perpetuate the policies he has labored for; and this turns usually into an urge for the continuation in power of his party and of those in it who will see his unfinished program completed.

Since the president has great ends in view, means he would not attempt to defend otherwise seem to have a curious morality of their own. Because they cannot be justified in any general sense, he tends to employ them either secretly or without recognizing them as related to his personal principles of conduct.

He probably knows that this often approaches the ethically doubtful, and may be dangerous; but usually he got to be president by being a successful political strategist. This implies that he has joined in the political game; he is aware that he has been its beneficiary and that it has brought him to a position of power. Distinctions tend to be blurred: between ends and means, between long- and short-run tactics, and almost always between

NOTE. This essay appeared in the *Western Political Quarterly*, volume 6, number 2 (June 1953). Reprinted by permission of the University of Utah, Copyright holder.

public and personal interests. To a mature man, who has survived and has come to a commanding position, such means as have accomplished it are likely by then to be regarded as allowable because practically effective. As he comes to grips with the exigencies of office, the accepted way of getting things done does not seem wrong. There are no ready alternatives; and political survival is a defensible end.

As difficulties multiply, and he has to rely on subordinates, means are likely to be still more carelessly adopted. His deals and maneuvers are carried out by secondary staff who are given tasks to do—the conduct of enormous administrative agencies, the securing of legislation, the gaining of approval for appointments, the bargaining for reduction in specific or general opposition—and who are instructed only as to ends. Subordinates are under even more compulsion and have less reason for restraint. This behavior is the stuff of daily political life in our system.[1]

It may be that these unlovely procedures would generally be approved, if they came to the surface and were discussed. The American penchant for practicality conduces to understanding, to forgiveness, even to praise—particularly if the ends sought are approved and if the tactics succeed. Then the methods are not too closely examined for their long-run consequences, or for their compatibility with professed principle. When there are legislative investigations or reporters' exposures, they are conducted with such bias as to have about them strong odors of hypocrisy, as if the examiners possessed quite different terms of reference; and, of course, they do not.

Doubtful means, however, do have inevitable consequences, even if they are not brought to light. They may even link up into a system. When there is proper hostility, there may well be a kind of revulsion among those who accepted gratefully enough results favorable to themselves; but consequences do inevitably take shape and ultimately have to be recognized.

Such periodic exposures are not so revealing about the com-

1. Marriner S. Eccles, speaking of his role as amateur in government and the difficulties encountered by a subordinate, has remarked: "He is always under pressure to do the expedient thing rather than pursue a course that he believes in the long run is in the public's best interest. He may, in fact, sacrifice his public career if he balks at expediency and chooses instead the unpopular course—not as an expression of a contentious nature, but as the logical application of what he believes is right in principle and fact." *Beckoning Frontiers* (New York: Alfred A. Knopf, 1951), p. 141.

promises of politics as are distant judgments as revelations occur, assume a kind of pattern, and become history. At such times it is possible to see that the means used—and the approval given—were justified or were not justified. They were wrong because means and ends could not be separated and because means have a way of becoming even more important than ends; or they were right because both ends and means merged to achieve consequences important to the public interest—a result perhaps more important, it will be said, than adherence to professed principles. This is one strange effect of democratic institutions. It tends to separate private from public morality and to justify behavior by different tests.

When Lincoln rejected the advice of those who said that Grant was a doubtful choice for commander-in-chief of the Union forces because he had a drinking problem, his reply is said to have been that he wished his other generals used the same brand of whiskey. That is a story Americans have retold endlessly and with the warmest approval. So long as battles were won it was a small matter that the general should have been a man of uncertain character. But his weaknesses were inevitably registered in the scandals of his administration when he succeeded, as a popular hero, to Lincoln's office. Both in 1868 and 1872 the people approved the man who had won his battles above others whose integrity was unassailable.

There is something of an analogy, certainly, in Roosevelt's choice of a running mate in 1944. The sacrifice of Henry Wallace, who had been Vice President between 1940 and 1944, to the exigencies of compromise gave the United States at a time of crisis, six years later, an administration tormented with the demeaning incidents of cheap corruption. These had been going on for some time and were not by any means a pattern peculiar to the Truman regime. They went deep into the structure of support Roosevelt had used to underpin his domestic and especially his foreign policy—his ends. To meet the challenge of the Nazi-Fascist threat from 1936 on seemed to him so overwhelmingly the most important objective that compromise, even the sacrifice of other objectives if it was really required, was a presidential duty.[2]

2. If I seem to identify compromise with expediency it is because compromise was so frequently, in the Roosevelt case, made in the interest of immediate ends, was practical, and involved a giving up of items in an integrated program. This is the way it was: the

It may have been worth the price; but only as later events unfolded could it be seen what that price really was—and its precise measure would never be known because it was possible, for instance, only to speculate about the kind of president Henry Wallace might have been. It was clear, however, that far more was paid than was indicated by giveaways. This kind of thing led inevitably to minor turpitude in and about the White House and in the executive agencies—the unworthy acceptance of gifts and favors for the use of influence. The presence of fixers and influence-peddlers among the entourage of the presidency constituted evidence of an irresponsible carelessness concerning the integrity and dignity of a great office. This carelessness in Truman's time did not concern the president's powers; but it did show that ends and means had been hopelessly confused. If this carelessness did not involve the nation in controversy concerning more than the proper conduct of the presidential office, it revealed a habit so persistent as to indicate a continuing dilemma for all its occupants: how much could justifiably be given for much wanted support?

It is possible to argue that Roosevelt used doubtful, even costly, means to achieve his results; but it is possible, also, to assert that he was never irresponsible about what he was doing. For such departures, it can be seen or inferred by the serious student, he had well-weighed reasons. If there were unfortunate consequences it was because he had deliberately chosen what he believed to be a lesser evil. His wide experience, his deeply felt responsibility for welfare and stability, may have weighed too heavily in his mind; he may have underestimated his ability to command response and get his way without consenting to such serious sacrifices. The choices he made can be weighed now with more sympathy,

---

President and his helpers, facing crises to be surmounted, reforms to be gained, came eventually in each case to the point of dealing with those who must allow enabling legislation to be passed. There they met those who knew what opposition would be offered by affected interests; and who, to make their task easier, or perhaps expressing a latent opposition of their own, demanded modifications. The President would be advised, gravely, that not so much could be done; this point and that point would need to be given up or weakened. Coming from legislators like Garner, Robinson, Harrison, Rainey, and other conservatives who in New Deal days were in the strategic positions, these represented urges toward "common sense," and orthodoxy; and the word "practical" was very often used. What businessmen wanted was always "practical." Roosevelt knew that these objections had to be met somehow; it was easiest to make a preliminary "deal," and long-range objectives could be deferred.

however, because it is so clear, as it was in the case of Lincoln's support for Grant, that what he believed to be necessary in the public interest was actually paramount. Also, he succeeded. The depression he inherited was lightened; a succeeding one in 1937 was aborted; and the Nazi-Fascist conspiracy to dominate the world by force was defeated. These were the great objectives of his policy and they were attained.

This need not prevent a reassessment of the situation he faced. We are bound to examine the other consequences involved, and to speculate concerning the possibilities of lesser or different compromises. The results of his surrender enlarged themselves to frightening size as time went on, and finally involved not only lesser deviations from a moral code but the integrity of the presidency itself. The minor irresponsibilities of hangers-on during the Truman administration, the weaknesses of a regime riddled with small corruptions, were not in themselves so significant; but these and other signs of degeneration weakened the office itself at a time when leadership was necessary to national survival. The minor stigmata were evidences of major failure. In the end constitutional principles themselves were involved. Truman finally found himself without the prestige to do what needed to be done. A president speaking from an impregnable moral position as the chosen leader of his people would not, for instance, have placed his office in jeopardy to legislative aggression and then have allowed his military chiefs to take over the argument concerning national policy—not military strategy, but high political decision. The controversy between MacArthur and Generals Marshall and Bradley that took place under congressional auspices in the spring of 1951 ought never to have happened.

Does the frequency of similar occurrences in our history indicate a weakness in the system? Or does it have to be said, rather, that the president has to be allowed a freedom of maneuver in which moral decisions are inappropriate, and that the only allowable judgment is to be reached by weighing gains against sacrifices as only he is in a position to do?

Two of the compromises made by Roosevelt were among the more serious: they grew out of his reliance on the city machines for political support after 1940, and his acceptance of private industry's methods of preparation for the world conflict finally entered in 1941. At the time it was difficult to see how he could have done otherwise. Both seemed necessary in the circumstances. Yet now it seems not at all certain that the decisions were wise. There were other choices he might have made. At least it is interesting to speculate about his alternatives.

The road to the presidency runs inescapably through preliminaries to nomination; and to a degree not understood by the uninitiated, this road is controlled by local politicians. This is far more true of a first term than of a second. It is usually conceded that presidents can be nominated for a second term because they have become leaders of their parties and have been able to place their own men in strategic positions—particularly in the national party offices and in administrative positions with benefits to confer.

During these first four years, there has not yet been time for serious party disunity to set in, for dissidence to get well started, and for competing aspirants to establish themselves. It is not strange that Roosevelt sailed into his second term with hardly any vocal opposition, or even that he was able to strengthen his mandate by aggressive affirmation of his intentions. There were, of course, the Liberty Leaguers, and the almost unanimous opposition of the press. But all that counted for rather than against him with the electorate—a matter hard to understand in the heat of the contest but obvious in retrospect. Such opposition was confirmation in voters' minds that their candidate had been effective.

However, a novel set of problems was presented by the nominations for third and fourth terms.[3] In the Roosevelt history these third- and fourth-term experiences have considerable significance. By 1940, disaffection had bitten deep. The constant hammering of the opposition newspapers had had another effect than that of confirming him as a progressive leader. The middle-income group had widened with returning prosperity and had taken on conservative color. Its members had, in effect, returned to their Republican affiliations. In consequence, the Democratic politicians, most of them conservatives, were looking for some means of appeasing the demand for an end to the "bold

3. These will not arise again so long as the constitutional amendment limiting presidential service to two terms remains in effect.

new experiments." This sensitivity was heightened by the growing alienation among the southern Democrats, most of whom dissented from the policies of the past eight years and disliked all those who were responsible.

Much of this antagonism centered in a professed opposition to the departure from custom represented by a third-term bid. What lay beneath was a welter of dislike for various Roosevelt policies. The Supreme Court fight of 1937-38 still rankled; the bitterness remaining from the disestablishment of the National Recovery Administration was still strong; powerful farm organizations had turned hostile; isolationists were conscious that European involvement was being covertly arranged; and businessmen were convinced that the administration disapproved of the close government-business relations they had been so long in perfecting and considered essential to their existence.

It was very widely believed, even by many of those close to Roosevelt, that he himself would not again be a candidate, but would exert his influence to insure a like-minded successor. One frustrating difficulty, felt both by his supporters and by opponents, was that no obvious successor had appeared who seemed at all likely to carry on the New Deal. For lack of a popular Democratic candidate a good deal of attention centered on a most unlikely person—Secretary of State Cordell Hull. This elderly gentleman from Tennessee would have suited the professionals in every respect except the vital one that he could not possibly win. The professionals felt they needed a candidate who would promise to keep labor's gains and who, at the same time, would not offend the conservatives. Since such a man did not exist, Roosevelt could override the objectors. His support was massive among the voters.

He had not taken the necessary care to build up a possible successor of his own sort. Robert H. Jackson, for instance, might have been made governor of New York in place of Herbert Lehman; but when James A. Farley—who had ambitions for the same office—objected, the matter had not been pushed. There were some indications of a build-up for Harry Hopkins; but if a build-up was intended it obviously did not catch on; and, anyway, no one so committed to the Roosevelt policies as Hopkins could be forced on the dissident elders.

When the 1940 convention approached there was no possibility that such a successor could be nominated. Roosevelt had either to take the nomination himself or abandon it to someone like Cordell Hull and invite almost certain defeat for his policies as well as his coalition. Moreover, the situation was complicated by the disaffection of Farley, the national chairman, whose successful cultivation of the party bosses had given him large ideas about his own availability. Roosevelt was in the position of having to take the nomination in spite of the professionals' reluctance and he did not have Farley to manage things for him at the convention as had been done in 1932 and 1936.

At Chicago, Hopkins, sheer amateur, negotiated a deal with the big-city bosses, a practical one for both sides. They were to support the nomination and work for the election; and in return they were to be recognized as the disposers of local patronage and other benefits. Flynn of New York, Hague of Jersey City, Kelly of Chicago, Pendergast of Kansas City—these were the types. They abandoned Farley; and Flynn was made national chairman. The nomination went through, and the election was won. Henry Wallace for Vice President was the Roosevelt gambit for the preservation of the New Deal in spite of the bosses' reluctance. Thus Roosevelt found the support necessary for going on into his great years as a war leader and as the nemesis of Nazi-Fascist totalitarianism.

His memory is not enlarged by pretending that a high price was not paid; and there is even doubt as to whether the price was too high for what was gained. This will be an interesting exploration for future students. One exaction was the demand of the bosses that Truman be substituted for Henry Wallace in 1944. This was not all; the costs continued to mount. There were a good many shocking reminders of the deals of 1940 and 1944 in the revelations of the Kefauver crime-investigating committee in 1950-51. These carried inevitable recollections, for all those who were old enough to remember and for those familiar with social history, of similar incidents in the early years of the century and even of those further back in the days of Boss Tweed and his infamous colleagues. They recalled, as well, the fairly recent Teapot Dome scandals in Harding's time.

The lesson was that civic virtue is an end not won by unvirtuous means. The municipal corruption fought by Tom Johnson and

Brand Whitlock and revealed by the muckrakers was not extinguished by exposure, but by municipal ownership of the public utilities. The corruptionists would not let these alone as long as there was money to be made from them; and the officials did not stay uncorrupted so long as there were favors to sell. All during those decades everyone concerned knew well enough that any means of purification short of the drastic one of expropriation would be insufficient. Yet none of them quite dared to say so or to risk their political futures on so uncompromising a policy. It was not until municipal services became unprofitable that American cities took over—at a good price—the utilities so long the center of repeated scandals.

Meanwhile the corruptionists had other fields to cultivate—not new ones, but ones growing immensely more profitable as America grew fabulously more wealthy. Vice, crime, gambling, and racketeering were repeatedly exposed. Many a political reputation—including that of Thomas A. Dewey—was won by investigation and prosecution of the participants. Nothing, however, was done to purify the sources. It has to be admitted that Roosevelt covered these politicians and their machines with the New Deal mantle when Hopkins made the deals for renomination in Chicago in 1940; and the deal was confirmed in 1944 by the substitution of Truman for Wallace as vice presidential candidate. The consequences became available for examination when the Kefauver Committee's report was made.[4]

As Roosevelt approached World War II, the implementation of his grand strategy required an enormous expansion of industrial productivity. He had to consider how it could be obtained. Part of this history will be found in the accounts of various participants.[5]

4. In Chapter I of *This I Remember* (New York: Harper and Brothers, 1949), Eleanor Roosevelt had this to say: "Franklin was a practical politician . . . I often heard him discuss the necessity and role of local political organizations, but he recognized that certain of them were a detriment to the party as a whole. He never got over his feeling against Tammany Hall or any boss-ridden organization, though he acknowledged that some were well administered and valuable." Or, she might have gone on to say, "that some were so necessary as to be indispensable."

Other revealing comments on the President's relation to local political organizations will be found in James A. Farley's *Behind the Ballots* (New York: Harcourt, Brace, 1938); and Edward J. Flynn's *You're the Boss* (New York: Viking Press, 1947).

5. See, for instance, Donald M. Nelson's *Arsenal of Democracy* (New York: Harcourt, Brace, 1946); General H. H. Arnold's *Global Mission* (New York: Harper and Brothers,

None of these, however, throws much light on the decision to entrust existing business organization with the task. It is taken for granted that no alternative existed and that mobilization was merely a matter of farming out to large organizations appropriate functions and entrusting to them any further subcontracting. Perhaps this was the only feasible procedure. It was certainly so in the minds of the President's administrators, few of whom had gone through the struggles with business in the early days of his administration. In view of that struggle, and the influence it must have had on Roosevelt's mind, this interpretation seems far too simple. There must have been uncertainty before he made the deliberate decision to proceed as he did.

When President Wilson was shuddering at the prospect of war in 1917, he said to his Secretary of the Navy, Josephus Daniels: "There are two reasons why I am determined to keep out of war if possible. The first is that I cannot bring myself to send into the terrible struggle the sons of anxious mothers, many of whom would never return home. The second is that if we enter this war, the great interests which control steel, oil, shipping, munition factories, and mines will of necessity become dominant factors, and when the war is over our government will be in their hands. We have been trying, and succeeding to a large extent, to unhorse government by privilege. If we go into this war all we have gained will be lost and neither you nor I will live long enough to see our country wrested from the control of monopoly." This Daniels is known to have cited to Roosevelt at the outbreak of World War II, saying: "If our country should be drawn into this maelstrom, the benefit of your reform measures will be lost and our country will again fall into the same quagmire witnessed in 1921-33."[6]

This passage evokes recollections of Secretary Daniels' valiant opposition to these same interests during the Wilson administration. The purveyors of steel, oil, and other naval materials had firm relationships with procurement officers in the navy, and the Secretary's efforts were largely futile; but he did on several occasions reject outrageous identical tenders from steel and oil

1949); and Robert E. Sherwood's *Roosevelt and Hopkins: An Intimate History* (New York: Harper and Brothers, 1948).

6. These remarks are quoted in the first volume of Frank Freidel's biography of Roosevelt. The original is to be found in the Daniels manuscripts in the Library of Congress.

companies; and he never missed an opportunity to oppose what he believed to be sinister influences on naval policy. Roosevelt was the assistant secretary at that time and a little impatient with his chief, who was lumped in his mind with William Jennings Bryan and others as "dear, good people," but hopelessly unrealistic.[7] The younger man evinced very little concern about the issues Daniels viewed with such righteous indignation. All his thoughts centered in the necessity for getting on, for "efficiency," and he was far more influenced by admirals' views than was Daniels.

His impatience with his chief, so evident in his private letters at that time, was a source of embarrassment to him later on. He came to see that Daniels' scruples had been justified; and he must have developed in time a rather sorry picture of himself as a gullible young xenophobe. When he became President, the older man was made ambassador to Mexico and was in every way possible shown the honor due a mentor who had been proved right. Wilson, quoted so approvingly by Daniels, was amply justified. The postwar era *was* a quagmire, and it *did* end in a debacle, and those same interests were solely and inescapably responsible.[8]

Still Roosevelt could see no way to get the nation back on its feet when he inherited the Hoover depression in 1933 except by restoring business to "prosperity." This was what "recovery" meant. Yet there had to be some admixture of "reform" in the recovery. This was the product of the dear, good people's scruples. It did not go far, no further than would make the system operate

7. This characterization was made in a letter to his wife from Washington, dated August 2, 1914. It is published in *F. D. R.—His Personal Letters, 1905-1928,* ed. Elliot Roosevelt (New York, Duell, Sloane and Pearce, 1948). "These dear, good people, like W. J. B. [Bryan] and J. D. [Daniels], have as much conception of what a general European war means as Elliot has of higher mathematics."

8. Roosevelt had learned to value the older man long before that, and very evidently regretted his earlier criticism. The letter he sent in good-by on August 6, 1920, was affectionate beyond any formal need; it also acknowledged a debt. "You have taught me," he said, "so wisely and kept my feet on the ground when I was about to sky-rocket—and in it all there has never been a real dispute or antagonism or distrust . . . Hence, in part, I will share in the reward for which you will get true credit in history. I am very proud—but more than that I am very happy to have been able to help . . . please let me keep on coming to you to get your fine inspiration of real idealism and right living and good Americanism." *Personal Letters,* chap. 11. The attitude of Secretary Daniels toward his Assistant Secretary is very cautiously approached in the volume of his reminiscences titled *The Wilson Era* (Chapel Hill, University of North Carolina Press, 1946). But of course these were written after the Roosevelt presidency and after Daniels had served as ambassador to Mexico. Daniels was a kindly man and he had something like a fatherly attitude toward his younger colleague.

tolerably; and even this was bitterly resented. Every item of "reform" had to be fought for inch by inch; and the fight grew harder as recovery proceeded and the renewed profits of business could be poured into its lobbies, its control of mass-communication media, and its resistance to change of any sort. This resistance perverted NRA; it hindered labor legislation, higher taxes, unemployment relief, and social security. Finally, with some gains registered, Roosevelt's changes were brought to a full stop as the price of adequate preparation for an obviously oncoming world conflict. The epitaph was provided when "Dr. Win-the-war" was acknowledged to have taken over from "Dr. New Deal." The occasion was a press conference in December 1943.

Daniels was watching from his post in Mexico; and when he reminded Roosevelt of Wilson's fears and of how they had been justified by events, he must have recalled to the younger man's mind not only the means used for victory in World War I but also many intervening events reinforcing such a warning. He must have mentioned, for instance, the incidents associated with the minor economic recession of 1937. Even after the events of 1929-33 and the subsequent partial recovery through government action, the big businessmen had learned nothing. Neither, it seemed, had some of the cabinet members. Farley and Morgenthau in particular were bitterly opposed to "compensatory spending," largely because it seemed unorthodox to the businessmen they consulted. Their suggestions for recovery were the same ones that had proved inadequate before; but they were quite as determined to try them again. Acceding to this demand, it was the "restoration of confidence" that Roosevelt spoke of in his special message to the Congress on November 15, 1937. He had been reluctant. Morgenthau had said to him: "What business wants to know is: are we headed toward state socialism or are we going to continue on a capitalistic basis." And Roosevelt had answered, wearily, "I have told them again and again." But he did once more reiterate, with whatever reluctance, the futile formula.

Subsequently, as Morgenthau admits, even he was shaken when, a few days later, he spoke to the Academy of Political Science and was received with open skepticism and hostility. "On each side of me sat a Morgan Company partner. The audience was filled with the wealthiest and most conservative businessmen in New York

City ... I told the audience of businessmen: 'We want to see capital go into productive channels of private industry. We want to see private business expand. We believe that much of the remaining unemployment will disappear as private capital funds are increasingly employed in productive enterprise. We believe that one of the most important ways of achieving these ends at this time is to continue progress toward a balance of the federal budget.' The reception of my New York speech almost convinced me that he [Roosevelt] was right. The audience of leading businessmen openly tittered and hooted when I tried to set forth the Administration policy."[9]

Morgenthau was not the only member or friend of the administration to be thus humiliated. Roosevelt himself was not immune. "Confidence" was not restored. Recovery from incipient depression required policies opposed by the businessmen. As a result of the campaign of 1940, when Dewey headed the Republican reaction, the split between the "monopolists" and the President's followers was opened wide. They were his enemies and the enemies, as he believed, of national progress. How, then, could he subsequently have contemplated calmly entrusting to the same businessmen the preparations for war, with all the opportunity this would offer for consolidating their power over the economy? He must have had the gravest misgivings.

Yet that is what, finally, he felt compelled to do; and when he died, as the war was ending, these doubtful associates remained in all the strategic places of power. From those places they proceeded at once to oust from the administration all the remaining Rooseveltians, to institute a new "red hunt," and to drive into political exile all those who might furnish any opposition. Truman, the bosses' man, allowed it all to happen.

If Roosevelt had been asked directly at any time during the war what he felt the future position of Germans and Japanese in the world ought to be, it seems probable that he would have spoken

9. Henry Morgenthau, "The Struggle for a Program," *Collier's*, October 4, 1947, pp. 20f. It might be noted that Secretary of the Treasury William G. McAdoo in Wilson's cabinet was treated in much the same way by the New York financial fraternity. The story of his struggle to gain their consent to the Federal Reserve legislation in 1913 is told in his *Crowded Years* (New York: Houghton Mifflin, 1931), pp. 240f. But business confidence did not bulk so large in McAdoo's estimation as in Morgenthau's.

for their reinstatement in the family of nations. There might be difficulties. Some guarantees were certainly due France and China, he would have said; and some were due also the long-suffering victims of dictatorship. But he would neither have lost his Christian conviction that the vanquished ought to be saved for civilization nor accepted the conclusion that all Germans and Japanese were involved in the guilt of the ruling groups.

Yet it is difficult to see how these humane ends could be found, even implicitly, in the means adopted to achieve military victory. The same question arose—still does arise—over the Darlan incident in connection with the African invasion. But longer consequences attach themselves to certain other decisions, such as that for the terrible mass bombings of both nations, for "unconditional surrender," and finally—but this after he was gone—for the use of the nuclear bomb at Hiroshima and Nagasaki. Looked at in sequence, these constitute a kind of progression. One more terrible means followed another until the genocidal weapon was finally resorted to. The nation would not soon recover from these abandonments of moral scruple. At best they left a deep wound in the body of Western principle and made it impossible for the Christian nations to occupy the position traditionally assumed as they confronted the wholly "practical" Russian colossus. Stalin's purges were not worse than Hiroshima.

As time goes on the conclusion seems more and more inescapable that the means resorted to in achieving the immediate end of victory very seriously compromised the attempts to organize for permanent peace. There are echoes in the Rooseveltian "unconditional surrender" of Wilson's "force, force to the utmost"; and there is the further suggestion that Roosevelt's United Nations, like Wilson's League, may have been thought of as an overriding way to expunge the record of doubtful means. Perhaps that may turn out to be the case; perhaps, also, the war could not have been won without the use of genocidal weapons. This last appears now not to be true. On the contrary, unconditional surrender, mass bombing of civilians, and the use of the atomic bomb seem either to have contributed much less to victory than was at first thought, or actually to have prolonged the conflict. It was almost immediately seen by many that this was true of unconditional surrender, since the demand bolstered the resolution of the bombed population and deepened their sense of identity with their rulers instead of contributing to the divisiveness which might have weakened resistance. The atomic bomb did put an end to wavering Japanese resistance. But in spite of the Stimson and Truman justifications, it is doubtful whether the full-scale invasion of the home islands, with its consequent million American casualties, would actually have been necessary. The Japanese had been trying to surrender for many months. The decision to use the bomb was partly, although not wholly, implicit in the almost completed preparations for using it; and so Roosevelt shares the blame. From April to August in 1945 nothing really important occurred except the tests at Alamogordo determining its practicality.

It may be said that the choices in all these instances have to be judged as they must have presented themselves at the time and not as they appear in the light of subsequent events. Of course, this is true. Yet with the exception of mass bombing, done under intense provocation, these were decisions taken without strict necessity. Unconditional surrender was presented as the United Nations' aim at about the same juncture in World War II as was Wilson's "Fourteen Points" program in World War I, and it stands against the latter in dramatic contrast. Unconditional surrender could not have been thought of as a tactical concept; it must have been adopted with a view to the situation after the victory; but it did, in fact, prolong the war, and was recognized by many dissenters at the time as likely to have this effect.

The Assistant Secretary of the Navy in World War I had felt that easy treatment of the aggressor would be a mistake. A passage in one of his letters[10] written before the declaration of war in Europe in 1914 seems to foreshadow the intransigence of 1943. "Rather," he said, "than long drawn-out struggle I hope England will join in and with France and Russia force peace *at Berlin.*" He was very evidently possessed of a conviction that humiliation was called for, divesting Germans of pride and destroying their national unity. The peace of 1918 had not been forced at Berlin. This had been a mistake, Roosevelt felt, and ought not to be repeated. At Casablanca the United Nations were committed to another course.

This decision was consonant with Lord Vansittart's reasoning,

10. Dated August 2, 1914, written to his wife. *Personal Letters,* chap. VI.

prominently discussed just then. He claimed to have the only practical solution of the German question. This began with the premise that all Germans were equally responsible, along with Hitler and his Nazi associates, for degenerate national behavior, and proceeded to the conclusion that they must be exterminated, or if not quite that, punished severely enough to be forever purged of similar temptations to aggressiveness.

The other possible source, perhaps more likely for Roosevelt, might have been the Old Testament. An eye for an eye was an understandable demand of the Jews who had suffered so terribly from Nazi persecution; but it was questionable as public policy. Still Roosevelt also lent himself to the so-called Morgenthau plan for reducing Germany to a rural country with no industrial potential for further war-making.

There would thus seem to be a pattern. And it could be argued that it persisted through the decision to break up the Reich into three occupation zones, and even to have been responsible for the forcing on West Germany of an atomized federal government.[11]

At any rate the wartime slogan of unconditional surrender certainly resulted in such a destruction of German cities that it would have been impossible to establish a successor government. There was then no alternative to the costly and inept Allied military occupation. The occupation—soon recognized as a mistake—was involved in the destruction of German unity; but so also was the power vacuum, into which the Soviet government at once tried to rush. It is certainly arguable that if a conditional surrender had been arranged, as in 1918, and a successor government recognized, the worst of all the sources of conflict between the Russian and American imperia might have been avoided.

11. J. L. Kunz, in a discussion of the status of occupied Germany (*Western Political Quarterly,* December 1950, pp. 538f), has shown how little doubt there can be that the destruction and dismemberment of Germany was considered a necessary course in American administration counsels. There was, of course, the "Morgenthau Plan" outlined in the first pages of *Germany Is Our Problem* (New York: Harper and Brothers, 1945) by Henry J. Morgenthau himself; also Sumner Welles, in *A Time for Decision* (New York: Harper and Brothers, 1944), advocated dismemberment. That these ideas were entertained—although they were perhaps moderated on reflection—by Roosevelt was shown by his proposal at Teheran for partition of Germany into five "autonomous" states and two internationally controlled areas. Actually a Commission for the Dismemberment of Germany was set up. Secretaries Stimson and Hull were opposed, however; and so was Stalin. Roosevelt lost his enthusiasm; but Germany was in effect dismembered, and West Germany was provided with the weakest possible central government.

Another quite different instance of allowing means to compromise ends is furnished by the course taken to meliorate the financial crisis of 1933. It has to be admitted that most of those who have studied the events of that period have felt that Roosevelt could not have done other than he did. The events have been described as practically inevitable by Moley and others who took part in it. Even Harold Laski argued at length that to have adopted an alternative would have been impossible because so foreign to American habit. I did not share this view and still do not agree. Judged by the test of consequence it will become clearer, I believe, that the agreement to reinstate the old banking system was a mistake and was not compelled by any necessity.

Those who argue that nothing else could have been done minimize the discredit the system had then fallen into; they also forget the readiness of a frightened people to accept any solution offered by a bold leader. Even if the hypothetical character of this argument is admitted, the alternatives may still be considered. The financial collapse of 1933 could have been remedied in at least two ways dismissed by those who prevailed. One was nationalizing the banking system and the other was the use of national credit as a balancing mechanism. I argued for these, although I was not included in the financial planning of the crisis weeks. Banking never became a public system, although the Banking Act of 1935 tended in that direction, and Marriner Eccles, whose counsel I had strongly recommended to the President, was largely responsible for its shape. Orthodox private handling of the government's credit did finally, if reluctantly, give way to the balancing concept; but the opportunity of March 1933 was wasted.

If Roosevelt, rejecting Baruch's, Ballantine's, Harrison's, and others' advice, had asked at once in 1933 for legislation transferring the closed banks to public ownership, he could have got it. If he had abandoned the dogma of annually balanced budgets and had used more effectively the taxing power, there would not have been more disaffection in the business community than occurred anyway. He was, as we know, persuaded to follow "practical" advice.

Then there was the matter of "inflation"—bringing up the price level so that activity could resume at old levels after the massive load of debt had been discharged. It became obvious within a few months that exhortations not to fear fear itself had not been enough; nor had the "restoration" so urgently wanted by the bankers and businessmen. Again, there was "practical" advice from Charles Warren, professor of farm management at Cornell, abetted by Henry Morgenthau, now Secretary of the Treasury. At their urging the futile experiment of manipulating the price of gold was undertaken and had soon to be abandoned. Not until after the appointment of Eccles to the chairmanship of the reorganized Federal Reserve Board did fiscal policy become more nearly effective. The alternatives had been thoroughly weighed; the practical course had been followed; gradually and embarrassingly it had had to be abandoned. Inflation was doubtless better than stagnation. If planned rebalancing had to be rejected, inflation was a possible recourse, although it was a dangerous national habit to acquire. Eccles was opposed to NRA, thus proving more realistic than those of us who expected too much from it. He would have taken more immediate measures for rebuilding purchasing power and for reorganizing the credit system, and these measures were taken, but too slowly and too late.

The confusion, the delay in recovery, and the suffering of the unemployed and their families in the years immediately following cannot be measured; but they allowed the distresses of the preceding years to linger on until preparations for war began in the late 1930s. They must be charged to the "practicality" of the business leaders as against the "radicalism" of those of us who would have acted differently, though we did not precisely agree with each other. Our general remedy had in the end to be accepted, even if in modified form and with an admixture of noxious inflation. Much of the history is told in Eccles' *Beckoning Frontiers*. The account offers a really illuminating instance of compromise with "common sense" and "orthodoxy" on the advice of practical men. If measured by long-run results it certainly was the worst possible course to have followed.

These are illustrations of the operating method inherent in give-and-take politics. Roosevelt is often spoken of admiringly as a supreme practitioner of the art of compromise, and those most qualified to speak are the most admiring. Reference might be made to many other instances. Among them is the decision to administer social security through state agencies, with consequences running far beyond the mere ineffective administration of the system. This was a "practical" decision, one intended to lessen objection of local political interests operating on congressional leaders. Again, it seems certain that even if a federal regionalized administrative organization had been decided on as public policy seemed to require, the act would not have been rejected. The time had come for that kind of thing; it could not have been resisted.

Still another instance is the course followed in the development of the Tennessee Valley Authority. This was an opportunity for a spectacular demonstration in rehabilitation. The land was exhausted; the people were deep in rural and urban poverty; and all this had resulted from remediable causes. Nothing seemed more deplorable to Roosevelt than this degeneracy of America's land and people. He had studied and experimented in New York State with solutions. When he assumed the presidency, the way had been prepared by years of discussion for such a venture as he proposed. There was opposition—open from the power interests who were old enemies, and latent from the local politicians who wanted no disturbance—but there were powerful allies, too, like Senator Norris who for years had fought to preserve the resources of the valley for the people there and for the nation. With him was the considerable cadre of progressives in Senate and House, Roosevelt's natural allies. The dramatic announcement of the plan was received with general acclaim and with only muted and cautious disapproval from those who were opposed. The enabling act passed; the administration was set up; and then erosion set in. The decline of the TVA is a long, involved, and sad story.

In the end the announced intentions of conservation and rehabilitation were defeated.[12] The compromises were practical ones intended to appease the disaffected and to reduce objection. They ended by making the TVA little more than a public corporation for the production of power. The wider intention of rehabilitating a whole countryside was very largely lost. The TVA,

12. Further explored by R. G. Tugwell and E. C. Banfield, "Grass Roots Democracy— Myth or Reality," *Public Administration Review,* Winter 1950, pp. 47f.

if measured by the original objectives, stated eloquently in the preamble of the enabling act, was a far less significant demonstration than it might have been. What the cost of the necessary support for a firmer policy would have been is, as usual, difficult to say; but the sacrifices cannot really have been necessary except in the most grossly expedient sense and at the cost of an imaginatively conceived device.

These illustrations suggest the conclusion that expediency did usually result in immediate success, a smoothing out of difficulties. If, however, success is measured against the possibility of a harder attack on the opposition and the possible results of that policy, the results seem leaner not richer. Concerning the TVA, judgments will differ, varying because of firm or weak belief in the intention. There are those who do not believe that the TVA was a good idea, just as there are those who do not believe in a system of social security. So far as they are concerned, any degree of emasculation is so much to the good. But it was Roosevelt's intention to shape a strong means for an intended end in both instances; and in both, compromise went a long way to attenuate the means and so to defeat the ends.

The extreme complexity of the everyday maneuvers centering in the presidency does have to be considered. Issues do not present themselves singly or simply. It is often necessary—or it seems necessary—to sacrifice the important for the essential. That this may degenerate into the making of choices for momentary convenience is true; and some decisions have to be forgiven out of sheer sympathy for the harassments of office. Others are made to secure ends often known only at the central deciding point, and there is no record of the process to be examined later and by others.

Critics who have attempted assessment of presidents, especially those who have presided over national crises, have rarely had sufficient information to make their conclusions really credible. How important was it in the early New Deal days—in 1934-35—to relieve Senator Pat Harrison's mind about a possible challenge from his rival politico, Theodore Bilbo, at home in Mississippi? Harrison was majority leader. There was legislation to be passed. He found it objectionable; but he would support it in return for relief from Bilbo's rivalry. So Bilbo was given a useless job in

Washington and kept away from the hustings in Mississippi. It was a humiliating—even an immoral—arrangement; and it did no more than postpone Harrison's crisis. However, it did provide support Roosevelt had to have at the moment, or thought he had to have.

Another example of political compromise, whose costs are so often neglected by historians, relates to myself. My confirmation by the Senate as Undersecretary of Agriculture was requested by President Roosevelt in 1934. It was clear that the appointment to a higher post, just created, would raise a first-class storm of protest against the author of the "Tugwell bill" for the stricter regulation of the trade in food and drugs; against one of the authors of AAA and NRA; against the advocate of more generous relief to be paid for by higher taxes; and, beyond these offenses, against a member of the amateur "Brains Trust" so heartily detested by the professionals. I thought and said that my usefulness was too slight to justify the expenditure of much political capital. Yet Roosevelt chose to invest at least some in my promotion. In the process I became even more notorious, having been subjected to senatorial inquisition and having been publicly castigated by several Democratic senators. Farley had to be put to work. When it was over, the President, smiling broadly, said to me: "You will never know any more about it, I hope; but today I traded you for a couple of murderers." I do not to this day know precisely what the deal was with Senator Smith of South Carolina. I suspect it was for the appointment of federal marshals with doubtful records. Whether the result was worth the price I am not the one to say; but it was deplorable that *any* price should have been exacted. Senator Smith could have been overridden.

The president is in a position to know better than anyone else the virtues of the merit system. No one suffers so much as he from the divided loyalties owed to congressional control of jobs in the administrative services. Nevertheless he is also bound to use whatever powers he has to secure needed legislation. Without the use of patronage he would lose one of his best holds on legislative leaders and a convenient means for consolidating his support. President Wilson gave in to the arguments of his Postmaster General, Burleson, who was the political boss of that administration, in the interest of his legislative program; and other presidents had always done the same thing. Roosevelt, being practiced in political finesse, deliberately withheld the distribution of jobs during the special session in 1933, much to the anguish of party politicians.[13] The faithful were then rewarded when the most essential laws had been passed. He must have had second thoughts when he saw how discipline declined once the hungry were fed. The price he had to pay even for small favors rose at once. Evidently—though on such matters he did not comment—he considered the results worth the cost. At any rate he continued to use the same methods even when they were far less effective. Farley, who arranged the deals, had no doubts: when the system failed it had merely been unskillfully used.

If patronage should be outlawed altogether in favor of the merit system, the president would be deprived of historic means for getting his own way. This possibility, however, has to be weighed against consequences seldom recorded because not measurable. It is quite possible that more is lost than is gained. I thought this true in Roosevelt's case. For, in spite of sedulous cultivation of political means and their skillful use by a masterly team, his power declined at crucial times and compromises of essential substance had thereafter to be made. Much of the New Deal had finally to be abandoned in a grand finesse to gain consent for strengthening the military in preparation for a war he saw coming but others did not. Domestic reform was then traded for a national purpose. That was when TVA was attenuated, when conservation and rehabilitation were given up, when the fatal concessions, so feared by Josephus Daniels, were made to the "monopolists." Even this deal was successful only by the slimmest margin. In 1940, the draft bill was renewed in the House by a majority of one, and when the war did come the margins of safety during its first two years were terrifyingly slim.

There exists a persisting interest among Americans—and, for that matter, among other people—about Roosevelt as President. The interest grows rather than declines. Along with the simple sorrow of those who lent themselves to his leadership, who trusted him to be their better selves and gain their better ends, a much more sophisticated interest prevailed for years with its center in the place prepared by the President himself at Hyde Park. There were gathered not only the mementos of his personal life—the ice boat

13. As is frankly recounted in that engaging account of Farley's *Behind the Ballots*.

he used on the Hudson, the *choiserie* from his desk, his various extraordinary collections, even his favorite furniture—but also mountains of paper. By analyzing these, political historians are trying to learn something of how the presidency is achieved and how it is managed. This last, no less than the uncritical reverence or ordinary folk, goes on and on. It is not likely to develop any certainties, perhaps not even much wisdom, for future statesmen. It has, however, dispelled some myths that rather cloud than clarify his contribution—such, for instance, as that he was a political miracle worker who had to do little to gain much.

Some of his uncritical followers would even perpetuate if they could the conclusion that he made no mistakes and no unworthy deals. What is emerging from more realistic assessment is the portrait of a man who maneuvered endlessly for political preferment, learned his trade in professional fashion, rose to the presidency by compromise and conciliation, and then had to struggle just as endlessly, with the means he had and understood, to gain the ends he saw as imperative to the nation's future. The struggle was a political one; it was neither clean nor pretty. His opponents were unscrupulous, powerful, and determined. He had to get his way against odds, often, and always against potentially powerful opponents. The voters judged that he succeeded. The methods he used they were not aware of; mostly, they were not interested. He had no support for niceness and scrupulousness. If he adhered to such standards it was because another course offended something inside himself, not because he feared any disapproval.

Roosevelt did have scruples. They came from his parents, his school, and his church; but experience taught him that they had to be diluted in politics. Fire had to be fought with fire; but if he could speak to those who remain behind him, I imagine he would hesitate to gloss over the ordeals he avoided, or the base struggles he often had to carry on. He might still claim that his ends were noble enough to justify his means. He would admit that perhaps he had sometimes been mistaken, but he would say that with what he had to do with at the time, he had done his best. He himself would have a sufficiently realistic judgment of the results. They were less than they might have been but still more than Americans ought to have expected from a practitioner of their kind of politics. This might have to be said for him. I am willing to say it.

12

THE EXPERIMENTAL

ROOSEVELT

The New Deal was mostly a convulsive struggle to overcome the great depression. Many of its characteristics, however, developed out of traditional progressivism and its devices had long been accepted items in a general program of reform. Progressives were provided with an opportunity by the crisis; they were not by any means compelled to improvise measures for its solution.

The doctrinal differences between Republicans and Democrats (or, if it is preferred, between Hoover and Roosevelt) were not new; they were, indeed, as old as the nation. The party line-up had not always been as it was in 1932. Sometimes the progressives had been Republican—as in the days of La Follette and Theodore Roosevelt—but they had never seemed very much or very long at home with Republicanism; and their happiest presidential leadership had been found, before Roosevelt, in Woodrow Wilson, who was heir to William Jennings Bryan and populism, and who was much influenced by Justice Brandeis.

It has to be said that progressives consorted very uncomfortably with the conservative elders among the Democrats; and it was always difficult for Wilson, as it was to be later for Roosevelt, to bring his program into legislative being. It would almost be true to say that the New Deal of the thirties consisted of postponed items from Wilson's program, abandoned in favor of preparation for war in 1916.

That there is an actual continuity here is sometimes forgot; for Roosevelt had been a very active junior in the Wilson administra-

NOTE. This essay appeared in *The Political Quarterly*, Spring 1950.

tion; and he had been an admirer as well as a distant (fifth) cousin of Theodore Roosevelt, his predecessor by a generation. He could quite legitimately think of himself as the inheritor of a tradition, and that he was very conscious of this all his close associates were aware. It is not too surprising, in view of all the circumstances, that he tended to accept the rules rather literally, somewhat as generals are said to begin all new wars by using the tactics of the last one.

The central tenet of American progressivism had always been the perfecting of laissez faire rather than the development of collectivism (though hard practicality had dictated the public ownership of municipal utilities). The post office was publicly owned in America, but the telegraphs and telephones, the railways, and the facilities for producing power were not. To meet the abuses of overcharging and poor service, the break-up of big corporations and regulation of the rest was relied on. The regulatory commission was one of the favorite progressive devices. It had an approved embodiment in the Federal Trade Commission; but it was best developed in states like Wisconsin and Minnesota, where progressives had been politically powerful. It was part of their scheme, in fact, that the central government ought not to be too powerful or active, a prejudice handed down from frontier and agrarian days when all government was considered to be oppressive and the more remote and larger governments the worst of all.[1]

Most of the nation's ills quite naturally seemed to Governor Roosevelt to have come from not having carried out the Brandeis-Wilson program. Big businessmen had abused their trusts; their organizations ought to have been broken up, and, where that had not been feasible, they ought to have been more closely regulated. If they had been, the depression might have been avoided. It had

1. The Democratic platform of 1896—the one on which Bryan first ran—had an emphatic declaration to this effect in its preamble: "During all these years the Democratic Party has resisted the tendency of selfish interests to the centralization of governmental power, and steadfastly maintained the integrity of the dual scheme of government established by the founders of this Republic of republics. Under its guidance and teachings the great principle of local self-government has found its best expression in the maintenance of the rights of the States and in its assertion of the necessity of confining the general government to the exercise of powers granted by the Constitution of the United States." Theodore Roosevelt's "New Nationalism" took another line; but it did not impress itself deeply on the progressive tradition; that was still one of decentralization.

not been done when it should have been done; so it must be done now. This was Roosevelt's immediate reaction.

The ills of 1932 were very nearly fatal ones. The depression that began in 1929 had failed to "run its course," as in conservative theory it ought to have done. It seemed to deepen as the months and years passed. Since the administration was Republican, and since the Republicans had purged themselves of all radicalism and were stout defenders of the status quo, such abuses as must have caused the depression still existed. Nothing had been done to abate them. The alternative program was obvious; and if the Governor of New York should become President, as it seemed more and more likely that he might, it would be quite expectable if he should turn out to be thoroughly and orthodoxly a progressive one. He would favor business regulation because it would seem to him that conspiracies to restrain trade had strangled industry, and because prices had been held too high and had restricted consumption; he would be against "the money power" because the financiers had a monopoly of credit which they withheld from small business, and used, or allowed to be used, in unrestrained gambling on the stock market. Aside from this, he would be against strengthening the central government, and conversely for enlarged state powers. He would want expenses and taxes reduced and most government functions decentralized and assumed by the states and local authorities.

This was in fact the kind of program Roosevelt contemplated. It was the furniture of his mind down into 1932; and his mind was never entirely purged of these preferences. If what was done during his administration is examined, much of it will be seen to be consistent with this inclination. There were, as time passed, many departures from the pattern. Indeed, some of the measures adopted almost at once, in the haste of crisis, were quite out of harmony with it, and obviously owed their origin to an entirely different tradition; but as President, he did not adopt the alternative ideology, perhaps never quite understood it; he was, in fact, inconsistent. He consented to such measures as AAA and NRA—as well as to some later ones—with misgivings, in an experimental mood because orthodox measures were so clearly inadequate, and because initial agreement among the interests involved had been secured. To other measures, such as the building up of a federal (central) relief organization, he gave only the most grudging consent and got rid of them as soon as possible; and when a permanent social security system came to be worked out, he settled an internal argument in his official family by coming down on the side of state rather than federal administration. This was a momentous and revealing choice; it showed what side he would always prefer to be on if he could.

It would not be inaccurate to describe what went on in the inner circles of the early New Deal as a struggle between old-fashioned and new-fashioned progressivism. There was developing a new conception of the nation as an organism having a gestalt whose integrity must be respected. The technological developments since the First World War had made this newer conception seem inevitable to some of us; but it was very far from having wide acceptance. Other conflicts, particularly of a political sort, were more easily seen; and sometimes inconsistencies were so confusing that no one could be certain about Roosevelt's commitment. To the collectivists it was clear enough, however, that Roosevelt could be persuaded to depart from the old progressive line only in the direst circumstances and then only temporarily. Even then he felt it necessary to make for himself a satisfactory rationalization.

This doctrinal faithfulness to a view of things symbolized by Justice Brandeis' name—because Justice Brandeis was a literal believer in fractionalization, and because Frankfurter, Thomas G. Corcoran, Benjamin V. Cohen, and other valued assistants were his disciples—led Roosevelt into numerous cul-de-sacs. There was the abortive early economy drive, given up with the greatest reluctance; there was the rehabilitation, without reform, of the banking system within the regionalized Federal Reserve framework; there was later the enormous undertaking of reforming the securities exchanges; there was the evasion of definition in setting up the TVA so that it had to be substantially surrendered later to local interests; there was the hand-to-mouth handling of relief so that satisfactory administration could never be achieved.

These and a dozen other items of the program owe their peculiar, often tortured, contradictory, or abortive character to the struggle of those early days, with one side at times dominating policy in some specific respect and the opposite side at other times winning out, but each usually securing some concession. In all that happened, however, the dominant philosophy was traditional, and as time passed and the crisis lightened, progressives of the older, more orthodox persuasion became the more trusted helpers. These were the Second New Dealers. By the end of 1934 the First New Dealers had mostly departed and with them the conception of an organic economy.

There is reason to believe that Roosevelt came to suspect the efficacy of recourse to the antitrust-plus-regulation devices. Partly this was the discipline of the office, and partly it was the approach of war. The war, even when it was only a distant probability, began to affect Roosevelt's view of domestic matters a long time before the monstrous prospect was taken seriously by others. When actual conflict was seen to be imminent, it quickly became absurd to regard supply organizations of the scale Brandeis would have sanctioned as adequate to the enormous demands. The insatiable appetite of the military for every commodity being made, and many not yet heard of, could be satisfied only by undertakings larger than even big business had ever imagined, and certainly far beyond the most horror-struck conception of the antitrust believers. The fears of the progressives were laid aside. Big business and "the money power" were enlisted as partners, if not wholly trusted ones, in the national effort. But, of course, laissez faire in America was of two kinds: the one that existed only in economists' texts, and the one that was actually practiced by big business. A business able in any degree to manage its prices was by so much limiting free enterprise. Many American products were sold at managed prices, and a competitive market did not exist. The long deception had worn very thin. The real question was: who was to do the managing? And more and more, public discussion turned on this issue rather than on the question whether big business should be tolerated at all.

This question of central importance would have to be returned to after the war; but not until then. From the first clear intimations of crisis a need for vastly expanded production was so pressing that delays were regarded with impatience by everyone concerned. The result would soon be a welter of waste and inefficiency, partially resolved by an allocations system (as often disregarded as honored), but no permanent institutions for management.[2]

It is not of much use to personalize the struggle of ideologies. The first phase began when the Columbia University group was invited to Albany in the early spring of 1932; but its engagements were in the mind of the man who was about to become President. Although each view had its protagonists, who urged, when they could, the turning of policy in the direction they believed it ought to take, and although they sometimes seemed to prevail here or there, what actually happened was that the tough Dutch mind with the final responsibility eventually came to grips with each issue and resolved it in accordance with his personal criteria. The secrecy of the Roosevelt inner operations chamber was extraordinary. The greatest pains were taken to guard it from penetration; and artful devices were invented for the confusion of the curious.

This explains the diverse—not to say contradictory—accounts, by various associates, of Roosevelt's attitudes, convictions, and choices. Not even Eleanor Roosevelt, who made a lifelong study of the matter, could suggest anything very helpful about the mind whose decisions made more difference to a whole generation than any other. It is doubtful, for instance, whether she—any more than many others with what they must have thought adequate knowledge—thought of him in early Albany days as a presidential probability. There was real doubt about his capacity as a responsible statesman. This is certainly a notable characteristic of most contemporary comments on his approach to the office. Even the politicians, Farley and Howe, who did think the presidency possi-

2. Still, the War Production Board, together with the overhead organizations in the Office of Emergency Management—the Office of Economic Stabilization and the Office of Mobilization and Reconversion—would be sufficient recognition that national life could not proceed on the theory that big businesses could be broken up and that the resulting little ones would make goods and fix prices fair to the consumer. If Roosevelt had himself furnished the continuity from war to peace it seems unlikely that he would have scrapped the institutions for conjuncture which had begun to take effective shape. He might have had to compromise under congressional pressure and give up some of them. But it is logical to think that he would have resisted. If he had, and had been able to reshape these devices to peacetime uses throughout the fourth term which he only began, he might have recognized that he had mistakenly resolved the ideological battle of the Brains Trust against their successors in 1933. For that had been the issue then; and what the Brains Trust had wanted for peace was not only useful for war. America would have to come to it sooner or later.

ble after his gubernatorial victory in 1930, had no idea of the Tartar they were catching. A surface agreeableness, a charm, combined in the Albany—and even in the later—years with complete domination of his grave physical disability, led almost everyone, his intimates included, to underestimate the extent of his commitment to certain objectives. They were even unaware, in many instances, that he *had* objectives.[3] And as for the method he used in reaching the ends unveiled from time to time, somewhat as lightning flashes from an innocent-appearing summer cloud, there were no clues of much use to his would-be helpers. The fact is that none of them really knew what he intended.

The New Deal was a Roosevelt construct, not that of a Brains Trust, of an inherited tradition, of Brandeis and Frankfurter, or of anyone else or any other group. It would not be true to say that as Governor, as candidate, or as President he did not borrow a good deal or even, on occasion, allow his "advisers" (a word which made most of those intended to be included in this class smile somewhat wryly) some latitude. Numerous speeches in campaign days and early in the first term contain phrases, sentences, even whole paragraphs of mine. I am sure that Adolf Berle would have recognized as many; and, of course, Raymond Moley could identify even more. But it is important, I think, that many passages I can identify are not in the intended context. My phrase, sentence, or paragraph was usually tortured or persuaded, as the case might be, into a larger whole and perhaps with a changed reference.

It was more or less the same with legislation. There were at least a dozen people who were quite certain that they were the principal authors of the Economy Act, the Agricultural Adjustment Act,

3. There were exceptions I would make to this. Missy LeHand, his secretary, was always aware and watched with amused tolerance the dashing of many hopes. Both Rosenman and Moley were sensitive enough, and had experience enough, to know how mysterious a center the Roosevelt outer agreeableness really had. Harry Hopkins found out later. But all three of these associates were peculiar in that they sought to be only projections of the Roosevelt intention if they could find out what it was. They had no desire to shape it. I doubt if any of them ever helped him to make it up, or even sought to. Moley's departure was occasioned by Roosevelt's change of mind. The President's message to the London Conference was a letdown to one who thought he was being the perfect reflection of his principal's intention, and he never really recovered from it. Nor did Roosevelt. He can hardly have looked at Moley after that without some feeling that he had ill-used a faithful helper.

the National Recovery Act, and the other measures in the "Hundred Days" after inauguration. Sometimes the case is good. For the Agricultural Adjustment Act did include authorization for the favorite programs of several different groups. Some of these had histories, in the sense of having been previously proposed, embodied in legislative proposals, made part of political platforms, or pushed by the Grange, the Farm Bureau Federation, or the Farmers' Union. The same was true of the National Recovery Act. Several familiar ideas for rationalizing industry, making its competitions less chaotic, and providing an overall guide to its activities were included; also thrown in were wage and hour provisions and the prohibition of child labor; then there was added the whole separate title authorizing public works and relief. Worse hotchpotches than either of these twin acts can hardly be imagined.

All this was not carelessness on Roosevelt's part, any more than were the loose-jointed, cliché-filled, overly comprehensive speeches of the campaign. He often felt that if many panaceas were authorized in a measure, the sponsors of each would at least not object; and it would be accepted by the Congress with a minimum of agrument or delay. Once the bill was passed one or another or maybe several of the emodied schemes could be tried and discarded if they failed. So far as Roosevelt was concerned, the scheme was of no importance, however much it meant to its doctrinaire authors. He was interested only in results —and grand results at that. He often had to pacify disgruntled zealots or those who had interests involved in one device rather than another; but this he counted a lesser evil than staging a knock-down fight in the Congress—especially when he himself had no settled convictions about method.

As some of us gradually came to understand, he had in mind a comprehensive welfare concept, infused with a stiff tincture of morality. These were, in most respects, like those of the progressives who had preceded him. But he had a more practical eye for results and less sentiment about ways of doing things than any of them had had—with the single exception of Theodore Roosevelt. Most of the others—Bryan, La Follette, and Wilson, for instance— had been evangelical (Bryan), contentious and cocksure (La Follette), or arbitrary (Wilson). Roosevelt was none of these.

This is not a very satisfactory statement since I am certain that he had intentions, and quite definite ones. They were simple, too; in fact one of the clues to his procedure was that, however devious and seemingly confused his own maneuvers or those he allowed his associates to use, the ends he sought were quite confidently carried in his mind, as clear as precepts are to a child. He wanted all Americans to grow up healthy and vigorous and to be practically educated. He wanted businessmen to work within a set of understood rules. Beyond this he wanted people free to vote, to worship, to behave as they wished so long as a moral code was respected; and he wanted officials to behave as though office were a public trust. It is possible to be speciously profound about Roosevelt, and no doubt many historians will be; but it is my belief that everything he ever did or allowed to be done was, in the circumstances and in his view of them, calculated to bring about one of these simple and admirable ends.

He often did not know how to accomplish what he wanted. A complicated economic system had gone all to pieces since the fall of 1929, and there were phases of its behavior that he had never had occasion to analyze. This was especially true of the money and banking system, at the center of his earliest troubles in office. When a business system breaks down, the paralysis is registered not first but with the most inconvenience in the banks. And the banker behind his desk refusing to make loans to start things going, unable to meet his own obligations because he has been too careless (as it suddenly appears) in the past, seems like the devil in the headquarters of this particular hell. His colleague, the investment banker, shares this guilt. He has saddled all his correspondent banks, and through them the nation's savers, with securities everyone concerned should have known were thoroughly speculative, but were supposed, somehow, to have been guaranteed by the underwriter. It seems, at first, to the amateur—and Roosevelt, in spite of having been a downtown lawyer for a bit, and having been briefly an officer of a Wall Street financial house, was a complete amateur—that bankers involved in such disasters ought to be punished. He assumed that they had abused a trust, had gambled with other people's money and had led investors to take unwarranted risks. He wanted to make such behavior impossible in future. The belated realization that the problems were too serious for such remedies to have much immediate effect brought on a succeeding impulse to treat the symptoms directly. If bankers would not now make loans enough, government must make—or guarantee—temporary ones for the emergency. If currency was short, more must be printed. If debts could not be paid because prices had fallen and what was to be paid back was more in value than what had been borrowed, the units of value must be cheapened and prices raised. Debts could thus be cleared away and confidence restored. Then there could be reforms.

Roosevelt, in the spring of 1932, when he had no further responsibility than that of writing speeches to give people confidence in his presidential candidacy, listened to everyone who might have anything revealing to say about the crash whose debris was piling up all around him. He consulted the financiers. The men from Wall Street came, and their apologies were unconvincing. Those who assisted Carter Glass in preparing the Federal Reserve Act were sent for, among them Professor H. Parker Willis, who had thought that what had happened was impossible. His remedies, like those of the bankers, were indistinguishable from current practice—deflation until slow recovery set in. Professor James Harvey Rogers was lucid about causes and even sympathetic to monetary manipulation as a remedy, although he knew that this alone was not enough. Then there were the unorthodox, from Irving Fisher to George Warren. Roosevelt could not understand the Fisher commodity dollar; but in Warren he met a man to whom everything seemed satisfyingly simple. The country was on a gold standard; vary the amount of gold in the dollar, and the price level would be run up or down, stabilization could be achieved, debts would be paid, and business would be resumed. Warren's complete assurance appealed to Roosevelt's preference for a simple solution and gave him more confidence than he had felt about any other scheme.

Roosevelt said remarkably little about all this. He could not sort out satisfactorily the differences among his visitors; and he realized that the bankers would be horrified at the thought of actually trying the Warren remedy. Meanwhile, the Reconstruction Finance Corporation made enormous emergency loans and the

Farm Board desperately attempted to stabilize the depressed prices of farm products. Still trouble piled on trouble. Loans to businesses and banks seemed to sink into the sterile economy like water into desert sand; wheat and cotton were bought and stored by the millions of carloads and prices did not respond. It was evident that these remedies were not enough. Finally, with the election over, and with inauguration approaching, the financial system began to disintegrate. Paralysis was complete. On Inauguration Day, every bank in the land was closed, and no one knew whether any of them would ever open again.

Roosevelt by now had heard much talk from every kind of person who thought he knew anything at all about money and finance, but at inauguration time it was apparent to him that he would have to temporize and experiment. He did not know what to do and no advocate of any remedy had been entirely persuasive. So he asked for and got from the Congress consent to take any measures he decided on. He did not dare try the Warren plan at once. That would induce more panic. He must have had sessions with himself in the few waking moments he could steal in those days; what he concluded seems to me entirely characteristic. He must first cut the nation off from the sinister speculators in London, Paris, and Amsterdam; he must make the banks safe for depositors; he must enlarge loan funds; he must cheapen the dollar. Then the unemployed must be put to work, meanwhile being sure at least of relief.

His first responsibility, however, was to encourage people in thinking that something would be done, something remedial. This was what he did. And presently he tried the Warren remedy, making Henry Morgenthau Secretary of the Treasury to see it through. The plan was, of course, futile, and in January 1934 it was given up. It had done little, if any, good. Gold was less crucial as a medium of exchange than he had been led to believe and manipulation of its price did not greatly affect the prices of other commodities.

When the crisis had passed, the nation could not tell what had caused the revival any more than it had been able to tell what had caused the depression. Nothing much was changed; but the system was beginning to run again. An opportunity for reform had been missed, but not one Roosevelt had heard about from any of the numerous financial experts. Not one of them had suggested a genuine national banking system. And if he ever thought of trying to establish one he must have given up the idea quickly when he considered whether anyone could be got to run it. Was he satisfied? I think so, because his larger intention had been carried out. The hungry were being fed; the jobless were getting work; fear no longer haunted men who ought to be free from its compulsions; children went to school decently fed and clothed.

Also the men who had been greedy, irresponsible, and careless had had a terrible lesson. A watch would be put on them now, and if they became greedy again they would be punished. This was all good. The nation was returning to security, freedom, and decency. Roosevelt knew well enough that these values were not established once for all. They were administered virtues, requiring leadership; but he was prepared to go on giving it. If people would thenceforth yield him their trust as a protector he would see that remedies were found.

This illustration—the muddling through the financial crisis—shows, as others might, I think, what Roosevelt was determined to bring about and how he was only interested in devices as experimental means to his ends. There were occasions when those who had been, as they thought, very clever in creating some institution to meet a need had come to regard it as an extension of their personalities. They must defend it, they felt, against any and all detractors and competitors. These were, aside from the businessmen who were in extreme anguish from loss of confidence (which they bitterly blamed the President for not restoring), the worst sufferers of those days. Some of them ought to be used as cases for study. They were not always what somewhat later came to be known as "empire builders" either; they might not be possessed of that peculiar expansive compulsion which Ickes was affected with and which became the secret vice of Harry Hopkins (while he made grand gestures to show how free of it he was), which brought Leon Henderson's Office of Price Control into discredit during the war, and was carried to the most absurd extremes by the businessmen who became bureaucrats. Quite often, in fact, they were pure idealists, so pure that any shading or compromise was for them quite impossible, and any political trading affecting their enterprises, such as went on in the White House, seemed the basest of betrayals.

Secretary Hull existed in permanent depression because of Rooseveltian carelessness about the sacred principles of free trade. George Peek died a lingering official death rather than consent to farmers being helped in any way except the one he had supported so long. Frances Perkins seldom had a serene moment because of the President's tendency to think in terms of national rather than local administrative units. And General Johnson had a period, at the height of the excitement over the goings-on under the aegis of the blue eagle, when he ran to the White House almost daily for reassurance. The New Deal was a hectic time for these marshals of recovery. Some of them lived long enough to see the nation recover without their aid. That may well have been the bitterest experience of all.

Roosevelt had a remedy he used in such cases, for experience soon taught him that his carelessness about means would frequently bring agonizing helpers to his desk. He called its homeopathic phase "holding hands"; and when this proved insufficient he resorted to promotion. He devoted an unconscionable amount of time and thought to these affairs, although the victims could never be persuaded that he cared in the least, and often went away complaining bitterly about him. These tirades came from deep down in injured egos and were often recklessly uttered. Those who were tougher, less committed, who shared, perhaps, the presidential carelessness about means, or who were simply personally loyal (as Howe, Rosenman, Early, McIntyre, Lowell Mellett, and Frank Walker always were and as Harry Hopkins came to be in his and Roosevelt's last years), or who were working politicians (as Farley was until the party elders tempted him with suggestions of preferment) were thus able, from a central position in and about the White House, to observe an extraordinary procession of sensitive and dedicated natures coming up out of obscurity, being revealed momentarily in the presidential sun, and declining again into baffled obscurity.

These individuals seldom turned up again. Roosevelt had done all he could to repair the damage, but his failure always rested on his conscience, making the sight of one of the defectors most unpleasant. He never "fired" anyone. There was, out of all the possibilities, only one case of contumacy. That, of course, was Arthur E. Morgan, first chairman of the Tennessee Valley Authority. The rest perished with their works, or such of their works as were no longer in favor. They went because matters became intolerable for them. The squeeze was permitted to go on until the tortured victim cried out in pain—meaning that he made a speech or a statement attacking his competitor or detractor—and presently even he could perceive the impossibility of his position. He would become the momentary hero of the opposition press; he would be "taken up" by the old Washington settlers, whose dislike of New Dealism was positively phobic; or the Liberty League, the Republicans, or Wall Street would, figuratively speaking, cultivate his company. The unsuitability, then, of further associations with the White House would be obvious. He might even attack Roosevelt as a last gesture when retiring into the shadows.

When there was a squeeze going on—as when first Jerome Frank for one reason, and later George Peek for another, were forced out of Secretary Wallace's entourage—the President was well aware of what was happening. Those who understood his dislike of grasping nasty nettles knew from small signs that he was peeking through his fingers. And when the blow-up came, they knew that it was not, as it seemed to be, a painfully unexpected occurrence. Sometimes they even suspected that there was a little presidential malice involved. Hopkins said to me, after we had watched one of these proceedings run its course, "You know, he *is* a little puckish." That was not far from right, perhaps, although the observation failed to reach the source: an essential carelessness about the means—and about people as their defenders.

His favorite remedy of promotion characteristically led to finding for the victim another, even more honorable, employment; but sometimes he kept people by him who had been injured, but who would stay because their loyalties were greater than their hurts. Jerome Frank was one of these. He later became the distinguished chairman of the Securities Exchange Commission and then an even more distinguished federal judge—both by Rooseveltian appointment.

This does not imply any lack of presidential interest in devices calculated to reach an end. On the contrary there was an omnivorous interest; but being committed to any of them would have been unacceptably limiting to one so doggedly determined to attain certain ends. Even those closest to him were sometimes confused about his maneuvers. They often mistook means for ends, shuddered at the wrong crises and were amazed that expected presidential reaction failed to take place. I once offered to bet Harry Hopkins fifty dollars that the President would find a way to complete the Passamaquoddy power project. The private power interests and the politicians between them had succeeded in stopping it half built; but I was sure the completion of this scheme (as well as the Florida Ship Canal) ranked as an end. I was quite wrong. But so was Hopkins; he refused the bet.

If, to future historians, the New Deal seems an unusually confused and heterogeneous approach to sociopolitical problems (recovery from economic depression and the regeneration of national morale), it may be helpful to recall that recovery was only part of the intention and that morale was important too if the country was to go forward in the ways Roosevelt envisaged. He conceived that when the country emerged from its economic paralysis, it might become what Bryan, La Follette, Theodore Roosevelt, Wilson, and Brandeis had hoped for. The means approved by the old progressives, however, never seemed adequate when the crisis was really at its worst. Recourse was then had to means whose origin was in a general concept of national integration: one nation, one people, held together by his leadership.

Historians will find, I think, when they move on from the years of the First New Deal into the period of preparation for war and then of war itself, a very different kind of Roosevelt. In this endeavor he was not tormented by counsels or those committed to laissez faire progressivism; even those at his elbow stopped reproaching him. It was plain to everyone that the marshaling of the nation's whole strength in one mighty thrust was necessary if the Nazi-Fascist threat was to be overcome. The steady assurance of his progression toward the domination of allied strategy showed him at his best, just as his fumbling with the early New Deal showed him at his worst. He had to overcome popular reluctance before he could proceed from step to step; but looking back, it can be seen that his course was not only consistent, but, for its end, correctly conceived. His sense of timing, always good, was in this instance even better. He waited as long as he had to, but not so long as would be disastrous, before making each move. Frequently, especially in the early stages, he got his way by the smallest of margins; but always, once he had won, and events had moved as he had said they must, people were compelled to acknowledge his rightness.

The mistakes made in moving the nation toward war seem now to have been remarkably few. Because he saw so clearly the ultimate intention, and because he was free to adopt the most suitable means, he operated at his best. During the New Deal his intentions, although firmly held, were far less concretely visualized, his moves far less sure. Victory, or a permanent international organization of nations, are much more easily objectified than are freedom, security, and social justice. And if the ends become specific more easily in the one case than in the other, so do the means.

Some of the progressive means for attaining the ends that Roosevelt was from the first determined to attain in domestic policy had been tried and had failed. Antitrust legislation had been on the books for forty years and had again and again been strengthened after successive failures to achieve results. There had been a Federal Trade Commission since Wilson's time and, measured by its terms of reference, its achievements had been miniscule. So strong, however, was orthodoxy's hold on men's minds, especially when it had been crystallized in political controversy and defended as a cause, that practical failure had had no effect. Even in the debacle of 1933 believers in free enterprise were on hand to urge the old remedies not only as recovery measures, but as the reforms needed to prevent the recurrence of such disasters.

Roosevelt's departures from the old solutions were not happy ones for him; and he knew very well how unhappy they would make populist legislators. When he was urging congressmen to vote for measures they liked no better than he, in this traditional sense, his discomfort was obvious. It was so, for instance, in the message accompanying the submission of the Agricultural Adjustment Act, whose very name betrays the assumption of a federal duty to "adjust"—that is, to bring within government control the economic forces bearing on agriculture. The traditional remedy had always involved attacking the "middlemen," breaking up their conspiracies, regulating their activities, and forcing them to be fair to farmers. No New Dealer loved meatpackers, millers, and other processors; but it was obvious that the ten-year depression in agriculture had causes deeper than middlemen's sins. So it was decided to attempt the raising of prices by reducing the acreage of staple crops.

Roosevelt accepted the decision; but he said in his message to the Congress recommending the measures: "I warn you that this is a new and untrod path." He went on to say that if it proved to be the wrong one, he would be the first to acknowledge it. He may have been the more doubtful for knowing that there were several ways of reaching the adjustment we all talked of, and for not being sure which was likely to be most effective, or for that matter, which one we would finally decide to use. He did not add that he would be glad if we had to give all of them up, but he might have. I have no doubt that he would have been glad at the time; but I think he changed. And I think I know why. I believe the actual experience of the presidential office made him, as time went on, less and less a believer in the careless autonomies of laissez faire and more and more conscious of presiding at the center of a vast living organism, the Nation State. On one occasion when we met at Hyde Park to discuss the approach to some problem, perhaps a dozen of us, he began a little facetiously by saying: "Well, fellow socialists . . ." And I thought it not so facetious, really, as a sudden welling into voice of an unconscious recognition of what the nature of the presidential task was leading to.

I am moved here to say something everyone knows but very few seem to keep in mind. The discipline imposed by the presidency changes those who assume its responsibilities. Hardly any position in the contemporary world can so penetrate and alter personality and mold it to the national use. The director of the American government's multiple functions is in addition the leader of a victorious party, but also the head of a formidable and expanding power. With the torrents of converging energy sweeping in upon him from the continent's enormously productive mines, farms, factories, and systems of distribution, he has daily to reconcile a hundred urgent demands and turn their energies, if he can, toward what he conceives to be the national good. He is required to give direction to the most willful productive complex ever known. He is even required to keep it going when it shows signs of faltering and to smooth the way for its usefulness to the people. He would be a strange man, indeed, who, with these demands stretching his capabilities, would be able to remain quite the same person he had been before.

One who becomes president has presided over a tumultous political victory, and he is the acknowledged disposer of many thousands of fates. He may not have been the political boss of his party—in fact, few political bosses ever reach important elective offices of any kind—but after his election in a nationwide referendum, his prestige will be so enormous as to be almost beyond comprehension. More millions of votes will have been cast for him by free choice than any man ever attracted before. And if he may not have been well known to many of those millions of voters before the campaign began, when it is over, and they have voted for him, he will be their chosen man. Many of them may have a proprietary interest in his fortunes. They will wish him well because he represents their judgment. Such an elected hero, supported as he is by that massed backing, not a passive, lethargic election-day kind of approval, but an interfering, vocal, and very active kind of possessiveness (as can be told by studying the White House mail and telegrams, listening to commentators, and reading what appears in the press), can no longer behave as he did before this deification happened to him.

Added to the enormous powers of chief executive and of political leader there is the third: those of a chief of state. There must necessarily surround him, in this capacity, however simple and even shy a man he may be, all the circumstance appropriate to the nation's prestige. The ceremonial of so exalted an office is necessarily highly formalized—it must be if embarrassing discriminations are to be prevented. And the president can never depart from the formality expected of him as the living symbol of his country's position. His life must be a kind of public show, lightened a little here and there by touches of his own personality, by rather pathetic attempts to break out of his confinement and circumvent formality—never very successful and growing less and less so as he becomes more and more the embodiment of his office. The American people are inconsistent and demanding in these matters.

They require commonness and at the same time an almost unattainable elevation.

The result of this discipline is that many presidents cease to be human creatures at all, however human they must have been to have had the political appeal required for election. Then too they must have reached a mature conception of the nation's future to measure every decision they may make. This is not something they may reveal, except in bits and patches, since that would expose it to attack by those whose interests it did not suit. Besides, like any working plan, it has to be changed as conditions require and as the processes of judgment operate. It is therefore kept in the background; but if it does not exist it will make the life of the executive and politician almost impossible. He will again and again fall into inconsistencies; the judgments he must make many times a day will presently be seen to have no intelligible orientation; and ultimately he will lose the confidence of those who expect him to be their protector.

For democracies do demand such leadership; and under the Constitution only the president—the people's own man, *all* the people's own man—can supply it. He must persuade them, almost bully them, often, into doing things they are most reluctant to do. They have interests, prejudices, irresponsible preferences; they listen to gossip, are advised by a press they do not really trust, and by leaders they know to be incorrigibly local. They expect their president to be free from any interest or prejudice, to think singly of the national good, and to rally them to its support. He must force the Congress, against its will, to do what has to be done, and he must often do it by raising the people—who want nothing so little as to be raised—against it.

This is what the American presidency is and what it requires of its incumbents. It came to a full flowering with Roosevelt.

The presidency had not always been so demanding. To find comparable expectations centering there it would be necessary to go back to Lincoln's time, when the fatal compromises concerning states' rights had come to resolution in an appeal to force, likely, it seemed, to shatter the Union. It was Lincoln's task to prevent a threatened dissolution, even if it required the ordeal of conflict. Until the great depression revealed that capitalism was not a system at all, and finally, after its failure to cure its multiple fractures, demanded new leadership, the presidency had never embodied, to quite the same extent, the hopes and fears of the whole nation. Even Wilson, drawing back from the war and hating it, finally embracing it as the fire in which a lasting peace might be forced, had not had so massive a responsibility. Before becoming president, Roosevelt, in contemplative moments, must have shuddered at the immensities of the task.

One of the realities about the presidency is that those who come to it have then to be educated, and this can be a very expensive business for the nation. It sometimes seems almost providential that this period has never been fatal, unprepared and clumsy as some of the new presidents have been. If they have come from the legislature they have had to learn that there is inherent in the Constitution an opposition between the Congress and the President, and that a period of appeasement may enable the Congress to take such advantage that presidential leadership can never be reestablished. If they come from governorships, they are apt to be inclined toward the view that states still have the rights they had in the 1780s; and before they recover from these illusions they may have damaged the presidential power so severely that it can never be repaired in their time. So it goes very often; but with Roosevelt this, at least, was different. He knew what he had to work with and he intended to use its full capabilities. He was aware of congressional hostility; he knew that cabinet members are not always trusted executive subordinates, but are often rivals for power; he had had practical experience of the states' weaknesses, and was the less apt, because of that, to concede responsibilities they could no longer carry with any success; he knew that he had to be president of the whole nation and not only of those who had voted for him.

It is possible to go on at some length about Roosevelt's advantages of this sort over those of most presidents before him. Nevertheless, it is well to recall that, like Lincoln, he was not omniscient or even always wise; that he had to find his way through confusing fact and conflicting counsel; that he had inefficient and sometimes disloyal administrators; and that, although his principles were simple and clear, the exigencies he faced were such that expedients had to be found by costly trial and error. Not all of these experiments would prove even relevant to the problems they were meant to solve; and some would exhibit that difference between private and public ethics democracies learn to expect.

Everyone knows how Lincoln fumbled with his problem, only gradually and painfully finding his way to the winning of his war and, what was more important, the reestablishment of the Union; how one general after another failed him; how he had to struggle against the Congress and members of his cabinet for the liberty to shape strategy toward the softening rather than sharpening of the issues; how he had to bargain and compromise; and how fortunate it now seems that he was able finally at the bloodiest battlefield of all to talk of "binding up a nation's wounds."

We are not far enough yet from Roosevelt for just judgment; or perhaps the earlier, and less happy Roosevelt has been obscured by the more certain war leader. In the first conflict with depression, the fumbling pattern of 1860-63 was reproduced. Roosevelt found no generals who were both dependable and always wise. More and more his intentions had to be contemplated in secret because fewer and fewer of them could be realized. He attained a kind of victory, as Lincoln did, but it was far from a clean-cut or final one; and it might have gone to peices if the vast digression of war had not swallowed up and hid all its half-failures and distressing withdrawals. Still, he did possess an inner serenity anchored in the belief that expedients were necessary to good causes; for him their failures were never really heartbreaking.

I went with him one time to the little parish church at Hyde Park for a Sunday morning service. I cannot now recall how I happened to be alone with him that day; but I recall well enough why I was at Hyde Park. The National Recovery Administration had fallen into an awful chaos. After a spectacular flight, the blue eagle's plumage was torn and ragged. General Johnson had become a pathological problem, the temperamental, ranting, irresponsible head of an agency so subverted and rogue-minded that ending it seemed the only possible way to expunge the embarrassment it represented. Roosevelt had given the general carte blanche, had allowed him liberties so extravagant that no excuse seemed possible.

We had been talking all the day before, with some others coming and going, about the debacle of the NRA and about what could be done. He was frank about his errors, but, of course, he could not be frank in public. There had to be a relatively quiet withdrawal. One part of the problem was to dispose of Johnson, whose cantankerousness and volubility made most of the usual possibilities unsuitable. The other, much more important, part was determining what ought to be done about NRA. By this time it was offensive to those who, like myself, profoundly distrusted big business, however much we felt it represented a necessary technological advance; and the progressives were disaffected, being against bigness in any case and horrified by the very suggestion of partnership between business and government.

The NRA could have been administered so that a great collectivism might gradually have come of it, so that all the enormous American energies might have been disciplined and channeled into one national effort to establish well-being. That had been what I had had in mind in making my contribution to the Act setting it up.[4] But the law as amended in committees had also included, as was the congressional fashion, the ideas of the big businessmen themselves, who saw in the situation the possibility of a great supertrust, manipulating supplies, controlling prices, and establishing narrower and narrower rules for what competition remained. They had no idea of admitting government to partnership except as a cover. Johnson was Bernard Baruch's handyman—had been for years—and he had run away with the whole administration. Roosevelt had allowed this: he had indeed shut all the rest of us off when we had tried to object; and he had sheltered Johnson from the critical appraisal likely to modify the progress of industry toward domination of the whole administration.

He now had to get out of a bad situation as best he could. Talking to me, in this instance, was I suppose a kind of confession. By repeating the objections I had been urging whenever I could for a year or more, and pointing out where Johnson had got to in his coddling of the businessmen who had collected about him as deputies, code administrators, and so on, he let me know, and through me those others who thought as I did, that he had been quite wrongheaded and even persistent in his wrongheadedness. He did not say he had been as pleased as Johnson had been to see all

4. I had elaborated this in *The Industrial Discipline and the Government Arts* (New York: Columbia University Press, 1933).

the "fat cats," as he called them, flocking to Washington and taking part in the recovery effort. He did not mention, though in a bitter moment I did not hesitate to point it out, that he had sent word to Secretary Roper, after the Recovery Board (of which as Secretary of Commerce he was chairman) had made some objections, not to have any more meetings. This had meant that there were thenceforth to be no intermediaries between Johnson and himself. It could be said after that, I told him, with more truth than when it had been said earlier about Moley, that if an appointment was wanted with Johnson it could be had only by asking the President to arrange it.

The fact was that no one could be blamed but himself; and by having me at Hyde Park for a weekend and talking freely about getting out of the trouble he was in, he was making amends. I knew well enough that others were trying to devise something too—Frances Perkins, for instance, who wanted NRA abandoned except for its labor provisions.

I awoke on Sunday morning and lay a long time. There was no doubt that Roosevelt was overly given to artful contrivance and was now unhappy that some means had suddenly turned into ends—as he could see that NRA had done—but there was also no doubt about his being essentially a whole, perhaps an intended, President. He was not a made President, but a born one. He came to the manipulation of powerful forces and vast interests as naturally as I had to studying them. He accepted into himself the collective personality of the American people in the same way, I thought, looking out at the meadows, that that old oak over there accepted into itself the whole arrangement of nature just here and now, and lorded it over the field and its creatures with an unmistakable, unconscious, perfectly modest majesty. No monarch, I thought, unless it may have been Elizabeth or her unruly Tudor father, or maybe Alexander or Augustus Caesar, can have given more sense of serene presiding, of gathering up into himself, or really representing, a whole people. He had a right to his leeways, he had a right to use everyone in his own way, he had every right to manage and manipulate the palpables and impalpables. He would only do it for his country's good. He was part of a guided ordering of affairs. He had the secure innocence that comes of resting on a bosom broader than most of us ever find.

As I started to say, I was going with him that morning to the Sunday service. The church at Hyde Park is hardly more than a small, stone-walled, ivy-covered chapel; but it exactly suited Roosevelt. We had been talking in his bedroom—he in his old sweater, with the morning papers scattered about, and one cigarette after another being fitted into the long holder he used. He was telling me how he meant to bring the government into better order—not that he used such words. What he said was, "We ought to do more for the poorer farmers" and "more to expand the forests" and "build more dams for power" and "put a floor under wages" and "make the planning board more effective." The broad and deep implications of such remarks as these needed, by now, no discussion between us. There were many things not yet done. Even his new people, Corcoran, Cohen, and the others, and the old helpers like Berle and myself could agree on these well enough. There were, however, some the other crowd would never agree to. They were after him, I knew, to scrap NRA, having the excuse of its outrageous mishandling; but I wanted it kept. It could still be the industrial counterpart, I thought, of the Agricultural Adjustment Administration. This, whatever its human defects, was rapidly knitting up American agriculture into a system. I would have liked to see industry become a system too, although not one managed by Baruch's friends or any other private interest. We had only to call up the original intention of self-government for industry but with government supervision.

He knew how all this stood well enough. And he was wondering, I thought, whether the nation was ready to become so self-conscious as I suggested it might, an organism, eliminating many of the wastes of competition, gaining the advantages of plan and purpose. There was plenty of contrary evidence. The very thought of such direction turned the stomachs of the party's elders and made congressmen shudder. Theirs was a life of caprice called freedom. It was what had caused the breakdown his bold words had pushed into the background. The clamor for a balanced budget was rising to heaven from those businessmen who lived by its unbalance. They opposed relief for the unemployed even though it supported an economy they could then exploit. There was no sense in them. It really did not seem as though an integrated system could be established with such people still in places of power. At the least, it would take inspired leadership. To do it, Roosevelt must be clear in his mind and must have the kind of instrument NRA was meant to be.

He was deciding whether he would undertake it. He could not yet quite see the structure he would need. Those who preached the virtues of littleness and the restoration of competition were always nagging at him. For one of them he had deep respect: Brandeis. Some he was taking for his working team: Frankfurter, Corcoran, and Cohen. Yet I could see that the presidency had done its work on him. He saw the nation, as none of the others did, whole; he saw part working with part, all functioning together: the men in the cities, the men on the farms, the men at sea, all working for each other as they worked for their families; and he the conjunctural center. He could not make the nation over. He could not make it other than it was. He could only make it more consciously what it had been trying to become. Moreover, he had tried an experiment. The NRA was my kind of thing. He pointed out that I had approved his choice of Johnson to administer it. I returned that I had thought it would have no chance at all unless Baruch was in on it—hadn't he himself reminded me that Baruch "owned sixty congressmen"? Also, I said, it was quite possible that Johnson had run away even from Baruch, for that old-timer was at least discreet. I pleaded, in other words, that because the experiment had gone badly it did not prove what the fractionalists were saying. It simply had not been a good experiment. I begged for renewal—with a governing board for balance and sanity. This was one place where such control was indicated. Before he had begun to get ready for church he had been trying that over in his mind, wrestling a little with his dislike of boards. I gave him a name or two, and he liked them. He said we must talk of it more, but now it was time to go.

We lifted him into the back seat of the big open car—it was one of the few times I was allowed to help. He patted the seat beside himself. I got in and we rolled down the drive to the Albany road, with the Secret Service car following cheerfully in the morning sunshine, and the presidential cape blowing a little in the wind. We came up to the door of the chapel, and after his usual trouble with the braces we went in. He worshiped, singing the hymns, reading the responses, listening attentively to what seemed to me a meaningless sermon by a young man in vestments. I found it obscure because I did not have the hang of the Episcopal language and did not understand the doctrinal issues he preached about. Also I was bothered a little by getting up and sitting down—which amused him because he had a special dispensation in that respect. As the quite moments came while the young man talked and I looked sideways at him, I felt that I had lost. I was asking too much. It was not only NRA, it was the whole organic conception of the living nation, equipped with institutions for foresight, conjuncture, and balance. It was not yet time for it. He himself would go on doing what he could of this by main cleverness and personal manipulation. He had no feeling of being possessed by any lesser objectives than those he was in direct touch with here in his church—the brotherhood of man in the fathership of God. With anything not indicated directly for a Christian gentleman he would temporize, experiment, tentatively put forward if it seemed to go in the right direction; but he would not give it or its administrators any kind of loyalty, bind himself to its history or to their fortunes. He would not go far to persuade people of its desirability or risk much of his political capital to establish or maintain it.

So I knew that NRA was done for; and I hardly expected to see another attempt of the sort in my lifetime. I might have been full of lament. But somehow what I had perceived had communicated itself to me and I had borrowed a little of his equanimity. It can be imagined that this was for me a political event of the first importance. I had learned to understand more than I had before not only about a President but also about the presidency. I would spend a long time in future wondering if it had to be that way in a democracy.

Shortly after inauguration, Roosevelt gave me the advice I have on occasion repeated to my own helpers. I call it the parable of the truckdriver, not because of any intended disparagement of that calling, more because I admire the toughness required to carry it on—as no doubt the President did too. It was intended, besides bracing me, to illustrate the necessarily tentative nature of essays in administration. I came into the oval office one day late in the fall of 1933 looking, I presume, tired and perhaps a little wan, as though things were getting to be decidedly too much for me—as, in fact, they were. I had been at it now since the very early spring of 1932, much of that time immersed in outsize problems quite beyond any experience I had ever had before; and for several months had been carrying almost the whole administrative burden of the old Department of Agriculture—while we tried to find ways of reforming it—the Secretary necessarily spending most of his time on organizing the Agricultural Adjustment Administration. I was also serving on half a dozen interdepartmental boards in the Secretary's stead, the most important being the National Recovery Board and the Public Works Board; and I was still doing a certain number of jobs for the President—acting as his familiar in the now diminishing Brains Trust relationship. Probably, also, I was beginning to feel the unrestrained hammering of the press, begun almost as soon as the panic of the bank holiday had subsided. At any rate, I was in a state of noticeable discouragement.

The President looked that day, as he did all through the first term, quite leisurely in his seersuckers, and, with his good brown color, healthier than any physically immobilized man had any right to look. The sun streamed through the doors open to the lawn and a breeze crept around the walls, where by now all his ship pictures were hung. His enormous shoulder and chest development fairly loomed over his almost empty desk—empty, that is, except for gadgets—hiding the shrunken legs below. The impression, too strong to miss, was one of enormous power and confidence. He leaned back and blew out a long cone of cigarette smoke. "You will have to learn," he said, "that public life takes a lot of sweat; but it doesn't need to worry you. You won't always be right, but you must not *suffer* from being wrong."

"But," I said, "I have to make the most awful decisions for an amateur like me. And I always have to make them too soon. It gets me down."

"If you have decisions to make," he said, "what do you think about me? And I sleep nights. I'll tell you what you can think of. If you had been a truckdriver, just installed in your office, 50 percent of your decisions would be right on average; they would have to be. But you aren't a truckdriver. You have had some preparation. Your percentage is bound to be higher. So long as you keep it over 50 percent I won't get rid of you and send for a truckdriver." He laughed one of those laughs which could be heard all over the West Wing in those days and which made harassed people out in the waitingroom, newspaper correspondents lounging in the lobby, secretaries with problems they could not fathom, look at each other and smile in sympathy. Those laughs echoed in the pervading gloom of that year from California to Pennsylvania and made everyone in the whole nation feel better, all except the sour reactionaries, who were already busy whispering that it was a sign of approaching mania—"the lousy bastards," as Harry Hopkins used to say.

Outside, the reporters surrounded me as usual. They knew I would not repeat anything I had been told but, as Fred Storm said, they could always hope, couldn't they? "What had he been laughing about?" they wanted to know. I was too enraged at their employers by now and too conscious of unrelenting malice to dare tell them, as perhaps I should have. It may be that the nation, hanging on Roosevelt's words as it was in those days, might not have liked to hear that its servants in Washington, who pretended, as far as seemed congruous, to be infallible, were only expected by the President to be as right as the law of averages required—a little righter than a truckdriver, hauled in and put down behind a desk. Besides, by that time it had occurred to me that one of my wrong decisions might be more important than all my right ones; so the average he spoke of was illusory. There was, after all, something amiss with the parable, even if it did illustrate the tolerance of an Executive who did not value any decision too highly. Most decisions were about matters only important at the moment. He genuinely did not worry lest they be wrong. He had a source of support beyond the reach of ordinary judgments.

Roosevelt certainly had a feeling of being guided, but only generally. He had to make his own decisions and he had no expectation of being absolved from mistakes. So he kept the faith as he went along. He thought others ought to do it too, although he got enormous enjoyment out of their aberrations and laughed at their inability to behave. That this applied to nations as well as men, we all had occasion to learn. The issue of the war debts, it will be remembered, was all mixed up with the phenomena of the depression. If the farmers in Iowa were embittered about their debts to their mortgage holders (whom they roughly called "the money power"), the French and British were equally embittered about the debts they owed the United States. "Uncle Shylock" they called us.

For several centuries in similar circumstances, European nations had foreclosed on various parts of the world; but their sole response to repeated duns in these years was a press campaign picturing a hardhearted colossus. Hoover had been brought in 1932 to a moratorium, and before inauguration a preliminary conference in Geneva was to be held to fix the agenda for a full-scale conference later. The Europeans intended to use this occasion to get their debts forgiven, and E. E. Day and J. W. Williams, Hoover's emissaries, were quite prepared to cede the point so that some international monetary stability could be reached.

President-elect Roosevelt in Albany had had different ideas. He was, in fact, outraged. We were, he said, being put in a hopelessly false position. Anyone would think that we owed them an apology. This was not the naiveté of Coolidge, who, when the debts were mentioned, said, "Well, they hired the money, didn't they?" Roosevelt felt that both Coolidge and Hoover had been treated with intolerable arrogance. He meant to have things go differently. And if historians are puzzled still, as I understand they are, as to why the President that summer blew up the London Economic Conference when the Europeans thought they had things nicely fixed with Hull, and even Moley, they might consider Roosevelt's habit of differentiating means and ends, his carelessness about the one and his adamant holding to the other.

The issue of Russian recognition furnishes another illustration. It was to be expected that the new and more liberal regime would give up the stiff and prejudiced attitude set by Secretary of State Hughes in Harding's time and maintained through twelve unyielding years. To Republicans communism was sinful, and they had never wavered in their determination that the United States should take no official notice of it. Even before his inauguration Roosevelt had given some intimation that his attitude would be a different one. I noted from time to time his various remarks when the subject arose and I could see that on this matter he had reached a conclusion. I naturally wondered, as in other instances, what it was and how he had arrived at it. After a good deal of waiting and watching, I reached what I thought was the answer; and from then on I was even more interested to see whether I had been right. The confirmation all through was so ample as to be overwhelming.

In this one instance I had succeeded in working out a useful formula. I had learned from the hard experience of the campaign how little committed he was to any economic system or device, even to one affecting a whole nation. So he had toyed with the idea of a new national banking system, with self-government for industry, and with other collective devices. He had been willing to have all of them, as I had hoped, but he had approached each of them as gingerly as a cat might approach an oversized rodent it had cornered. He found them interesting to speculate about; they appealed to his highly developed manipulative faculties; he even worked out political preparations and administrative procedures. But his interest was that of a workman who might choose the kind of wood to go into a piece of furniture or the kind of fertilizer to put on a field. The wood or the fertilizer might have technical qualities of a fascinating sort, but if what was wanted was a certain result it was only sensible to let the wanted result dominate the choice of material. Also the President of the United States must measure or determine results in different terms from anyone else. They first had to be good for the nation and then had to be accepted by it; only after these criteria had been satisfied could the more strictly managerial judgment be allowed to have its way.

When once I had caught on to this formula, I was much more satisfied, whether the decision went for or against the system or device I felt was necessary. What more could anyone ask than that? I thought at the time and, being stubborn, have continued to think that a determined leader could have put into operation all the devices I have mentioned (as well as others I have not); but I never felt in the least disgruntled about it and I never went on trying to arrange a situation in which he would find himself committed to something his judgment had gone against—one of the particular vices of those in subordinate positions. This was a loyalty I know—because he once told me—that he valued.

I thought Russian recognition had been tried over in his mind and determined on as expedient. The economic prejudices of his predecessors weighed not at all with him in spite of his progressive predilections; but another prejudice did, and it might have affected his decision except that he found himself able to denature it. That involved, of course, the Communist attitude toward religion. He went into this thoroughly with me as he must have thought since, although it did not occur to me at the time, that his decision was partly determined by the belief that recognition would be helpful to religious Russians in the various ways any imagination can conceive.

It was that experienced hand Maxim Litvinov who was sent by the Politburo to negotiate when the President's decision became known. He related the event to me immediately afterward (he told others too, for they in turn reported it to me). When the signatures were affixed and Litvinov was about to leave, the President said to him: "There is one other thing; you must tell Stalin that the antireligious policy is wrong. God will punish you Russians if you go on persecuting the church." I ought not to put this remark in quotation marks, because I cannot be certain of its literal accuracy; out I am certain that it is almost exactly what he said.

Litvinov was taken aback. It was altogether unexpected. And when he thought it over he realized the significance of the way it had been put. The President had not said that the Russian antireligious policy would alienate opinion and create diplomatic difficulties. He had said it would precipitate divine punishment. Litvinov related this incident to others in a puzzled way. He spoke of it because he thought it had no diplomatic significance and so could be talked about; but also he was astounded and curious. He wound up by asking: "Does he really believe in God?"

That, at least, I could have answered. This, I knew for certain, was an end, not a means.

INDEX

Adams, Henry, 86
After Seven Years, 101, 121, 140, 150n
Agricultural Adjustment Administration, 91, 124, 249, 294, 302
Agricultural problems, Roosevelt's interest in, 18-19, 123
Agricultural relief, 199, 200-204
American Civic Association. 85
Anti-Trust Act, 62
Atom bomb, 269-270
Awalt, Francis G., 140, 220

Banks, 140, 149-150, 204-205, 217-218, 225-226, 272-273, 289
Baruch, Bernard, 136, 140, 172, 243, 303
Bean, Louis, 91
Bell, Daniel, 219
Berle, Adolf A., 92, 95, 100, 105, 114, 124, 129, 138, 172, 177
Bilbo, Theodore, 275
Bonus March, 184, 187-194
Brains Trust, 92, 96, 105, 125, 138, 276
Brandeis, Louis, 74, 279, 282
Broun, Heywood, 121
Brownlow, Louis, 81, 91
Bryan, William Jennings, 279
Bryce, Lord, 75
Budget, federal, 80, 88-90
Burgess, J. W., 80
Byrnes, James F., 138
Business, Roosevelt and, 143-146

Calloway, Cason, 26, 27, 28
Campobello, 37, 51
City Planning Commission, 85
Civil Service Reform Association, 86
Civil Service Reform League, 87

Civilian Conservation Corps, 123, 136, 249
Cleveland, Grover, 237
Cohen, Benjamin V., 282, 302-303
Conference for Good City Government, 87
Confidence, business, 150, 217, 230, 267
Construction Council, 169-170
Coolidge, Calvin, 94, 211, 307
Corcoran, Thomas G., 282, 302, 303
Coxey, Jacob B., 187

Daniels, Josephus, 74, 265-267
Davis, Norman, 141, 214, 246, 250
Day, E. E., 212-213, 307
Delano, Franklin, 82, 85
Delano, Frederick, 91
Deficit spending, 159
Depression, 100, 126, 130, 174, 181-183, 226-230, 279
Dewey, Thomas A., 264, 268
Disarmament, 250-251
Douglas, Lewis W., 89, 118, 138, 159, 215-216
Dows, Olin, 37-38, 54
Dunlap, R. W., 221-222

Eccles, Marriner S., 257n, 273
Economic planning, 106, 107, 117, 138, 174-175, 208-209, 245-247
Eisenhower, Dwight D., 156, 191, 237
Ezekiel, Mordecai, 91, 122, 201

Farley, James A., 79, 120, 262, 267, 276, 291
Farm, Roosevelt's, in Warm Springs, 3, 11, 19, 22, 27, 55